LANCIA
FLAMINIA & FLAVIA

ISBN 978-1-84155-429-7

CONTENTS

Lancia Flavia, Sporting Motorist, 1960	2
A History of Lancia, 1964	4
Lancia Flaminia, Road Test, 1958	12
Lancia Flaminia Coupe, Road Test, 1960	16
Lancia Flaminia Zagato, 1960	20
Lancia Flavia, Road Test, 1961	22
Lancia Flavia, New Cars, 1960	26
Fessia's Flavia, Road Test, Road and Track, 1961	28
Lancia Flavia, Road Test, Road and Track, 1961	30
Lancia Flavia Coupe 2000, 1963	34
Lancia Flavia, Road Research Report, Car & Driver, 1961	35
Lancia Flavia Coupe, Twin Test, 1962	42
Lancia Flaminia, Road Test, 1962	44
Lancia Flavia 1.8 and Lancia Flaminia 2.8, 1963	49
Lancia Flavia Coupe, Road Test, 1964	50
Lancia Flavia 1.8 Coupe, Road Test, 1964	55
Lancia Flaminia Coupe 3B, Road Test, 1965	58
Lancia Flavia Zagato Sport, Road Test, 1965	64
Lancia Flaminia GT, Road Test, Road & Track, 1962	69
Lancia Flavia Sport, 1964	71
Lancia Flaminia versus Flavia, Car & Driver, 1964	72
Lancia Flavia, Italy's First Front Wheel Drive, 1960	83
Lavish Lancia, 1966	86

The appearance of the Flavia is clean and practical without catching the distinction of many contemporary Italian bodies

A new Lancia—the Flavia

At the Turin Show

THE Turin motor show following hard on the heels of Earls Court presented as usual a dazzling array of cheap and not so cheap motor cars, clothed in scintillating bodywork by the best coachbuilders in the world. Whereas the specialist British coachbuilders have faded away or become absorbed in manufacturing concerns, their Italian equivalents have flourished and carved for themselves a permanent and irrevocable place in the country's motor industry. Notably of course this applies to Farina, who is now a motor car manufacturer of some size as well as a custom and small-run bodybuilder, and his position as a probing experimentalist for the Italian industry was emphasised by his curious Model X machine with wheels disposed at front and back and both sides, and incorporating many other unusual features. We hope to cover this car at some length in a future issue.

Apart from the price cuts announced on the eve of the show by Fiat and Alfa Romeo, the palm of Turin undoubtedly went to Lancia who produced the only completely new car of this show, and one of the most interesting designs of the year anywhere in the world: the front-wheel drive, horizontally opposed, four-cylinder Flavia. Lancia had apparently felt for some time that there was an important gap between their 1100 c.c. Appia and their 2½-litre Flaminia ranges which required filling. Subsequent to the introduction of the Flaminia the company had acquired the services of Professor Fessia as designer, he having been responsible for the Topolino when he was with Fiats at an earlier time. Professor Fessia, moreover, has been engaged on experimental front-wheel drive designs for many years now and it was therefore natural that he should give Italy her first car of this type. As with most Lancia designs, the car is unusual rather than revolutionary, and is notable for the excellence of its engineering rather than the novelty of its design. The new horizontally-opposed, four-cylinder engine of 1500 c.c., with a bore and stroke of 82 x 71 mm., is quite a masterpiece of compact design even if it is expensive to produce. Apart from small size and weight which allows it to be placed in front of the line of the front wheels, the horizontally-opposed layout has allowed a very low centre of gravity to be obtained with consequent advantages in road-holding ability. The engine has a separate camshaft serving each pair of cylinders, operating opposed valves and driven by a duplex roller chain. The opposed valve arrangement follows the practice of the Aurelia with individual fulcrum shafts located transversely. The positioning of the valves has allowed them to be of unusually large proportions. The cylinders are surprisingly widely spaced, but this allows large crankshaft bearings and crank webs. The crankcase and cylinder block is die-cast in one piece from aluminium for each side of the engine; wet cylinder liners are located at top and bottom.

On a compression ratio of 8·3 to 1 the engine produces 78 b.h.p. net at 5,200 r.p.m. on a twin-choke Weber 32DCHI or a Solex 32PAIA3 carburettor. This is a lively output for a 1½-litre engine although such power is to a large extent counteracted in this particular version of the car by the high overall weight of a full six-seater body. A notable feature of the front-wheel drive is the use of constant velocity joints and Hardy Spicer ball and groove sliding splines. The expense of such an arrangement indicates a real determination on the part of the designer and manufacturers to give the best possible front-wheel drive arrangement. An added advantage of this system is that it allows the incorporation of an excellent steering

This is the front sub-frame assembly with engine installed but without radiator. It shows strikingly how the engine is positioned ahead of the line of the front wheels, while the double wishbone suspension and Dunlop disc brakes can also be seen

lock and contributes to light steering. The front suspension is by double wishbones and a transverse leaf spring, and the braking both at front and rear is by Dunlop disc brakes with servo assistance. A surprising feature of the rear suspension is the use of a very light beam axle and long quarter-elliptic springs. Anti-roll bars are used front and rear and telescopic shock absorbers are fitted all round.

Externally the car is neat without being unduly distinguished, and the body shape suffers somewhat from the efforts to provide a really roomy interior and a large luggage boot. In this effort, however, it is obvious that the makers have been eminently successful. A bench seat at the front can accommodate three people in comfort and is upholstered, as is the rear one, entirely of foam rubber which Lancia claim reduce vibration by a considerable amount. The backrest of the front seat is fully reclining so that the car may be used as a bed if necessary. A distinctive feature of the inside is the unusual facia board which groups controls in a semi-circular panel to the left of the steering wheel (in the left-hand drive cars at present in production) and instruments in a nacelle in front of the driver. A very slender gear-change lever is mounted on the steering column. Thin pillars and wide glass area ensure good visibility not only for the driver but for all other passengers. A very interesting feature for a car of this type is the inclusion of a revolution counter in the speedometer nacelle. The luggage boot has a very wide lid and large uncluttered interior of good carrying capacity.

Despite the use of integral construction with front sub-frame the car is, as mentioned earlier, surprisingly heavy at 24 cwt. For the sporting motorist this is discouraging, although it must be emphasised that the makers' obvious objective has been to provide ample interior accommodation and fullest equipment. Produced in a different form, with shorter chassis and close-coupled bodywork, the new Lancia is likely to provide some welcome opposition for the Giulliettas that so dominate the sporting scene in this engine category. Even on the present power output of 78 b.h.p. a lengthy stretch of road will allow 90 m.p.h. to be seen on the speedometer. If the weight can be trimmed by a third to some 16 cwt., which should not be beyond the bounds of possibility, the increase in performance will be startling indeed. Moreover the layout of the engine with its ample cooling passages, noble bearings, large valves and good combustion chamber shape should lend itself to some fairly liberal "tweaking", although the present compression ratio at 8·2 to 1 is quite high even by today's standards.

In all, the Flavia is a most welcome addition to Italy's and the world's range of cars. Interestingly conceived and superbly engineered it bears Lancia's traditional stamp of ingenuity and quality throughout its design. We look forward with interest to the time when it will be possible to drive a production version of the car, and we hazard a guess that at the next Turin show Lancia themselves or others of the Italian coachbuilding school will have produced some attractive variations on a G.T. theme.

SPECIFICATION:

ENGINE:

Four cylinders, horizontally opposed; bore and stroke, 82×71 mm. (3·23×2·79 in.). Cubic capacity, 1500 c.c. (91·6 cu. in.). Overhead valves operated by pushrods and rockers. Compression ratio, 8·3 to 1. Maximum b.h.p., 78 net at 5,200 r.p.m. Maximum torque, 82 lb. ft. (net) at 3,500 r.p.m. Twin-choke Weber 32DCHI or Solex 32PAIA3 carburettor. Bendix electric fuel pump; tank capacity 10·5 gallons. Full flow oil filter; sump capacity 11 pints. Pressurised cooling system, with pump, fan and thermostat. 12v. 40 amp. hour battery.

TRANSMISSION:

Single dry plate clutch. Four speed gearbox with synchromesh on all forward speeds; overall ratios: top 4·09, 3rd 6·71, 2nd 9·53, 1st 16·16, reverse, 18·0 to 1. Gear lever mounted on steering column. Hypoid bevel final drive.

CHASSIS:

Suspension: front, independent with double wishbones, transverse leaf spring and anti-roll bar; rear, rigid axle with semi-elliptic leaf springs and anti-roll bar. de Carbon telescopic dampers front and rear. Brakes: Dunlop disc, servo assisted. Steering: Worm and roller; turning circle 36 ft; two-spoke 15½ in. steering wheel. Pressed steel wheels with 6·50-15 tyres.

GENERAL DIMENSIONS:

	ft.	in.
Wheelbase	8	8·3
Track: front	4	3·2
Track: rear	4	2·4
Overall length	15	0·3
Overall width	5	3·2
Overall height	4	11·1
Ground clearance		5·0
Unladen weight	24 cwt.	

A HISTORY OF THE

THE BEST-KNOWN VINTAGE LANCIA is the Lambda, notable for i.f.s., an overhead camshaft vee-four engine with beautifully made valve gear, and a very modern ball-gate central gear-change. The Lambda was covered in great detail in MOTOR SPORT *for June 1942.*

BEHIND most technically advanced cars, there is usually one man who nurtures the design from an idea germinating in his mind, through the difficult days after the model is first launched on the market, to its ultimate commercial success. Although to every designer his assistants are indispensable, with certain notable exceptions, great cars are not the work of design teams, but the result of an individual's creative thought and determination. Such a car was the Lancia, distinguished, from the Tri-Kappa of the early 'twenties to the current range, by the narrow vee design of the engine— a record broken over forty years only by the introduction of the flat-4 Flavia in 1961.

When the F.I.A.T. concern was founded in 1899, it took over the Ceirano Company, a bicycle and *voiturette* manufacturer, on whose staff were two apprentices. These were Felice Nazarro and Vincenzo Lancia, the son of a soup canner, both of whom were destined to make their mark as racing drivers. In the still youthful motor industry, the merits of men of ability were quickly recognised and it was not long before Nazarro and Lancia were in the works racing team.

Among Lancia's successes were a win in the second Florio Cup, held in 1904, at the wheel of a 75-h.p. 4-cylinder F.I.A.T., which had chain drive and rather obvious Mercedes influence, and second place in the 1908 Targa Florio. His name appears far less frequently in records of the period than Nazarro, but Lancia was a most unlucky driver, constantly dogged by minor mechanical failures. Later in 1908 he severed his connections with Fiat (as it had been known since 1906) and set up on his own as a car manufacturer.

The first Lancia designs were conventional enough, but were known, somewhat confusingly, as the Alfa and Di-Alfa. The former had a 2,544-c.c. (90 × 100 mm.) side-valve 4-cylinder engine in a 9 ft. 3 in. wheelbase chassis, and in England in 1908 the quoted chassis price was £400. The Di-Alfa was identical in most respects, but had a longer, 10 ft. 8 in. wheelbase, and a 6-cylinder version of the same engine. These models remained in production until 1913, when they were both replaced by the Theta, broadly similar to the Alfa, but with a 4,951-c.c. (110 × 130 mm.) engine, developing 70 b.h.p. at 2,200 r.p.m. Few early Lancias have survived, but a beautifully restored Theta is owned in this country by Mrs. Jeddere-Fisher and another is in the very interesting and beautifully laid-out Turin Motor Museum. This model was continued after World War I with few design changes as the Kappa and Di-Kappa.

As a first indication of future design trends, Lancia produced in 1919 a 12-cylinder vee-type engine of 6,032 c.c. (80 × 100 mm.) —his first breakaway from the traditional "in-line" design. Conditions were not favourable for the marketing of such a luxurious and expensive design, so although a few engines were made, the design was not proceeded with.

The first production vee-engined design was the 8-cylinder Tri-Kappa made between 1922-25—in the latter year it was withdrawn to permit increased output of the Lambda. The Tri-Kappa had a capacity of 4,595 c.c. (75 × 130 mm.) and developed 98 b.h.p. at 2,500 r.p.m. This engine was fitted in a chassis similar to the Kappa and it looked like a larger version of the Lambda. Two notable features were the single horizontal twin-choke carburetter and the exhaust manifold consisting, for all eight cylinders, of a single outlet at the back of the head. Top speed was in excess of 80 m.p.h.

Although it is known that a prototype of the Lambda was being tested in 1921, with a body having four staggered seats and distinguished or disguised by a radiator reminiscent of a Bugatti, the model was not revealed to the public until the Paris Salon of 1922. Not only was this a considerable advance on previous Lancia cars, but it was also technically ahead of nearly all its rivals. It was never intended to be a sports car, but its robust if somewhat rough engine and taut road-holding gave it an appeal comparable to that of the Vauxhall 30/98 and the Bentley 3-litre. As the weight of the early 4-seater tourer was a mere 15 cwt., the Company was able to guarantee a top speed of 70 m.p.h.

Construction was of integral pressed steel, with deeply flanged sides, which formed the main body panels; there were riveted cross-members, which carried longitudinal tubular supports for the engine, gearbox and footwells. The Lambda was of much lower construction than was usual at that time and it set the style for the now universal central hump between the seats and concealing the prop.-shaft.

Although independent front suspension had been used on a very limited scale on the Edwardian Sizaire-Naudin, the Morgan 3-wheeler and certain competition cars, to Lancia must go the credit for marketing on a large scale a model so fitted. The beam front axle was replaced by a triangular tubular structure, which supported the radiator, and at each side were enclosed coil-springs and hydraulic dampers. This layout had numerous virtues, including low unsprung weight, much improved suspen-

STOLID WORTH.—The Lancia Kappa with open touring coachwork.

A 5th-series Lancia Lambda with unusual coupé de ville body.

sion (even if wheel movement was limited by modern standards) and a very good steering lock. Rear suspension was by long semi-elliptic springs and the brakes had small drums shrouded by the protruding hub centres and were cable operated; these were later replaced by very large aluminium drums. The wheelbase was excessively long, but this did not appear to affect road-holding adversely.

Vincenzo Lancia was able to lodge patents for his vee-4 engine, which for many years compelled designers seeking a very compact engine design to go in for a flat-4 layout. In planning this very narrow angle power unit, Lancia was aiming at building the very shortest engine possible, and he achieved this by staggering one pair of cylinders from the other at an angle of 13°; this angle refers to the selected position of the connecting rods on the crankshaft and the cylinder bores in relation to each other. The design is, in fact, more accurately described as a staggered four. Other advantages of this design were the short rigid crankshaft, well-dispersed combustion chambers and the square cylinder block and head, which permitted freer circulation of cooling water. Furthermore a single camshaft and rockers could be used instead of the two sets needed on a 90°-vee engine.

Production of the specialised components used in the Lambda was facilitated by the fact that Lancia had his own foundry, and the Company's reputation for fine castings has persisted through the years. The block was cast in aluminium, with steel liners pressed in and the crankshaft ran in three main bearings. The inlet and exhaust manifolds were bolted to the rear of the block and there was not much room for cylinder-head studs, so only six of these were used, resulting in more frequent than usual gasket failure.

A total of thirteen thousand Lambdas were built between 1922 and 1932 in nine series, but there is little distinction between the first six. These all used the original 2,120-c.c. engine, and series one to three and most of series four had a 3-speed gearbox with remote control centre-change and ratios suited to more undulating terrain than found in this country. Coachwork was angular in the extreme and available as an open 2-seater or 4-seater tourer, for which a detachable saloon top was offered. Marelli electrical equipment was changed for Bosch on the sixth series, the tourer was fitted with larger doors and the model was available with an even longer, 11 ft. 2½ in., wheelbase. The series seven introduced in 1926 was bored out to 2,370 c.c., with numerous other detail engine modifications, and a few of these were built with a separate chassis so that specialist coachbuilders could exercise their talents. A notable feature of this enlarged engine was the unconventional design of the connecting rods with

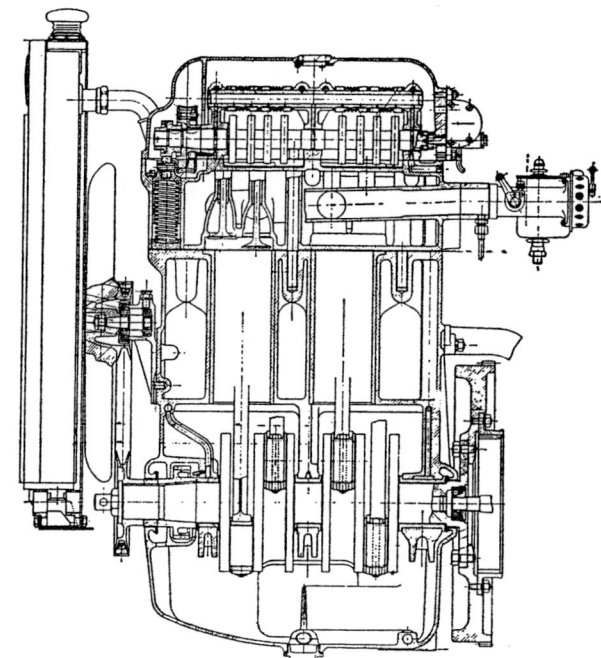

A sectional view of the Lambda "staggered-four" power unit and its coolant radiator.

offset shank. 16-in. brakes with shrunk-on alloy fins and lower-geared steering to match the new low-pressure tyres were now fitted.

A separate chassis was standard for the eighth series and the radiator was 3 in. higher; this series was especially popular in this country, with Weymann fabric saloon coachwork, which was angular in the extreme, true "early Gothic," with box-like rear boot, on which was mounted the spare wheel, and wicker seats. There was also seen on this chassis at the 1928 Olympia Show, one of the ugliest cars ever built. This was the "Airline" saloon, with a sharply sloping roof line and a protrusion, in which the third passenger, who was seated centrally, was supposed to accommodate his head. The final eccentricities were an air-speed indicator and a swivelling searchlight on the roof. The ninth series, differing only in detail from the eighth appeared in 1932, shortly before the model was withdrawn. Both these had a 2,570-c.c. engine, developing 69 b.h.p.

Although most Lambdas were good for 75 m.p.h. and the series eight and nine for 80 m.p.h., performance did not increase commensurately with power output, as weight rose, too, and many owners, not satisfied with the existing performance and finding the engine not very amenable to tuning, fitted seventh and eighth series engines into earlier chassis. Incidentally, very few of the early Lambdas seem to have survived, but there are quite a number of series five onwards about still, although unfortunately many have been "cut and shut," a modification which does not exactly improve handling. Certainly the Lambda was one of the great cars of the vintage era and affection for it is not based on sentiment alone.

Just at the end of the vintage period, Lancia supplemented the Lambda with the Di-Lambda, a rather larger and more imposing touring car. Chassis design followed closely that of the Lambda, but wheelbase was lengthened to 11 ft. 5 in. and the engine was a revised and developed version of that used in the Tri-Kappa. This was, of course, of vee-8 design, but capacity had been reduced to 3,960 c.c. (79.37 × 100 mm.) and power output was 100 b.h.p. at 3,800 r.p.m. The engine was cast in two blocks of four cylinders and the head was detachable.

The increased power output was countered to a considerable extent by increased weight—a typical tourer weighed around 38 cwt. Top speed was just under 80 m.p.h., with 55 m.p.h. obtainable in 3rd and a maximum in 2nd of 40 m.p.h. This early vee-8 had tone characteristic in common with the majority of its type, there being a remarkable freedom from vibration and engine noise.

A late-series Lancia Lambda in which a separate chassis enabled specialist coachwork to be fitted.

Another Lancia open tourer, in this case a Di-Lambda.

Rare bird—the 1,925-c.c. Lancia Artena.

Quite a large proportion of Di-Lambda production has survived simply because the model was toughly built. Apart from the maker's own Torpedo 4-seater tourer and saloon coachwork, a wide selection of bodies by specialist builders was available. The majority sold in the U.K. were saloons by either H. J. Mulliner or Weymann, but other available styles included a rakish cabriolet designed by Lancias and built by Mulliner, known as the "Bachelor's Two-Seater." The Di-Lambda was one of the less significant Lancia models and was withdrawn from general production in 1933; it was, however, available to special order until 1937.

Two new models, the Artena and Astura, were introduced in 1931, as successors to the Lambda, and were in fact identical apart from wheelbase length and engine type and size. The Astura used a vee-8 2,604-c.c. engine, based on the Di-Lambda unit, while the Artena had a development of the Lambda engine, but with stroke reduced to 90 mm., giving a capacity of 1,925 c.c. Standard features of both cars included the usual Lancia i.f.s., 4-speed gearbox and a central lubrication system.

The Artena never achieved great popularity and was quietly withdrawn from production in 1933. The Astura, on the other hand, sold well and in its various forms continued in production until the outbreak of war. There was little distinction between the first and second series, but the third series had much more modern styling. The fourth series, which was available in standard forms as a 4/5-seater pillarless saloon or as a drophead coupé, differed in a number of points from the earlier versions. The overall length of the chassis was slightly greater, and was now the type adopted for the Aprilia (to which reference is made later). Ground clearance was reduced by 2½ in. to 6⅞ in. and the brakes were Lockheed hydraulics.

The short-lived Artena was replaced by the Augusta, another model with a comparatively brief production life. Not only was the Augusta the smallest Lancia yet produced, but it was also a stop-gap model until the introduction of the design which was intended to be, and was, the successful climax to Vincenzo Lancia's career in the motor industry. Nevertheless the Augusta is a much-loved Lancia model.

Powered by a 1,196-c.c. (69.85 × 78 mm.) vee-4, developing a modest 35 b.h.p., the Augusta had a dry weight of only 17 cwt. and this enabled it to attain a top speed of 70 m.p.h. without fuss; 55 m.p.h. was obtainable in 3rd gear, but fuel consumption, at around 25 m.p.g., was expensive for such a small-capacity and light car. Apart from an indefinable charm, which makes the Augusta appeal to all who have driven it, there were such practical features as 4-door pillarless bodywork, which proved surprisingly rigid and durable and was to become an accepted Lancia feature. In addition, the usual Lancia i.f.s. gave it a considerable advantage over many of its rivals. Other good points were the excellent hydraulic brakes, a very nice centre-change and the comparatively modest price of £390.

Development work on the Augusta's successor started in 1934, shortly after production had commenced, but it was not until 1937 that the Aprilia entered production, a month or so before the death of Vincenzo Lancia. Although subsequent models had been good, none had achieved the popularity of the Lambda and Lancia's aim was to produce a small and light high-performance car that would do just this.

At first glance, the most striking feature of the Aprilia was the exceedingly neat and aerodynamic coachwork, but the mechanical features were equally intriguing. The engine was a 1,352 c.c. (72 × 83 mm.) narrow vee-4 unit, evolved from that used in the Augusta and largely of aluminium-alloy construction; this was used in conjunction with a 4-speed "crash" gearbox. Not only was there Lancia i.f.s., but the same system, combining torsion bars and a transverse leaf-spring, was applied at the rear. But for the introduction of the Issigonis B.M.C. designs, the writer would have stated categorically that the Aprilia had the best suspension of any small saloon, as it combined exceptional adhesion and almost complete freedom from roll; the springing was, however, a little on the harsh side, giving a somewhat pitchy ride.

The pillarless saloon bodywork had no separate chassis, but a flat steel "floor," with a streamlined underside (the only projection was the exhaust), to which the body was welded. Most vulnerable panels, such as wings, were bolted on and easy to replace. Styling was particularly clean and uncluttered, with a sloping roof and tail, in which a divided rear window and adequate luggage accommodation were provided. There were no running-boards and the headlamps merged into the wings.

In view of the small capacity engine, performance was quite exceptional and compares very favourably with many current 1½-litre models. Top speed, aided by the clean shape and low weight of 17 cwt., was an easy 80 m.p.h., with effortless sustained cruising in the 65-70 m.p.h. band. It would accelerate from 0-50 m.p.h. in under 13 sec., and could cover the standing quarter-mile in 21 sec. The speeds obtainable in 2nd and 3rd gears were 40 and 60 m.p.h., and fuel consumption rarely fell

A first-series Lancia Astura, with drophead coupé bodywork.

The flamboyant body on this series 4 Lancia Astura is by Carrozzeria Touring.

One of the outstanding small cars of all time—the 80-m.p.h., all-independently-sprung Lancia Aprilia.

below 30 m.p.g. The steering was light and high-geared and turning circle a mere 30 ft. It can be truly said of the Aprilia that it was one of the great cars of the 'thirties, with a specification and performance up to 1964 standards.

Two years later, in 1939, a Series-2 version with an enlarged engine of 1,486 c.c. replaced the earlier model, and this remained in production until replaced by the Aurelia in 1950. Other features of the Series-2 model were pierced wheels to permit better cooling of the brake drums and a fuel gauge consisting of a series of numbers, which lit up in turn as the tank level fell. The Aprilia was always available in chassis form, and a considerable number of drophead coupés were built on the pre-war chassis by Farina and Eagle; these were pretty enough little cars, but lacked the body rigidity of the saloon versions.

A really good Aprilia will still fetch close to £200, but the majority, as a result of the integral steel construction, are severely rotted, especially around the rear suspension mountings. Most Aprilias require, therefore, a complete body rebuild, an exceedingly expensive business but, in the writer's opinion, well worth the trouble.

The joint work of Gianni Lancia, the son of Vincenzo, and Vittoria Jano, former Fiat and Alfa Romeo designer, the Aurelia was the first new Lancia model introduced after the war and appeared at the Turin Motor Show in 1950. Over a period of eight years, the Aurelia was evolved from a modest 1¾-litre touring saloon into a quite hot Gran Turismo car with a top speed well in excess of 100 m.p.h. This evolution resulted in a bewildering assortment of engine sizes, but changes in chassis design and body styling were comparatively few. The original model closely followed Aprilia practice, with an integral body/chassis unit of 4-door pillarless type, pressed in sheet steel. The simple uncluttered lines were also reminiscent of the Aprilia, but with larger overall dimensions, the wings flush with the body sides and a curved windscreen and rear window; the boot lid was operated by a lever inside the car. Interior finish was somewhat austere, but practical, with rubber floor covers and cloth upholstery. A nice feature was the dipstick for the fuel tank.

The Aprilia as a sports/racing car, seen cornering characteristically, which means somewhat hectically, during the 1938 Donington T.T.

Another great Lancia model—the Aurelia, here seen in GT 2500 sixth-series form, a G.T. car capable of 110-115 m.p.h.

Mechanically the Aurelia was just as interesting as its predecessors; front suspension was independent on the traditional Lancia vertical coil-spring system. In unit with the final drive were the clutch and 4-speed gearbox, this creating good weight distribution and a favourable effect on road-holding. As the gearbox was controlled by a steering column change, the linkage was one of the longest ever, but, nevertheless, the change was very precise and one of the few of its type that is acceptable. Hydraulic brakes were fitted all round, inboard at the rear. The drive shafts passed through the hubs to outboard universal joints and the rear wheels were independently sprung on trailing wishbones and coil-springs.

The engine was a 60° vee-6 design, with a single light alloy casting forming the upper half of the crankcase and the cylinder blocks, and there were detachable wet cylinder liners. Each bank of three cylinders had a separate light alloy head and the overhead valves were push-rod operated.

This initial model was designated the B10 and had a top speed of just over 80 m.p.h. A year later, in 1951, both bore and stroke were increased to give a capacity of 1,991 c.c., and power output rose to 70 b.h.p. at 4,500 r.p.m., giving a top speed of 85 m.p.h., and this model was called the B21. Again in 1952 power was boosted to 90 b.h.p. at 5,000 r.p.m., and the model became known as the B22. Models B51 and B52 were separate chassis versions of the B21 and 22, for fitting with specialist coachwork. These various models remained in production concurrently until replaced by the Series-2 in 1954. Major differences between this and the earlier Aurelias lay in the larger capacity engine of 2,266 c.c. and an entirely new rear suspension. By increasing the capacity of the engine, it was possible to reduce the compression ratio to 7.4 to 1 and peak power (86.5 b.h.p.) was developed at a lower engine speed (4,300 r.p.m.). As weight was greater, there was no increase in maximum speed, but acceleration was much improved, because of the better torque characteristics of this engine.

The performance was excellent and the 80 m.p.h. obtainable in 3rd gear gives an indication of the high-gearing and long-legged gait of the Series-2 Aurelia. The steering was low-geared (4 turns lock-to-lock) but precise, and the turning circle was a quite compact 35 ft. The rear suspension was now of the de Dion type, suspended on semi-elliptic springs; the previous pattern had certain disadvantages, in that it had a slight oversteering tendency and in the wet one could never predict with accuracy when the limit of adhesion was reached. In addition, despite a ride control, it tended to give a rather bouncy ride.

The Aurelia blended into the motoring scene somewhere between the M.G. Magnette and the Riley Pathfinder (the styling of which it undoubtedly influenced); it was compact and comfortable, but with performance and road-holding vastly superior to most of its rivals.

A Gran Turismo version, designated the B20, supplemented the saloon in 1951. This had a capacity of 1,991 c.c. and developed 75 b.h.p. at 5,000 r.p.m. Bodywork was a most handsome 2-door fixed-head coupé, with basic lines similar to those of the saloon, but with a straight-through wing line into which merged a sloping roof. Weight was 1¾ cwt. less than that of its more sedate stablemate and it was 7 in. shorter. It was primarily a 2-seater, but there were occasional seats at the rear and a large boot. During the 1951 season the model was raced by the works and successes included second place in the Mille Miglia against very tough opposition from sports/racing cars, and victory in the

2-litre class at Le Mans.

In 1952 the Series-2 was introduced—the only important difference was an increase in power to 80 b.h.p. at 5,000 r.p.m.—and a year later the Series-3 was brought out with an enlarged engine of 2,451 c.c. and developing 118 b.h.p. at 5,300 r.p.m. As the works were now concentrating on the development of pure competition cars, they were no longer so interested in racing the Aurelia and most of its subsequent successes were limited to rallies. Especially notable were the late Johnny Claes' victory in the 1953 Liége-Rome-Liége Rally and that of Louis Chiron in the 1954 Monte Carlo event.

Six series were produced in all and although production figures fell after the introduction of the Flaminia, the GT model was only finally withdrawn in 1959. The Series-4 model was fitted with the de Dion rear axle, with the axle tube supported on semi-elliptic leaf-springs and located laterally by a Panhard rod; it was also the first model to have Vandervell bearings. In 1956 this was replaced by the Series-5, which had new-type camshafts, non-detachable cylinder liners, a Fitchel and Sachs clutch, and direct drive on top gear. The final model, the Series-6, made from 1957-9, differed only in detail from its predecessors. A Spyder open 2-seater, styled by Farina and designated the B24, was marketed from 1954 onwards; styling was very similar to that of the Alfa Romeo Giulietta Spyder, with pronounced rear wing line and half bumpers. On this model a central gear-change was standard, and although the column change was retained on the coupé, quite a large number have been converted by Nardi and other specialists.

The Aurelia was one of the most successful Gran Turismo cars of the post-war era and one of the most satisfying to drive. Top speed varied according to the back-axle ratio fitted and the length of unobstructed road available, but in standard form it was in the 110-115-m.p.h. bracket. The real merit of the Aurelia lay, however, in its general all-round excellence, a beautifully smooth motor that would surge up to 5,000 r.p.m., a genuine 80 m.p.h. in 3rd gear and excellent road-holding, both fully controllable under all circumstances and utterly predictable, with a slight inclination to understeer. Steering was a little heavy at low speeds (partly due to the Michelin "X" tyres fitted as standard), but improved considerably as speed increased, and the 3¾ turns from lock-to-lock did not require too much wheel winding. The clutch was definitely in or out and the steering column change was precise and silent in action. The GT model was exceedingly refined and free from vibration; even the exhaust note was subdued for a car of its type. Although costing new, with purchase tax and import duty, in excess of £3,000, a good 1954-5 example can now be bought for around £500.

In 1953 the 1,090-c.c. Appia, the second model to be evolved by Gianni Lancia, was placed on the market. This had a 68 × 75 mm. vee-4 cylinder engine, with the crankshaft running in two main bearings and developing 38 b.h.p. at 4,800 r.p.m. Although front suspension was by the familiar sliding pillar system first used on the Lambda, the more usual live axle mounted on semi-elliptic springs was fitted at the rear. The integrally constructed body had lines similar to the Aurelia, but scaled down and with the same pillarless construction. There was a 4-speed

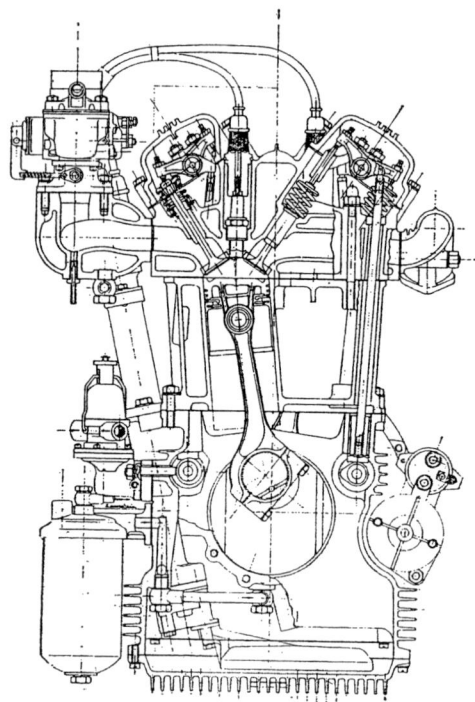

The Lancia Appia engine; note the long push-rod o.h. valve gear.

gearbox, with a reasonably satisfactory steering-column change and virtually unbeatable synchromesh. The aluminium drum brakes were exceptionally large, but disappointing features were the excessively low-geared steering and large turning circle of 36 ft.

Five years later the Series-2 model, with power output raised to 48 b.h.p. at 5,200 r.p.m. and slightly revised styling, replaced the earlier version. Top speed in this form was 80 m.p.h., with 40 and 20 m.p.h. available in 3rd and 2nd gears. Acceleration from 0-50 m.p.h. took 15 sec., a time bettered by the slightly larger Aprilia of twenty-one years previously. A coupé by Farina and a convertible by Vignale were also available; these differed from the standard versions, by having a 53-b.h.p. engine and a horizontal radiator grille in place of the traditional design. The Series-3 adopted the modern air intake, but otherwise was identical to its predecessor.

In a vain attempt to rival the success of the Alfa Romeo Giulietta, "Sport" versions of the Series-3 Appia were built, with lightweight Zagato bodywork and 60-b.h.p. engine. There was also available a Farina coupé with the same engine. The Appia was finally withdrawn from production in 1963, some little while after the introduction of the Fulvia. It had always been a tough, but rather expensive little car; perhaps its best virtue was reliability and this was more than confirmed by a test carried out in 1958 by an Italian magazine. A production model was driven over 100 laps of the Mille Miglia course—a distance of 97,200 miles—at an average speed of 43.6 m.p.h. Fuel consumption was 33.2 m.p.g. and no major replacements were required during or at the end of the test.

Despite conflicts with his fellow directors, Gianni Lancia, after reaching full age and assuming control of the Company, was determined on an exceedingly ambitious competition programme. He visualised this as both a means of improving the Company's production cars and as excellent publicity.

Initially the B20 Aurelia was entered by the works in a number of long-distance sports-car events, but soon a pure sports/racing coupé was evolved. This had exceedingly handsome fixed-head bodywork and used the Aurelia engine enlarged to 2,693 c.c., with a supercharger mounted in the vee formed by the cylinder arrangement and twin horizontal carburetters. Front suspension was by trailing links with a transverse leaf-spring and inboard mounted brakes.

At the rear, design closely followed Aurelia practice, with semi-trailing arms used in conjunction with jointed drive shafts, except that a leaf-spring replaced the helical coil-springs. The rear

A Lancia small car—Gianni Lancia's 48-b.h.p. Appia series 2 saloon.

The Formula One Lancia D50 as run at Barcelona in 1954.

The V8 2½-litre power unit of the Lancia G.P. car, said to develop 260 b.h.p. at 8,000 r.p.m.

A HISTORY OF THE LANCIA—continued from page 179

brakes were also mounted inboard and the gearbox was in unit with the final drive. After winning the 1953 Targa Florio (Maglioli) and finishing third in the Mille Miglia (Bonetto), a team of three cars were entered for Le Mans. Although at one stage Bonetto briefly held the lead, the whole team retired with various mechanical maladies.

By November of that year, the sports/racing car (now typed D24) had an unsupercharged engine of 3,300 c.c. estimated to develop 160 b.h.p., a de Dion rear axle and Spyder 2-seater bodywork by Pinin Farina—certainly one of the prettiest sports/racing cars ever conceived. A team of four, driven by Fangio, Taruffi, Castellotti and Bonetto, was taken to Mexico to compete in the Carrera Panamericana race. Serious opposition came only from a number of independent Ferraris, which were much faster than the Lancia. Surprisingly enough for an Italian team, the Lancia equipe was superbly organised and the D24 model won first three places, but Bonetto was tragically killed when, while leading the race, his car was in collision with a lamp column.

Early in 1954 it was announced that Lancia would be competing in Formula One events with a car designed by Vittorio Jano, now Lancia's Chief Engineer, and driven by Villoresi and Ascari. An earlier indication of Lancia's interest in this field of racing was revealed by the support given to the Lancia-Nardi Formula Two car. This used the 1,991-c.c. Aurelia GT engine, with four Weber carburetters, rear-mounted in a triangulated tubular chassis. Despite being tuned to give an output of some 130 b.h.p. the Lancia-Nardi was not a success and quietly faded from the scene.

Development of the Formula One Lancia was slow and the D50, as it was typed, did not appear until the Spanish Grand Prix, the last Grand Épreuve of the 1954 season. In the meanwhile the Company continued to race the D24 sports car with considerable success. After finishing second in the Sebring 12-Hours' Race (Valenzano/Rubirosa), victories were gained in the Mille Miglia (Ascari) and Targa Florio (Taruffi), as well as a number of less important events.

No entries were made at Le Mans on the grounds that a team could not be prepared in time. Unkind critics suggested that the real reason was a reluctance to meet up with the Jaguar D-type, hotly tipped as winner of the race. The lie was given to this suggestion when a team of four cars was entered for the 1954 Tourist Trophy. Two of these had engines enlarged to 3,750 c.c., a not very wise decision for a race run on a handicap basis, especially as Jaguar were running 2,482-c.c. versions of the D-type and David Brown refrained from entering the 4½-litre Lagonda. Just to confuse matters Lancia nominated all drivers as spare drivers to each other, but they took fourth and sixth places on handicap, with Taruffi/Fangio finishing second on scratch and Manzon/Castellotti third.

Whereas most constructors had adapted existing Formula Two cars to meet 1954 requirements, Mercedes-Benz and Lancia had the advantage of starting with clean drawing boards. Jano chose a t.o.h.c. 8-cylinder layout, with the sets of four cylinders at an angle of 90°; a bore and stroke of 73.6 × 73.1 mm. gave a capacity of 2,487 c.c. Estimated power output was 260 b.h.p. at 8,000 r.p.m. and dry weight was fractionally over 12 cwt.

In general, the D50 was much lighter, lower and shorter than its contemporaries, and it had, therefore, a superior power-to-weight ratio. Suspension was by double wishbones at the front and the de Dion system at the rear, in both cases using a transverse leaf-spring. The engine, which was mounted at an angle to permit the driver to be seated alongside the prop.-shaft and so reduce the frontal area, formed an integral stiffener to the light tubular frame. The 5-speed gearbox was in unit with the final drive and there were pannier fuel tanks mounted between the wheels.

For most of the 1954 season, Ascari and Villoresi were released to drive for Maserati and Ferrari, but in tests at Monza Ascari had lapped at 121.5 m.p.h., and, on paper at least, the Lancia was faster than the W196 Mercedes. At long last it was felt that the cars were ready to race and two were entered for the Spanish Grand Prix in October. Ascari made fastest time in practice and by the third lap was in the lead, but Villoresi had already retired with brake failure. A lap later Ascari made a pit stop, because of a slipping clutch, did another lap and then retired. A disappointing first appearance, but pre-race testing rarely reveals how a car will fare in the actual event.

Three cars were entered for the Argentine Grand Prix, but two were eliminated by crashes and the third retired with engine trouble. A very despondent Lancia team returned to Turin, without competing in the Buenos Aires City G.P. However, by March most of the problems had been sorted out and the team finished first, third and fourth in the Valentino G.P., defeating the works Ferrari and Maserati teams. The Lancia team followed this up by finishing second, fourth and fifth in the Pau G.P., after Ascari had led until a brake pipe broke; and Ascari had an easy win in the Naples Grand Prix.

The next race was the Monaco G.P., which became a four-cornered battle between the Mercedes of Moss and Fangio and the Lancias of Ascari and Castellotti. Both Mercedes retired, and as Moss slowed, Ascari shot into the Harbour *chicane* without realising that he was leading the race, a brake locked, and to the horror of spectators the Lancia slid into the Mediterranean in a cloud of steam. Both car and driver were safely recovered and Ascari was apparently little the worse for his dipping. The Lancias of Villoresi and Castellotti finished fourth and sixth.

A week later Ascari was dead, killed while trying out a Ferrari at the Monza Autodrome—his car had left the course for no apparent cause. Perhaps he was more shaken by the Monaco crash than he thought, perhaps an unsuspecting workman had crossed the track, perhaps it was because he was not wearing his lucky crash helmet—all these theories have been suggested as causes of the crash.

Lancia immediately withdrew from racing, shocked by the death of the 1955 World Champion, the pride of Italy. Castellotti was reluctantly permitted to run as a private entrant in the Belgian G.P. and held third place until a spin caused him to retire, but the Company never resumed racing. The expense of building and developing the competition cars had proved too much for the Company's resources. The final folly had been

The eye-catching Lancia office-block.

a 16-storey office block straddling the Via Vincenzo Lancia. Shortly afterwards the Company passed out of the family's control and a new management took over. The Lancia D50 racing cars were handed over to Scuderia Ferrari, who raced and modified them with Fiat finance, but that is another story....

The first indications of a change of policy by the new directors at Turin came with the introduction of the Flaminia as successor to the Aurelia saloon. This had appeared in prototype form at the 1955 Turin Show, where, in pillarless form and with a longer and lower line, it was exhibited by Farina as the "Florida" on the GT Aurelia chassis.

In production form the Flaminia had 6-light bodywork and forward hinged doors (the prototype was pillarless) and there were also a number of mechanical changes. Although the Aurelia GT engine was retained, the dimensions were revised to 80 × 81.5 mm. giving a capacity of 2,458 c.c. The traditional sliding pillar front suspension gave way to a system of coil and wishbones. In other respects the mechanical recipe was largely as before.

With a power output in its initial form of 100 b.h.p. at 4,800 r.p.m., the Flaminia could just exceed 100 m.p.h. and accelerate from zero to 60 m.p.h. in 15.5 sec. Since then power output has been raised to 110 b.h.p. and at the Frankfurt Show an enlarged 2.8-litre engine became available. Despite a price in its native country of some £1,650, the Flaminia was an immediate

A desirable combination—the Lancia Flaminia Sport with Zagato coupé bodywork.

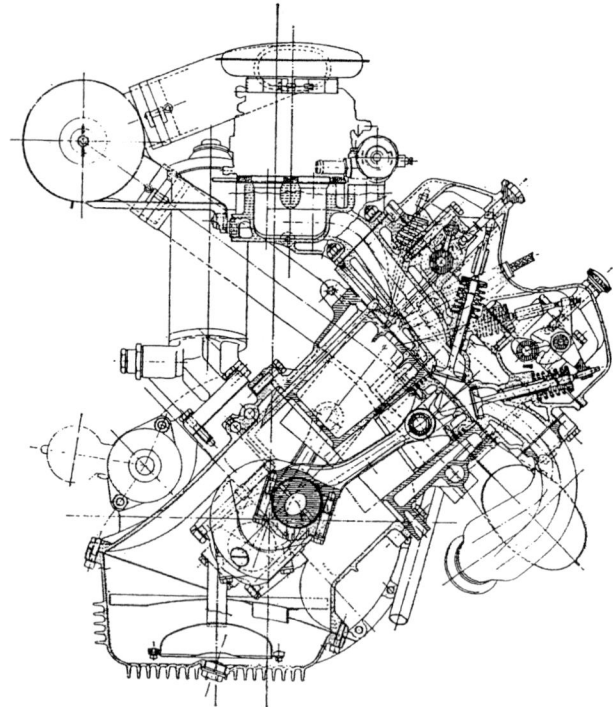

Reversion to the vee-four, and adoption of o.h.c. valve gear is apparent in the Fulvia engine.

success and by 1959 production figures had reached 100 a month.

Since 1960, shorter wheelbase versions with coupé coachwork by Farina and Zagato have been available. With triple Solex carburetters, 125 b.h.p. is developed at 5,600 r.p.m. and claimed maximum speed is 111 m.p.h. Competition experience with the very handsome Zagato coupé has led to the introduction of a much faster version with triple Weber carburetters, developing 140 b.h.p. at 5,800 r.p.m. and with a genuine top speed of 125 m.p.h. The tragedy is that such delectable machinery is beyond the means of the majority of British enthusiasts—it requires a true connoisseur to pay £3,388 when a car 50 m.p.h. faster is available for little more than half the price.

Late in 1960 the introduction of the Flavia made a complete break from traditional Lancia practice and the new model was completely new in every respect. The Flavia was the work of Professor Fessia, who had designed the front suspension of the Flaminia and that of the Fiat 600 and had been responsible for the pre-war Fiat 500.

The Flavia has a flat-4 horizontally-opposed 1,500-c.c. engine, mounted ahead of the front wheels and driving these *via* a 4-speed all-synchromesh gearbox. Independent front suspension is by double wishbones with a transverse leaf-spring and an anti-roll bar. At the rear there is a live axle with semi-elliptic leaf-spring and Dunlop disc brakes are fitted to all four wheels. Despite its conventionally low square lines and four headlamps, the Flavia contrives to look rather different from its rivals. With a top speed in excess of 90 m.p.h., performance is excellent for a 1½-litre car, but gearing is perhaps rather on the low side, and this is confirmed by a fuel consumption which rarely betters 25 m.p.g.

More pugnacious—a Flaminia Sport with Touring coupé body.

Sports versions of the Flavia with a 90-b.h.p. engine and either Farina coupé or Vignale convertible coachwork have since become available. In this form the model comfortably exceeds 100 m.p.h., and this performance is closely matched by the standard version with engine enlarged to 1.8-litres introduced at the Frankfurt Show. Like most Italian cars, the Flavia has been seen with a wide assortment of specialist coachwork and a number has been built for competition use with lightweight Zagato bodies.

The latest addition to the range is the Fulvia saloon, which, like the Flavia, has front-wheel drive, but uses a revised version of the Appia engine, with dimensions of 72 × 67 mm. and developing 60 b.h.p. at 5,800 r.p.m. This angular little car has only just come on to the British market, but the performance should be quite excellent.

Despite the ever-increasing car production, to cope with which a new factory has been recently opened at Chivasso, the Company markets a wide range of commercial vehicles. One of these is called the Beta, forming a last link with Lancia's practice of calling his models after letters of the Greek alphabet. More recently models have been given names of roads leading into Rome, which themselves are named after Roman Statesmen.

Professor Fessia's f.w.d. flat-four Lancia Flavia with Avanti-like Zagato body.

The present Lancia models are considerably different from the type of car built by Vincenzo Lancia, but, nevertheless, they are still beautifully finished, individual motor cars, soundly engineered, in many respects technically unorthodox.

SPECIFICATIONS OF LANCIA CARS

Model	Years Made	Bore (mm.)	Stroke (mm.)	c.c.	Vee Angle of Cylinders	Max. b.h.p.	r.p.m.	No. of Cyls.	Wheelbase	Weight (cwt.)	Standard Coach-work	Price	Notes
Alfa	1908-13	90	100	2,544	In line	Not available		4	9ft. 3in.	Not available	Various	Chassis £400 (1908)	Side-valve engine.
Di-Alfa	1908-13	90	100	3,816	In line	Not available		6	10ft. 8in.	Not available	Various	Chassis £560 (1908)	Side-valve engine.
Theta	1913-18	110	130	4,951	In line	70	2,200	4	11ft. 0in.	*25½	Various	Chassis £750 (1918)	Side-valve engine.
Kappa	1919-22	110	130	4,951	In line	Not available		4	11ft. 1½in.	*25½	Various	Chassis £1,175 (1919)	Side-valve engine.
Di-Kappa	1921-22	110	130	4,951	In line	Not available		4	11ft. 1½in.	*25½	Various	Chassis £1,050 (1922)	Side-valve engine.
Tri-Kappa	1922-25	75	130	4,592	22°	98	2,500	8	11ft. 1½in.	*25½	Various	Chassis £1,150 (1923)	
Lambda 1st-6th Ser.	1923-25	75	120	2,120	13°	49	3,250	4	10ft. 2in.	25	2-str. sports, 4-str. 4-door tourer or with detachable saloon top	From £625 (1926)	6th Ser. also available with 11ft. 2½in. wheelbase, straight tubular connecting rods.
Lambda 7th Ser.	1926-27	79.37	120	2,370	14°	59.4	3,250	4	10ft. 2in. 11ft. 2½in.	27			Offset connecting rods.
Lambda 8th-9th Ser.	1928-32	82.55	120	2,570	13° 40′	69	3,500	4	10ft. 2in. 11ft. 2½in.	27			I-section connecting rods.
Di-Lambda	1928-33	79.37	100	3,960	24°	100	3,800	8	11ft. 5in.	*23½	Various	From £1,175	Available to special order until 1937.
Astura 1st-2nd Ser.	1931-33	69.85	85	2,604	19°	73	4,000	8	10ft. 5in. 11ft. 4¾in.	*19 19¾	Various but usually 4-dr. sal. or d.h.c.	Chassis £625 (1933)	
Astura 3rd-4th Ser.	1933-39	74.61	85	2,972	17° 30′	82	4,000	8	11ft. 4¾in.	*20¾			
Artena	1931-33	82.55	90	1,925	17°	55	4,000	4	9ft. 8in. 10ft. 3½in.	*17 17½	Various, but usually 4-dr. saloon	Chassis £445 (1933)	
Augusta	1933-36	69.85	78	1,196	18° 15′	35	4,000	4	8ft. 8¼in.	16¼	4-dr. 4-str. saloon	£390 (1933)	
Aprilia 1st Ser.	1937-38	72	83	1,352	18° 6′ 40″	47.8	4,300	4	9ft. 0½in.	16¾	4-dr. 4-str. saloon	£298 (1937)	—
Aprilia 2nd Ser.	1939-50	74.61	85	1,486	17° 40′	48	4,300	4	9ft. 0½in.	17¾			Recognisable by pierced wheels.
Ardea	1939-50	65	68	903	19° 54′	29.2	4,300	4	7ft. 10½in.	16¾	4-dr. 4-str. saloon	Not available in U.K.	
Aurelia B10	1950-54	70	76	1,754	60°	56	4,000	6	9ft. 4½in.	22	4-dr. 4-str. saloon	Not available in U.K.	
Aurelia B21	1951-54	72	81.5	1,991	60°	70	4,500	6					
Aurelia B22	1952-54	72	81.5	1,991	60°	90	5,000	6					
Aurelia B12 2nd Ser.	1954-57	75	85.5	2,266	60°	86.5	4,300	6	9ft. 4½in.	23⅝	4-dr. 4-str. saloon	£2,862 (1955)	
Aurelia B20 GT 1st Ser.	1951-52	72	81.5	1,991	60°	75	5,000	6	8ft. 8⅜in.	22¾	2-dr. 2/4-str. f.h.c.	Not available in U.K.	
Aurelia B20 GT 2nd Ser.	1952-53	72	81.5	1,991	60°	80	5,000	6	8ft. 8⅜in.	22¾			
Aurelia B20 GT 3rd-6th Ser.	1953-59	78	85.5	2,451	60°	118	5,300	6	8ft. 8⅜in.	25	2-dr. 2/4-str. f.h.c.	£3,346 (1957)	Also available as B24 Spyder.
Appia 1st Ser.	1953-56	68	75	1,091	10° 14′	38	4,800	4	8ft. 1½in.	16	4-dr. 4-str. saloon	Not available in U.K.	
Appia 2nd-3rd Ser.	1956-63	68	75	1,091	10° 14′	48	5,200	4	8ft. 3in.	18	4-dr. 4-str. saloon	£1,588 (1961)	Also available as Farina coupé with Sport engine.
Appia Sport	1959-63	68	75	1,091	10° 14′	60	5,400	4	7ft. 8½in.	16	f.h.c. by Zagato	Not quoted	
Flaminia	Introd. '56	80	81.5	2,458	60°	110	5,200	6	9ft. 5in.	32	4-dr. 5-str. saloon	£2,847 (1963)	Original output 100 b.h.p. at 4,800 r.p.m.
	Introd. '63	85	81.5	2,775	60°	129	5,000	6				£2,945 (1963)	
Flaminia Sport 3B	Introd. '63	85	81.5	2,775	60°	140	5,400	6	9ft. 1in.	These details vary according to the body fitted, which may be by Farina, Touring or Zagato			Previous versions had 2,458-c.c. engines.
" " 3C						150	5,400	6					
Flavia	Introd. '60	82	71	1,500	Flat 4	78	5,200	4	8ft. 8¼in.	23¼	4-dr. saloon	£1,760 (1963)	
	Introd. '63	88	74	1,800	Flat 4	92	5,200	4				£2,075 (1963)	
Flavia Sport	Introd. '61	82	71	1,500	Flat 4	90	5,800	4	8ft. 1½in.	These details vary according to coachwork fitted, which may be by Farina, Vignale or Zagato.			
Fulvia	Introd. '63	72	67	1,091	10° 14′	60	5,800	4	8ft. 1½in.	19½	4-dr. 4-str. saloon	£1,389 (1963)	

* *Chassis only*

A crisp, neat appearance is in keeping with the character of the Flaminia. The rear bulwarks (for they are hardly fins) are very helpful for siting when reversing into a confined space

ITALIANS will tell you that the Flaminia is now their finest car; they omit more expensive Maseratis and Ferraris from the considerations because these they regard as competition models. The Flaminia is indeed a fine car technically, and in performance and appearance. Recently three new variants were announced, but the four-door saloon with body designed by Pinin Farina, which is the subject of this test, continues in full production. Flaminias are being made entirely in the Lancia factory at Turin at the rate of about 100 a month.

Only in special circumstances does *The Autocar* agree to test cars wholly abroad. The Flaminia is unlikely to be available in right-hand-drive form for some months to come; a L.H.D. example was, therefore, accepted in Italy, and tested over many kinds of roads, including *autostrade* and mountain passes. Right-hand-drive will be offered first on the new two-door short chassis Flaminias which have a floor gear lever.

A reminder of the unusual mechanical design of the Flaminia may be helpful. The engine is a 2½-litre, 60 deg vee-6 with push-rod operated valves and a Solex 2-choke downdraught carburettor. At 7.8 to 1 the compression ratio is relatively low; during the test no pinking was heard, although Continental premium petrol is usually of lower grade than that in the U.K. The engine differs in several respects—including the bore and stroke—from that of the Aurelia G.T.; in particular, it produces higher maximum torque at lower r.p.m. (141 lb ft at 3,000 r.p.m. compared with 126.5 lb ft at 3,500 r.p.m.).

In respect of front suspension the Flaminia breaks tradition by having wishbones in place of the sliding pillars of earlier models. Its directional stability at high speed benefits when compared with that of the Aurelia, for example.

At the rear, a de Dion axle supported on leaf springs is used, and in unit with the hypoid rear transmission are the gear box and clutch and two inboard drum brakes. Lancia refer to this as the propelling unit. Heavy mechanical components are thus divided evenly between the two ends of the car, and the transmission is sprung weight. This is, no doubt, responsible in part for the car's good traction and tenacity to the road. It is seldom possible to hear the transmission of the Flaminia.

This car was fitted with Michelin X tyres at 26 lb sq in front and 28 back—raised by 2lb all round above normal for the performance testing. The familiar characteristics were observed—outstanding tyre adhesion in all conditions, minimum of squeal, and thumping over serrations or studs in the road. Steering is commendably light, even at low speeds.

Without difficulty the Flaminia accommodates six people,

A modern, two-dial instrument layout is viewed through the wheel. The lower edge of the panel is padded and leather trimmed. Fitted rubber mats are used in the front only

for it is a big car, 15ft 11in long and weighing almost 32 cwt unladen. Its plain, artistic exterior makes it appear smaller but, when sitting inside, the driver gains a spacious as well as a bright impression of the car.

All but the very large will find a comfortable driving position by adjusting the seat on its rails and the seatback for angle. If there is a criticism, it would be that even with the seat fully back, the knees of a tall driver find hardly enough room under the steering-wheel rim when the feet are on the pedals. This is a little surprising because the wheel itself is set quite high and, in fact, the top of the rim would come into the field of vision of a short driver. For those who adopt the long arm position at the wheel the front seat needs to be on its back stop, in which setting the knee-room for rear seat passengers is marginal for comfort. The steering column is not adjustable for length.

We do not recall any car with a more pleasing column-mounted gear lever. If all could be as well engineered there would be less criticism of this position of lever on the majority of cars. It is more surprising on the Flaminia because the linkage has to be extended back to the gear box at the rear. Synchromesh is provided for the four forward speeds, the lever movements through the gate—with light spring loading down-column—are very short, and changes can be made as quickly and positively as with floor-mounted lever. The synchromesh proved to be unbeatable, even during extreme handling while obtaining acceleration figures.

First experience of the car was on the *autostrada* where its stability and ride-comfort quickly became apparent. It cruised effortlessly up to 90 m.p.h., reaching this speed quickly. On the rougher patches of road there was the minimum of pitching, and no road shocks were transmitted

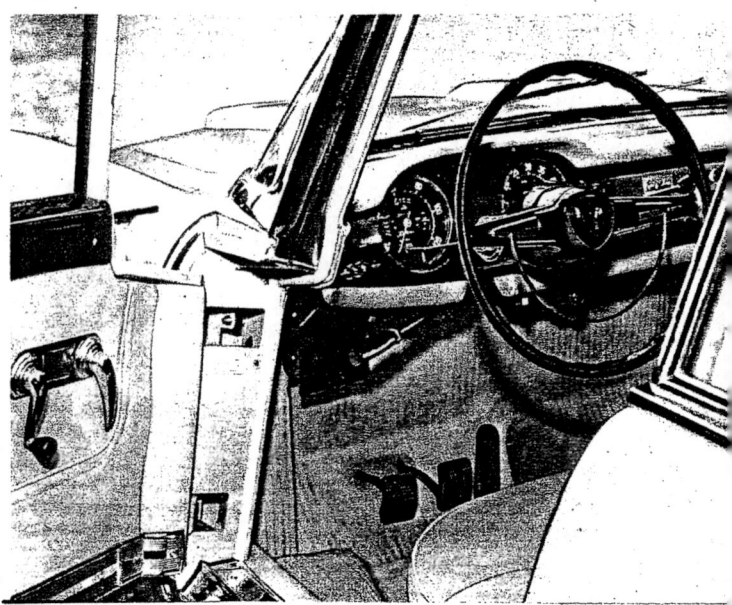

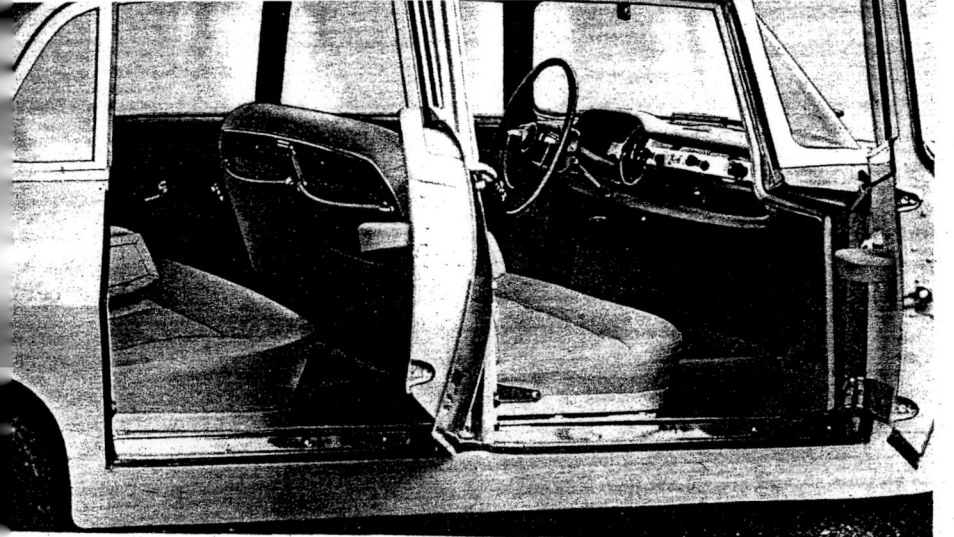

Lancia Flaminia

Wide doors with a reasonably high roofline give convenient access to front and rear seats. The rear quarter vents are vacuum operated

through the steering wheel. The silence and smoothness of the engine are apt to mislead as to the speed, so that the rapid rate of closing with other vehicles comes as a surprise at first. It would be an improvement if the engine cooling fan could be silenced; the whirring undertone it produces above 3,000 r.p.m. engine speed is the only disturbing sound when cruising at speed with windows closed.

When the car was driven fast through winding mountain roads, other qualities became apparent. Cornering is virtually roll-free, and the steering remains light right up to full lock. On cambered and rough-edged roads the car is unusually pleasant to control, because there is complete absence of free movement or spring in the steering linkage, and thus positive corrections can be made however small they may be. There is quite strong self-centring action, and this was welcome when taking successions of sharp or hairpin bends. In these conditions the light steering is appreciated, although a little less wheel-winding would be an advantage—there are 4½ turns from lock to lock. The lock itself is very good in both directions.

Conventional live axles are seen at their worst in climbing mountain passes; almost invariably wheel spin and some axle hop develops as a car so equipped pulls away from the steep part of a hairpin bend. The Flaminia's de Dion "rear end" apparently scores here; the wheels grip firmly and the car will come smoothly out of the corner at full power.

Because it is customary to comment on under- or oversteer characteristics, it is often assumed that all cars have one or the other. The Flaminia is neutral, exhibiting neither characteristic to a noticeable degree. It gives a better conception of its entirely orthodox handling to state that if the car is pulled round a corner excessively fast and with power on, the back end will slide first. Additionally, as with almost all cars, a corner is completed more satisfactorily with the engine pulling. Important, too, is the ability in an emergency to brake quite hard during cornering without throwing the car off its line.

Some kinds of regular cobbles cause rumbling in the car, but badly laid sets and potholes are taken very well indeed, whether slowly or quickly. Driven fast over surface irregularities of the rolling type, the car bottomed on the rear springs on two or three occasions, when carrying two passengers and luggage.

The precise nature of the gear change, already mentioned, is also an advantage both in the mountains and in traffic. The Flaminia has a 3.91 to 1 top gear, giving 21 m.p.h. per 1,000 r.p.m. It runs smoothly without snatching down to 18 m.p.h. in top, but a change down at about 25 m.p.h. is advisable, for there is practically no pull in top below that speed. Third gear ratio is 5.9 to 1, and the gap seems considerable; this ratio looks after most traffic requirements.

Drivers who use the full performance of the car would probably prefer a rather higher third and more than 68 m.p.h. at peak revs (5,200) in this gear. Both second and third gears are needed frequently for pick-up when driving fast. The engine is very free-revving, and it is easy to exceed the 5,200 limit in the intermediate gears. There is no additional noise, fuss or vibration to warn that 5,200 or even 5,500 has been reached.

If we may judge from this and previous Lancias tested, it seems that the makers favour a very gentle clutch. When attempting a rapid get-away from standstill, either clutch-slip or low initial engine speed must be accepted; acceleration figures are not appreciably affected either way. The car moves off quickly, and for all ordinary purposes the clutch is precise, light and smooth.

When the engine was hot there was a tendency to stall while idling in traffic. This responded to adjustment in part but not entirely. On the car tested, also, there was a moment of hesitation when the accelerator was depressed which made it difficult to obtain an entirely smooth pick-up from crawling speed or after a gear change. This could have been caused by need for a carburettor adjustment, by pedal linkage fault, or a combination of the two. The car was taken from ordinary works transport at the factory in Turin and had no special preparation for the test. It had already done 16,700 miles.

But for the advent of servo-assisted disc brakes, the Flaminia's four large drum brakes would have been described as very good; as it is, "entirely adequate" is a fair term. They pull the car up firmly with moderately heavy pedal pressure, and at no time did they fade. From high speed, braking produced some slight rumbling—felt through the pedal rather than heard. No definite attempt was made to fade them, and the weather during the test was mostly cool and wet, but it was noted that there was no deterioration after repeated applications down hill. Brake pedal travel increased in the course of the test, and towards the end it was sometimes necessary to pump the pedal once or twice to obtain normal pedal feel and travel. The hand

Left: A 60 deg vee-6 engine can be kept very short—note the space and accessibility. The battery cover is seen low down in front of the radiator. Below: The boot is large and neatly trimmed; its load line is low and wide. An exceptionally good toolkit is provided. Styled-in bumpers, though neat, are more easily damaged and transfer damage

brake is operated by a sturdy transverse lever under the dash; as adjusted on the test car it was not very powerful.

For owners who have to watch fuel consumption, a figure of about 22 m.p.g. for ordinary driving would be representative; on long runs perhaps 24 m.p.g. might be achieved. Hard driving brings this down to about 19 m.p.g. The overall consumption figure for the test of 1,380 miles was 20.8 m.p.g.

Many pages could be written about the equipment of the Flaminia and about its ingenious fittings. The doors are large and of heavy construction; they shut, fit and seal very well. It is easy to enter any of them, and the deep windows and screen provide a good view for all.

Light grey cloth upholstery is used in the test car, and this effectively prevents slipping. Folding centre arm rests provide for two or three abreast seating, both front and rear seats being of bench type.

Roof trim is in light plastic material, and the doors are cloth-covered, with bright metal and black enamel mouldings. Leather is used for the coaming over the instrument panel, for the spongy visors and the outer arm rests in front (which also serve as door pulls). Leather is applied also as piping for the seats and the edges of the door pulls, and to cover the padded lower edge of the instrument panel.

Pale grey moulded and fitted rubber matting is fitted over the floor in front, neat and practical, but not to everyone's taste in a luxurious car. The rear passengers are provided with pile carpeting.

The instrument panel is of high gloss black enamel with a bright metal band across it; there were no irritating reflections in the screen at night. A radio is neatly styled into its centre. The driver's instruments are grouped in front of him and are easily seen through the wheel (which has only two horizontal spokes and a lower half horn ring). A small locker with key is provided in front of the passenger.

Lighting and other controls take the form of unlabelled, similar black knobs below and beside the radio. Some twist, others pull or even pull, twist and pull again. They look neat enough, but can be confusing for quick use.

Incorporated in the screen wiper knob is a press button for the washer. The button automatically starts both the blades and the spray, and stops them again. If the spray button is used when the wipers are already twist-switched on, it stops the blades after spraying the screen. Although the windscreen is well wrapped round, most of the area in front of the driver is wiped by offsetting the blade pivots to the driving side.

Four more buttons, three to the left and one to the right of the steering column, respectively apply manifold vacuum to open the rear extractor quarter-lights separately, close them both together, and operate the electric rear window wipers, of which there are two inside and two outside in pairs. The rear window occupies the full width of the body and is flat, but the small anti-dazzle rear view mirror does not take full advantage of it to give an adequate rear view. There is a shelf behind the rear seats, and a second radio speaker is mounted there. Two interior lights are provided, one on each side, and these have courtesy switches on the doors as well as an overriding switch on the panel. There is a cigar lighter, and ashtrays are fitted at front and rear.

A very neat lamp arrangement has been devised; two head and two large side lamps are built in. A dipper lever is mounted on the left of the steering column, which also allows semaphore use when moved up or down, but only when the side lamps are switched on. This lever, moved at right angles, operates self-cancelling turn indicators. In practice this is not entirely satisfactory, because it can result in one or other function occurring inadvertently. The side lights also contain the signalling blinkers and yellow fog bulbs, all of which work independently. The white blinkers show clearly through the yellow fog lights. Small additional amber signalling repeaters are mounted on the sides of the body.

Frontal appearance typical of Farina's current production designs. The bonnet is hinged in front. The subsidiary lamps each include side, fog and indicator bulbs

There can be few cars with a more effective hot and cold air system. Over 30 m.p.h., ram effect gives an increasing blast of air—cold or hot according to the position of a central under-panel water tap. Two pairs of additional levers control the delivery of the air to the front occupants' feet or to the four screen slits, or to both. The inner screen slits have hinged deflectors which enable the air to be delivered up and over the screen or, by turning them over, back to the passengers. With this arrangement the screen can be demisted and, we should imagine, defrosted in seconds—or the passengers roasted. In slow traffic, a silent booster fan can replace the ram air flow. The heater control levers are all out of sight and must be felt for beneath the panel, which is perhaps not the simplest arrangement. No attempt has been made to cover in their cables nor, in fact, any of the other wires and leads under the panel.

A very large boot is somewhat obstructed by the vertically mounted spare wheel, but few people would need more accommodation. An above-average tool kit is provided, but there is no starting handle or provision to use one. The fuel tank holds only 12½ gallons, including 1¾ gallons in reserve, and thus gives a safe cruising range of no more than 230 miles. The reserve tap is on the floor in the front of the car; no reserve warning light is provided. There is a warning light to show that the choke lever is in cold starting position.

The exterior door handles, of the type with grip and separate thumb button, are neat and comfortable to use. Instead of the sharp edges on the inside of the grips which are found too often on cars these days, the Flaminia has a comfortable inlaid rubber pad. The driver's door carries the lock with key.

Under the front hinged bonnet (released by a two-stage catch beneath the facia) the short, compact engine, dominated by a quickly detachable, circular air filter, looks small, and the radiator block, with its thermostatically controlled shutters, sticks up like a tombstone in the spacious engine compartment. Easily reached ahead of the radiator

A slab-sided appearance is subtly and neatly avoided by shaping, and without recourse to strips or decoration. Twin wipers are fitted for the rear window. The wheel trims look attractive but are easily dented and make it difficult to apply airline or gauge

14

block and mounted, transversely, low down in the cold air stream is the 12-volt battery. There are two under-bonnet lights and alternative oil filters, one on each rocker cover, each with a breather pipe feeding into the air filter. The dip stick is easy to reach but, going in or out, it rubs No. 2 cylinder plug lead, to the detriment of the insulation. Everything beneath the bonnet is clean and accessible, and has an air of quality about it.

At present eight standard colour schemes are available, four being duotone and one metallic. Practically all the equipment is standard. Extra items involving additional cost are radio, leather upholstery, separate front seats and Saxomat two-pedal control.

The Flaminia saloon is a select model of international importance and appeal costing the equivalent of £1,650 in its native country. It combines in one car many of the requirements and desires of discerning motorists; accommodation for the whole family together with adequate luggage space within moderate exterior dimensions, the lively performance and impeccable handling for which Lancias are traditionally noted, tasteful Farina styling and a modest fuel demand.

LANCIA FLAMINIA

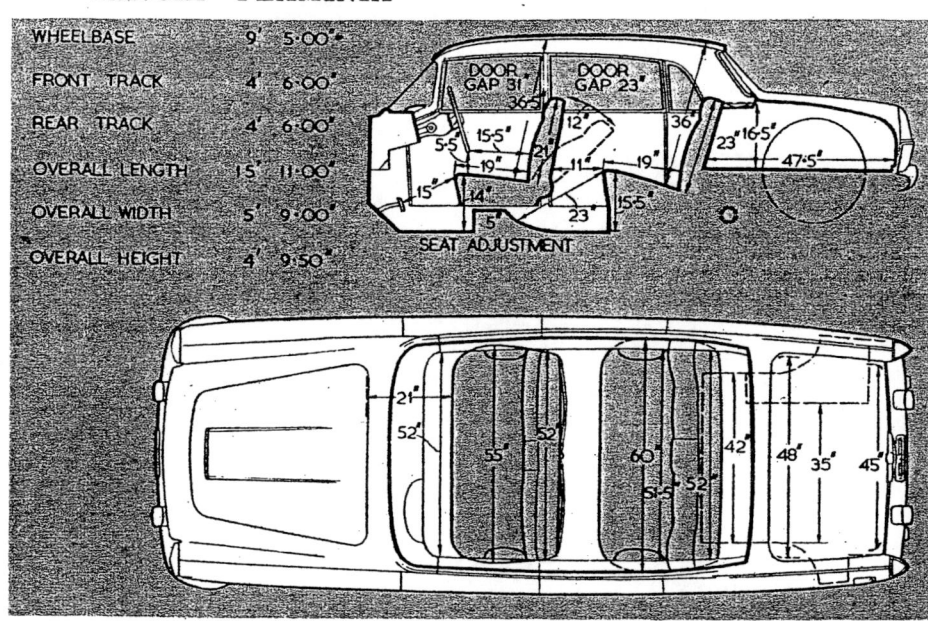

Scale ⅛in to 1ft. Driving seat in central position. Cushions uncompressed.

PERFORMANCE

ACCELERATION:
Speed Range, Gear Ratios and Time in sec.

M.P.H.	3.91 to 1	5.91 to 1	8.60 to 1	12.94 to 1
10—30	—	7.3	5.0	4.0
20—40	11.3	7.0	4.8	—
30—50	10.8	6.9	—	—
40—60	11.3	7.7	—	—
50—70	11.6	—	—	—
60—80	13.9	—	—	—
70—90	19.7	—	—	—

From rest through gears to:

M.P.H.	sec.
30	5.0
40	7.9
50	11.3
60	15.6
70	22.1
80	31.0
90	43.3

Standing quarter mile, 20.2 sec.

MAXIMUM SPEEDS ON GEARS:

Gear		M.P.H.	K.P.H.
Top	(mean)	102.3	164.6
	(best)	103	165.8
3rd	At 5,200 r.p.m.,	68	109.4
2nd	recommended	46	74.0
1st	limit	31	50.0

TRACTIVE EFFORT:

	Pull (lb per ton)	Equivalent Gradient
Top	207	1 in 10.8
Third	315	1 in 7.0
Second	467	1 in 4.7

SPEEDOMETER CORRECTION: M.P.H.

Car speedometer:	20	30	40	50	60	70	80	90	100
True speed:	19	28	38	48	57	67	77	87	97

BRAKES (at 30 m.p.h. in neutral):

Pedal load in lb	Retardation	Equivalent stopping distance in ft
25	0.09g	340
50	0.32g	94
75	0.63g	48
100	0.92g	33

FUEL CONSUMPTION:
M.P.G. at steady speeds

M.P.H.	Direct Top
30	38.2
40	35.5
50	32.6
60	29.6
70	26.4
80	22.2
90	19.1

Overall fuel consumption for 1,376 miles, 20.8 m.p.g. (13.6 litres per 100 km).

Approximate normal range, 19-24 m.p.g. (14.9-11.8 litres per 100 km).

TEST CONDITIONS: Weather: overcast, damp tarmacadam road surface, slight breeze. Air temperature, 62 deg. F.

Acceleration figures are the mean of several runs in opposite directions.

Tractive effort obtained by Tapley meter.

Model described in *The Autocar* of 27 April, 1956.

DATA

PRICE (basic), including heater, with saloon body, £2,500 0s 0d. British purchase tax, £1,215 7s.
Total (in Great Britain), £3,715 7s.

ENGINE: Capacity: 2,458 c.c. (150 cu in).
Number of cylinders: 6 in 60 deg. vee formation.
Bore and stroke: 80 × 81.5 mm (3.15 × 3.21 in).
Valve gear: o.h.v., pushrods and rockers, hemispherical chambers.
Compression ratio: 7.8 to 1.
B.H.P. 112 (gross), 100 (nett) at 4,800 r.p.m. (B.H.P. (nett) per ton laden 56.8).
Torque: 141 lb ft at 3,000 r.p.m.
M.P.H. per 1,000 r.p.m. in top gear, 21.

WEIGHT: (with 5 gals fuel), 32.1 cwt (3,610 lb).
Weight distribution (per cent): F, 48.7; R, 51.3.
Laden as tested: 35.1 cwt (3,946 lb).
Lb per c.c. (laden): 1.51.

BRAKES: Type: SABIF hydraulic.
Drum dimensions: F, 11.81in diameter; 2.75in wide. R, 11.0in diameter; 2.75in wide.
Lining area: 236 sq in (134 sq in per ton laden).

TYRES: 165-400mm Michelin X.
Pressures (lb sq in): F, 26; R, 28 (normal). F, 28; R, 30 (fast driving).

TANK CAPACITY: 12.5 Imperial gallons (includes 1.75 reserve).
Oil sump, 11 pints.
Cooling system, 18 pints (including heater).

STEERING: Turning circle:
Between kerbs, 38ft 4in L. 41ft 4in R.
Between walls, 39ft 7in L. 42ft 7in R.
Turns of steering wheel from lock to lock, 4¼.

DIMENSIONS: Wheelbase: 9ft 5in (287cm).
Track: F, and R, 4ft 6in (137cm).
Length (overall): 15ft 11in (485cm).
Width: 5ft 9in (175cm).
Height (unladen): 4ft 9.5in (146cm).
Ground clearance: 5.5in (14cm).

ELECTRICAL SYSTEM: 12-volt; 42 ampère-hour battery.
Head lights: Double dip; 45-40 watt bulbs.

SUSPENSION: Front, independent, wishbones, coil springs and Sabif telescopic dampers. Anti-roll bar.
Rear, de Dion-type axle, half-elliptic leaf springs, Sabif telescopic dampers. Panhard rod.

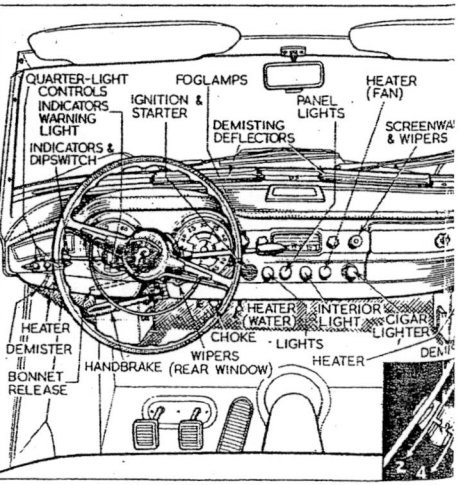

IN December of 1958 *The Autocar* published a road test of the Lancia Flaminia standard four-door saloon with left-hand drive, which was driven in Italy because none was then available in this country. Today one model in the Flaminia range is made with right-hand drive—the series production coupé by Pininfarina on the intermediate length chassis (9ft 0·7in. wheelbase). One of these was submitted for test by Lancia (England), Ltd. To put this type into proper perspective in relation to the rest of the Flaminia family, it seems appropriate to outline briefly its sister cars. In addition to the standard saloon on a 9ft 5in. base, there are three short-wheelbase (8ft 3·2in.) two-seater Flaminias in series production by specialist coachbuilders —the G.T. coupé and convertible by Touring, and the Zagato Sport coupé.

All models other than the standard saloon are powered by the G.T. engine, which develops 119 b.h.p. at 5,100 r.p.m., as compared with just over 100 at 4,800. Compression ratio of the G.T. engine is 9·0 to 1, whereas the standard ratio is 7·9 to 1. In view of its rather formidable kerb weight (29·2 cwt, including 5 gallons of fuel), the Pininfarina car has the same transmission gearing as the standard saloon, whereas the lighter Touring and Zagato cars are higher geared overall, and have closer ratio gearboxes.

Since the unconventional (by touring car standards) design and layout of the Lancia give a powerful clue to its magnificent behaviour on the road, a few basic technicalities are worth noting by anyone unfamiliar with them. It has a lightweight 2·5-litre pushrod o.h.v. engine with six cylinders arranged in a 60deg vee; a divided propeller shaft takes the drive right back to a chassis-mounted transmission unit comprising clutch, four-speed fully synchronized gearbox, and hypoid bevel final drive with exposed half-shafts to the rear wheels. These are joined by a de Dion tube carried on half-elliptic springs, and unsprung weight is kept low by placing the Dunlop disc brakes inboard, adjacent to the final drive casing. Front suspension is conventional, by coil springs and wishbones of unequal lengths. By these means weight is distributed unusually evenly over the car's four wheels, with the slightly greater proportion over the rear, and very high standards of mechanical engineering support the Lancia design team.

Sitting at the wheel of the Flaminia for the first time, the driver needs to be briefed concerning the minor controls, since none has visual means of identification; they are quite quickly learned, but this lack of marking would at least hinder a thief. For cold starts there is a rich mixture lever, hidden beneath the middle of the facia; a red lamp in the instrument panel remains lit while this is in operation. To start the engine, the ignition key is turned clockwise, then pressed in to energize the starter motor.

Weather during the test period was mostly mild, but some mixture enrichment was needed for a mile or two after a cold start. Effective carburation of the test car's engine at low crankshaft speeds was not a strong point, whatever the engine temperature—this being governed, incidentally, by thermostatically controlled shutters on the radiator. The pick-up was sluggish and often hesitant up to about 2,500 r.p.m., and sometimes there would be a complete lack of response when the throttle was opened at 1,000-1,500 r.p.m.

These comments are emphasized by a direct comparison with acceleration figures for the standard saloon, of which the engine has a wider useful torque range, and develops its greatest power at a lower crankshaft speed. The coupé cannot match the saloon's top gear acceleration to about 75 m.p.h., but thereafter shows an appreciable improvement up to a maximum some 3 m.p.h. higher. When accelerating through the gears from a standstill, however, the coupé can out-perform the saloon by virtue of the higher speeds obtainable in the indirects, the recommended peak of the G.T. engine being 5,600 r.p.m. This can be reached in all forward gears, including top, and in the indirects a watchful eye must be kept on the rev counter to avoid over-speeding, since there are no indications from under the bonnet that the engine has approached valve bounce or is falling appreciably from peak power.

Throughout its range the engine runs smoothly, although

Deep and fully trimmed, the roomy luggage locker carries the spare wheel vertically in a well. The lid is spring-loaded, and self-supporting

Lancia Flaminia Coupé . . .

Amber flashing signals behind each front wheel arch supplement those at front and rear. Bumpers and rubbing strips at wheel-centre height give all round protection for the body panels. Rather vulnerable against high kerbs are the bright metal rings fitted to the wheel rims

strictly controlled during very fast cornering indeed. For these reasons it is an unusually restful vehicle over long journeys for driver and passengers, and practically no road noise is transmitted through the body structure.

Taken at increasing speeds over a specially laid section of concrete corrugations, the Lancia passed through the inevitable vibration periods and settled down to 60 m.p.h. and over with equanimity; an incidental fault below this speed was that the gear lever developed such violent fore-and-aft vibration as to overcome the selector springs and throw it into neutral—a point which the makers would need to rectify before marketing these cars in countries where washboard roads abound. The car was equally impressive over a section of Belgian pavé, over which it ran on a mostly level keel and with practically no float at over 50 m.p.h.

Dividends of the clever weight distribution are paid off handsomely through the steering gear; yet the front wheels still have to bear nearly 14½cwt, so that there must be supplementary reasons for the remarkably light control. Indeed, the Lancia provides an object lesson to those who now consider power assistance necessary or desirable for cars of this weight. On the move it requires remarkably little effort, and even at parking speeds is as easy to manoeuvre as other cars weighing half a ton less.

When Lancia replaced the old sliding pillar suspension by coils and wishbones, they had to accept much wider turning circles, this car taking over 40ft between walls. Full lock to full lock requires 4¼ turns of the steering wheel; although the gearing is thus fairly low, surprisingly little movement of the wheel is called for when motoring fast along twisting roads. So precise and easy is control then that steering the Flaminia becomes almost instinctive, entailing practically no conscious mental or physical effort, so that one's attention may be focussed almost wholly on the other duties of a fast motorist. There is plenty of feel with little or no kick-back through the wheel, and the right degree of self-centring action.

After stepping out of more humdrum cars, it takes some courage to drive this one faster and faster round curves in search of the limit, for its cornering abilities are outstanding; ultimately the tail slides first, but not without warning, and the Lancia's quick responses to control make recovery straightforward.

there are vibration tremors at 75-80 m.p.h. originating, perhaps, from the propeller shaft of which the centre bearing is carried in an extremely flexible rubber mounting.

Up to 90 m.p.h. the car cruises very easily and happily, but above this rate increasing mechanical fuss and wind roar discourage one from maintaining speeds nearer the maximum. The exhaust note remains agreeably restrained throughout, in keeping with the car's sporting—rather than sports—character.

It will be seen in the performance data that the fuel consumption rate falls only just below 20 m.p.g. when a constant 90 m.p.h. is maintained, and that better than 24 m.p.g. was recorded at 70 m.p.h. On an 80-mile run over give-and-take roads, during which 60 m.p.h. was not exceeded, a figure of 27.2 m.p.g. resulted. Thus the makers' claim of 21 m.p.g. as a representative figure seems well justified. As for oil, exactly a quart was required to top up the sump after over 1,000 miles of rigorous test-driving.

Having made the point that the Flaminia coupé is more than usually dependent on its gearbox, even when one is in no particular hurry, this can now be praised very highly for the ease and precision of the changes, the complete freedom from any sounds of gear engagement, however quickly the lever is moved, and the quiet running of all gears. The final drive could be heard faintly in the overrun. While the indirect ratios may be ideally suited to road conditions in the car's native Italy, sporting drivers in this country might prefer higher gearing for second and third. In first, about 1-in-4 is the steepest gradient on which a start can be made from rest with two up, a process made rather tricky by the fact that the parking brake, as on most disc-braked cars, cannot hold the car on such a slope.

Where this Lancia scores over almost all its rivals, at any price, is in its wonderful combination of the essentials to safe and enjoyable road travel—springing and road-holding, steering and brakes. Even by today's generally high standards it represents a pinnacle of development in suspension, the more remarkable when one considers the orthodox basic components.

Although firm enough to avoid any suggestion of sloppiness, the Flaminia gives a supremely stable and comfortable ride on average road surfaces, free from pitch and with roll

Disc Brakes

To state that a car is fitted with Dunlop disc brakes is sufficient to reassure drivers who have experienced these; for the Lancia installation they are power-assisted by a Lockheed vacuum servo, and there are separate hydraulic systems for front and rear sets—hence the possibility of total failure is so unlikely as to be disregarded. During our tests the car would stop repeatedly from 30 m.p.h. on a dry surface in just over 30ft without wheel locking; it will be noted, incidentally, that moderately high pedal pressures are required at this speed, whereas from 50 m.p.h. a 0.90g stop (equivalent to about 33½ft from 30 m.p.h.) could be achieved with only 70lb pressure. This is quite normal behaviour for a disc brakes system, which achieves its peak efficiency from higher speeds. When braking hard on a wet, straight road the front wheels would occasionally lock up unexpectedly easily, so that some care had to be taken. One wonders, therefore, whether the rear brakes might be made to do a little more work in proportion, although it is noteworthy that already they have the larger swept area.

Opinions of the test staff were divided concerning the driving position, several finding the steering wheel set a little too high and intruding in their line of sight. Some would have preferred brake and clutch pedals to be set an inch or so higher in relation to the floor. These pedals are pivoted below their pads, and follow a more natural arc of movement than do most pendant arrangements. The organ-type throttle pedal is so placed that heel-and-toe downward changes while braking are possible. One appreciates the spacious floor area, obstructed only by a slender tunnel covering the propeller shaft.

Left. Squabs of the front seats are recessed to allow extra space for rear-seat passengers' knees, and contain large pockets. The back floor is trimmed with carpet, the front with moulded rubber. Right. Large windows make the interior light and airy. On the floor, just forward of the driving seat (not seen here) is a tap for a 1¾-gallon fuel reserve. Beneath the facia is a softly padded protection strip: the cowl above is not padded

In general, the finish of the Pininfarina body is good without being superlative, and with the exception of some indifferent detail work, including an excess of self-tapping screw heads. The tiny locker in the facia cannot hold a typical twin-lens reflex camera, and the lips of the door pockets are immediately beneath the armrests, so that they are made practically useless. A particularly practical and safe design of sun vizor was appreciated.

Attractive and luxurious to the eye, the front seats are frankly disappointing functionally, giving so little lateral support that one cannot reap full benefit from the car's exceptional cornering abilities. The cushions and squabs have raised side pads, but these are several inches too far apart to fit most people. Leather trim is now standardized in this country. The backrests are adjustable for angle over a limited range by screw-stops. An ingenious mechanism slides the cushion forward when the backrest is folded forward (to give easy access to the rear seat). A disadvantage of this design is that there is a tendency for the passenger to slide forward with the seat under heavy braking, unless the feet are planted firmly on the toeboard.

By recessing the forward backrests, adequate knee room has been provided for rear-seat travellers, who have more space and comfort than is usual in close-coupled saloons of this type. There is just enough head room for people of average size, and a folding central armrest is fitted. The rear side windows are hinged for ventilation, and have neat over-centre catches; when opened, they promote rather pronounced wind roar. Swivelling vents in the front door windows are limited to a 45deg opening. The winding windows lower flush into the doors; on the test car the handles were rather stiff to turn.

Minor Controls

At the extreme right of the facia is a pull-and-twist knob for side and head lamps, complemented by a two-way lever sprouting from the left of the steering column housing—a bit too far behind the wheel for true finger-tip control. This selects side lamps or dipped beams with the knob half out, main or dipped beams with it fully out. The same lever also works the self-cancelling direction signals; its movements should be better defined. For instance, at night the head lamp beams may be raised or dipped accidentally when the intention is merely to make a signal. No provision is made for signal-flashing the head lamps in daylight, nor is a reversing lamp supplied. Very full illumination is given by the Carello head lamps on both raised and dipped beams, and two fog lamps give an excellent short-range spread to the road sides. A half-ring in the lower sector of the steering wheel (where it does not obscure the instrument dials), with thumb extensions along the horizontal spokes, sounds two melodious, penetrating horns.

The two main instruments—large, easy to read and commendably accurate—are a speedometer, including trip distance recorder, and a tachometer reading to 5,700 r.p.m. An electric clock is included in this dial. Within the speedometer are an agreeably precise fuel level gauge, and three others to indicate oil pressure, water and oil temperatures. There is no ammeter. Small tumbler switches at each side of the steering column control the roof light and the fog lamps, the latter being in unit with the parking and signalling lamps, which keeps the frontal appearance of the car simple and uncluttered. To the left of the instruments is a pull-switch for the single-speed screen wiper motor, and beneath is a button for the suction-operated washer jets, that on the driver's side being placed on the wrong side of the wiper spindle so that it ejects mostly round the corner of the screen. The wipers are not wholly effective when the car is moving fast, and slightly longer blades to increase the swept area would be an improvement.

With temperature set by a tap beneath the facia, supplemented by a single-speed booster, distribution of hot or cold air is thereafter controlled individually by the driver and front passenger, above whose feet are rather clumsy-looking boxes with very stiff levers to proportion the supply between screen and car interior. Once the car has reached 30-40 m.p.h. these air streams become very powerful even without the booster which, incidentally, makes a subdued

Accessibility under the forward-hinged bonnet, lined for sound insulation, is excellent. Left of the shuttered radiator is an oil cooler, and the brake servo is in the immediate foreground. A transparent plastic bottle for brake fluid is seen beside the screenwash reservoir

Lancia Flaminia Coupé . . .

whistle which is somewhat reminiscent of a jet engine.

Twelve greasing points on the front suspension require attention every 2,000 miles, and the outer universals of the rear half shafts, easily reached by removing the wheel hub caps, should be lubricated at the same intervals.

Over many decades one has come to expect so much of a Lancia that one judges it inevitably by very high standards. Although it is now costly to buy in this country, protagonists of the marque recalling earlier days when, for instance, an Aprilia was priced for a short time at under £300, may console themselves with the knowledge that the current products remain fully worthy of their famous name badge. Representing the highest level in current Italian concept and workmanship, the Flaminia coupé has a strong and attractive character, underlined by impeccable road manners, which make it as rewarding to drive in this country as in its native land.

LANCIA FLAMINIA COUPÉ

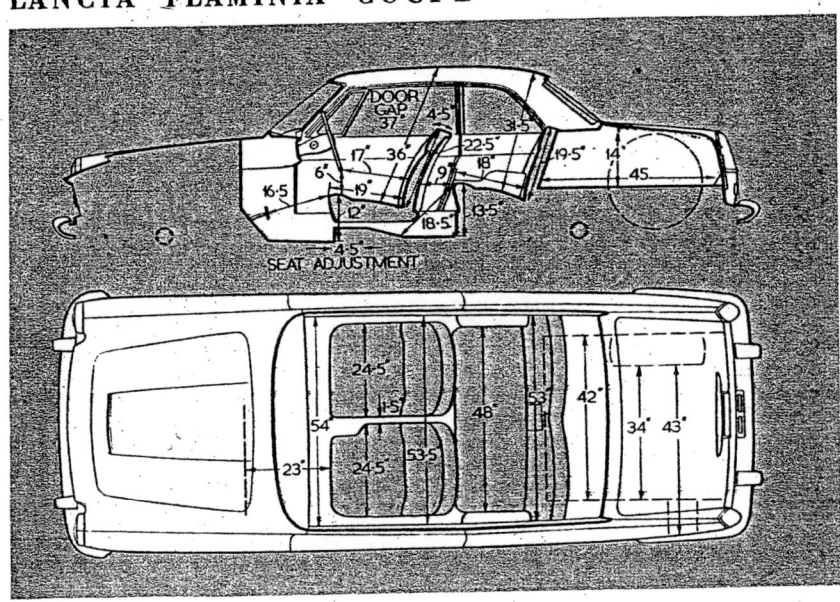

Scale ⅛in. to 1ft. Driving seat in central position. Cushions uncompressed.

PERFORMANCE

ACCELERATION TIMES (mean):
Speed range, Gear Ratios and Time in Sec.

m.p.h.	3·92 to 1	5·92¼ to 1	8·62 to 1	12·98 to 1
10—30	—	—	5·0	3·7
20—40	12·0	7·1	4·8	—
30—50	11·3	6·9	5·3	—
40—60	11·9	7·0	—	—
50—70	12·0	8·6	—	—
60—80	13·6	—	—	—
70—90	17·3	—	—	—

From rest through gears to:
30 m.p.h. .. 4·4 sec.
40 " .. 7·0 "
50 " .. 10·1 "
60 " .. 13·6 "
70 " .. 18·7 "
80 " .. 26·0 "
90 " .. 36·0 "

Standing quarter mile 19·1 sec.

MAXIMUM SPEEDS ON GEARS:

Gear		m.p.h.	k.p.h.
Top	(mean)	105·5	170·0
	(best)	107	172·3
3rd	..	73	117·5
2nd	..	50	80·5
1st	..	34	54·7

TRACTIVE EFFORT (by Tapley meter):

	Pull (lb per ton)	Equivalent gradient
Top	220	1 in 10·1
Third	345	1 in 6·4
Second	490	1 in 4·5

SPEEDOMETER CORRECTION: M.P.H.

Car speedometer:	10	20	30	40	50	60	70	80	90	100
True speed:	12	18	28	38	48	58	68	78	88	98

BRAKES (at 30 m.p.h. in neutral):

Pedal load in lb	Retardation	Equiv. stopping distance in ft
25	0·22g	137
50	0·47g	64
75	0·74g	41
100	0·84g	36
125	0·97g	31·1

FUEL CONSUMPTION (at steady speeds in top gear):

30 m.p.h.	35·1 m.p.g.
40 "	31·0 "
50 "	29·4 "
60 "	26·5 "
70 "	24·1 "
80 "	21·9 "
90 "	19·5 "

Overall fuel consumption for 1,052 miles, 20·1 m.p.g. (14·0 litres per 100 km.).

Approximate normal range 17-27 m.p.g. (16·6-10·5 litres per 100 km).

Fuel: Super premium grades.

TEST CONDITIONS: Weather: Occasional showers, mostly dry surfaces, 5 m.p.h. wind.

Air temperature, 68 deg. F.

STEERING: Turning circle.:
Between kerbs, L and R, 38ft 1in.
Between walls, L and R, 40ft 1in.
Turns of steering wheel from lock to lock, 4·25.

DATA

PRICE (basic), with two-door saloon body, £2,730.
British purchase tax, £1,138 12s 6d.
Total (in Great Britain), £3,868 12s 6d (Heater standard).
Extras: White wall tyres, £28 1s 8d (inc. P.T.).
Electrically-operated windows, electro-magnetic locks on front seat backs, rear window defroster, £122 10s 10d (inc. P.T.).
Woollen front carpets, £36 16s 8d (inc. P.T.).

ENGINE: Capacity, 2,458 c.c. (150 cu in).
Number of cylinders, 6, in vee formation.
Bore and stroke, 80·0 × 81·5 mm. (3·15 × 3·21 in).
Valve gear, overhead, pushrods.
Compression ratio, 9 to 1.
B.h.p. 119 (net) at 5,100 r.p.m. (b.h.p. per ton laden, 73·9).
Torque, 137 lb ft at 3,500 r.p.m.
M.p.h. per 1,000 r.p.m. in top gear, 18·7.

WEIGHT: (5 gals fuel), 29·2 cwt (3,266lb).
Weight distribution (per cent); F, 49·1; R, 50·9.
Laden as tested, 32·2 cwt (3,602lb).
Lb. per c.c. (laden), 1·46.

BRAKES: Type, Dunlop disc.
Method of operation, hydraulic, with tandem master cylinder, Lockheed vacuum servo.
Disc diameter: F, 11·5 in; R, 12·0in.
Swept area: F, 200 sq in; R, 236 sq in. (271 sq. in per ton laden).

TYRES: 175-400. Michelin X.
Pressures (p.s.i): F, 26; R, 31 (All conditions).

TANK CAPACITY: 12·5 Imperial gallons, including 1·75 gallons reserve.
Oil sump, 11·75 pints.
Cooling system, 18 pints (including heater).

DIMENSIONS: Wheelbase, 9ft 0·7in.
Track: F and R, 4ft 6in.
Length (overall): 15ft 4·5in.
Width: 5ft 8·5in. Height: 4ft 7·9in.
Ground clearance: 4·0in.
Frontal area: 17·5 sq ft (approximately).

ELECTRICAL SYSTEM: 12-volt; 42 ampère-hour battery.
Head lamps: Double dip; 45-40 watt bulbs.

SUSPENSION: Front, independent, coil springs and wishbones, telescopic dampers, anti-roll bar.
Rear: de Dion-type axle, half-elliptic leaf springs, telescopic dampers, Panhard rod and anti-roll bar.

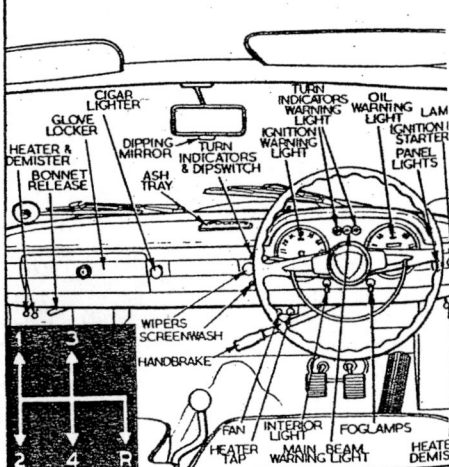

La Donna è Mobile

THAT'S the opening phrase of a song from Verdi's "Rigoletto" — you know, the one which goes "te-pom-pom-pom-pom-POMtepom." Literally, I suppose it means the lady is on the move; well, so she is figuratively, too, for *mobile* is Italian for fickle. That's the way it was with Miss Lancia Flaminia Zagato 340516-TO. One moment she was mobile, English-style, and the next she was *mo-bi-le*, Italian-style.

It wasn't really fair to rush her all the way from Turin to Venice and back, because she still wasn't looking or feeling her best after the Liège-Rome-Liège a few weeks earlier. But she looked irresistible; although wearing no jewellery like bumpers and hub caps, in other respects she was better equipped than other ladies of the same breed—extra fuel tankage, three screen wipers and special rally equipment.

Sitting beneath that low Zagato roof with its double-bubble section, and behind those almost horizontal screen pillars, one felt just like a Maglioli or a Frescobaldi, an effect accentuated by the full-throttle roar of air rushing into six chokes of three Weber carburettors. We made fast progress eastwards, mostly along fine *autostrada*—Milan, Brescia, Verona, Vicenza, Padua.... It is quite exciting to watch a speedometer needle sweep round to 200, even when one has to multiply by five and divide by eight to reduce kilometres to the more modest English miles—and perhaps even then to take 125 m.p.h. with a pinch of salt.

Right to its maximum on these roads the Lancia ran true as an arrow; just the pressure of one finger against the steering-wheel rim was sufficient to hold it on

When she was good she was very, very good ...

course. Off the *autostrada* and hurried round tight curves, she had some of the feel of a rear-engined car, with a pronounced tail swing; we were too short of time to experiment with different fore-and-aft ratios of tyre pressure. Steering was wonderfully light and positive, and the Dunlop disc brakes perhaps the best in lightness, sensitivity and efficiency that we could remember. Although the Zagato Sport body is mounted on the shortest of

... but when she was bad she was horrid

three Flaminia wheelbases (8ft 3·16i the car rode remarkably softly for a sp model, yet maintained a level keel.

And so we went to Venice where, course, the people all row about in Lagondas. Next morning the weather a bit overcast and dismal for the ret journey, and Miss Flaminia was in of her moods. When we drew up to our dues on entering the first stretch *autostrada*, her heart suddenly stop beating. The starter was dead, and horn wouldn't blow to let us warn escort car, which motored quie away.... Then the electricity all ca back again and we thought it was ju faulty ignition switch.

We rushed on to the end of that a strada, and her heart stopped again. the horn. And the starter. And lights—everything. We checked batt connections, loose wires under the da took out the ignition switch, stripped and put it together again. She fired away we went. Perhaps it was conne with the dynamo cut-out, and she wo stay lit if we didn't let the revs d below 1,000 p.m. Then, passing thro the next town, we blew the horn wl travelling slowly and the engine stopp Thereafter, pressing the horn button taboo. Next, an investigation of the h circuit, of all the fuses, of the ignit switch again.

Suddenly everything was live o more, and a fourth time she died, only come to life again for no clear reas Then, not far along the Milan-Tu *autostrada*, she cut at speed. Panic! Nowhere to pull off, it was dark and n pelting with rain. It *could* be the m fuel supply run dry, so we hastily tur on the reserve tap; after dropping tc tantalizing 15 m.p.h. she suddenly pick

All right, try the blessed starter!

up again, so maybe it really *was* fuel this time. Turin was still too far away to risk reaching it on reserve, so after a time we flashed lamps at the escort and pulled in at the next petrol station, where they wouldn't allow engines to be kept running. This time no amount of artificial respiration would bring her to life again.

We rang Turin. Would they please send an ambulance to the Chivasso filling-station to carry her those last twelve or so miles home? Yes, they would. The last view of her was through the back window of our escort car—a low, black silhouette merging quickly into the sodden gloom, *sans* volts, *sans* amps, *sans* watts, *sans* almost anything.

Back home in England they said: "Drive any nice cars in Italy?" "Of course," we replied. "A super this and a smashing that, and a wizard Lancia Flaminia Zagato which had competed in the Liège-Rome-Liège." "Was it the red one which went out with *electrical* trouble right at the beginning, or the white one which . . . .?" "Well, yes," we said, "it was red. . . ." R. B.

O.K., he's right on our tail again . . .

Damn, I thought it was too good to last . . .   You look at the fuses and I'll check the horn circuit . . .   Not again?

Lancia Flavia

Practicality has taken precedence over elegance in the Flavia. Below each pair of headlamps are parking and signalling lamps. Additional amber signals near the front wheel arches are of special value in converging streams of one-way city traffic

EVERY time a Lancia is tested, remarks are made about its unorthodox features and superlative engineering. This has certainly been true of four Aurelias, two Flaminias and one Appia tried during the last decade. Now the Flavia, latest offspring from the old-established Lancia concern, breaks with one family tradition by becoming the first Italian car with front-wheel drive and, for that matter, with a flat-four engine. A study of the engine, transmission and suspension unit (it was on display at Earls Court) would convince any engineer of the merit of its design and execution. In a road test, however, one is concerned with behaviour, not appearances, and in certain respects of mechanical refinement, silence and ride comfort this car is outstanding.

For those unfamiliar with the Flavia's make-up, its 1·5-litre engine has overhead valves operated by pushrods from two camshafts, and light alloy is used for the crankcase, cylinder blocks and heads. In unit with the engine is a single-plate clutch and an all-synchromesh four-speed gearbox with column change. On paper the front suspension might seem unenterprising, with a transverse leaf spring and each wheel carried on two wishbones. Neither would one suspect special merit from the rear suspension, a rigid, lightweight axle being carried on simple half-elliptic springs. There is an anti-roll bar at each end and—perhaps a point of some importance—de Carbon telescopic dampers are used for all wheels.

In the monocoque body full advantage is taken of the front-wheel-drive layout, by having flat floors and a steering-column gear change, to make the Flavia just wide enough for three-abreast seating, front and rear. With only 78 b.h.p. to command, such a full complement naturally has a considerable effect on performance. To fit it for the rare occasions when it might be required to carry six, the Flavia has bench seats fore and aft, without centre armrests. These are unexceptional in both appearance and comfort, providing practically no support to counteract roll and g during cornering.

As well as being adjustable for rake, the front squab can be let down fully to merge with the rear cushion and form a makeshift bed. The test car was trimmed in a thin plastic material, its pale grey colour emphasizing its dirt-absorbing properties; plastic trims are never so easily cleaned as one is asked to believe. Cloth trim, which is a same-price alternative, would be preferable. For leather, also optional, £112 extra is charged. The floor is covered with fitted matting of moulded plastic.

Detail finish of the interior is excellent, and where there is crash padding, it is firm enough for its purpose. Trigger-type interior door releases are recessed into the trim panels, on each door is a pull of transparent plastic, and the quarter-vents (in the front doors only) are worked by handwheels.

On pendant levers, the brake and clutch pedals are set at unrealistic angles. Although without visual identification, the four two-way switches on the curved keyboard are handy. Beside the ribbon speedometer is a round-dial engine revolution indicator

Lancia

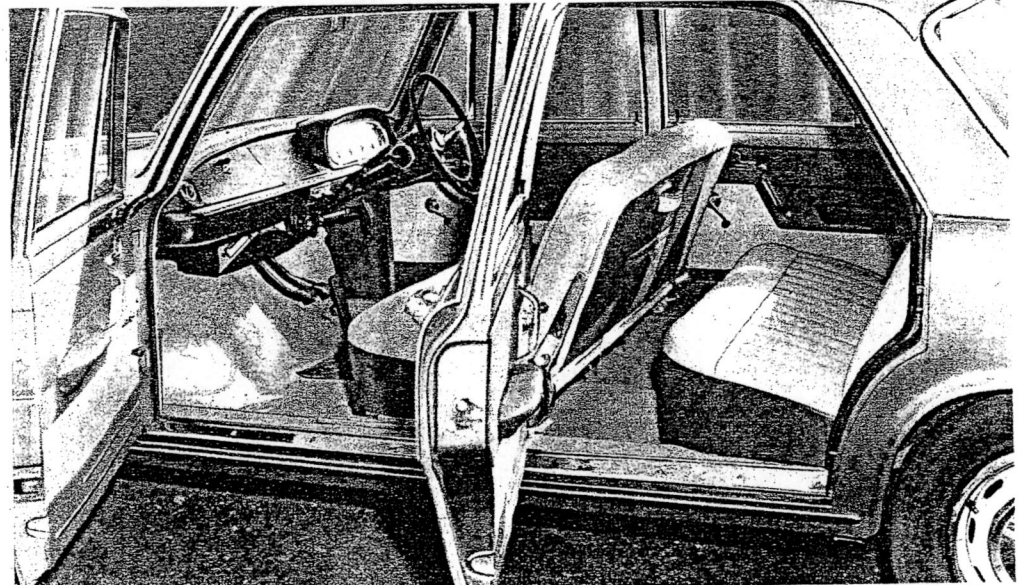

Three-abreast seating, front and rear, is unhampered by transmission tunnel or wheel arches, and leg room is adequate for all. Adjustable to suit the individual driver, the front seat squab also hinges down to form a bed. In the trailing edge of each front door is a red lamp, lit when it is opened

Although these are low-geared and take time to move, they are obviously thief-proof and can be screwed up so tightly as to eliminate wind-whistle.

As with certain other cars which rush through the air remarkably quietly at speed with the windows closed, the Flavia's reactions to an opened quarter-vent or winding window are excessive noise or draught respectively. The best compromise for warm weather ventilation is to open the small butterfly valves at each end of the facia and to wind down the back windows an inch or two. In our view, more effective extraction would be provided if the fixed quarterpanes in the back doors were hinged. Incidentally, the door windows have a pronounced curvature in the vertical plane. An interesting detail is that a red lamp in the trailing edge of each front door is lit when it is opened—even in daylight. There is no such provision in the rear doors. An effective fresh-air heating system is standard.

A lever for cold start rich mixture is found under the facia, a warning lamp remaining lit until this has been pushed fully home. Running temperature is partially controlled by radiator shutters, which mask only a section of the cooling element, but the bonnet must be opened to reach their adjusting lever. With these closed—even in mild end-of-summer weather—engine temperature remained rather low except when cruising very fast on M1. Until the unit warms up there is a low-speed flat spot, but there is no tendency to stalling unless the mixture control is dispensed with too soon.

From the moment it starts, the engine reveals unusual characteristics for a flat-four. It is quite remarkably smooth at any crankshaft speed from 1,000 r.p.m. to beyond the maximum recommended, 5,400 r.p.m., so much so that in this range one could not readily distinguish it as a four. A combination of inherent mechanical quietness, clever engine mountings and well-planned sound insulation keeps the passenger compartment somehow quite aloof from the working parts.

While the Flavia is not a star performer in respect of acceleration, and in our collective view would benefit greatly from an increase in engine capacity and hence torque, yet it can slowly reach and then hold an unexpectedly high maximum—in the lower or middle nineties, depending on wind direction. Thus it is admirably suited to long journeys on *autostrada* and their international equivalents.

Certainly, for use in this country, it is very seriously restricted by a choice of gear ratios which is difficult to understand. Thus the makers stipulate maxima in the indirects of 25, 42 and 60 m.p.h. respectively, corresponding to approximately 5,400 r.p.m. On the test car, incidentally, the true speed in third at these indicated revs was 56 m.p.h.; thus the instrument was presumed to be in error and 5,800 r.p.m. indicated was considered the maximum. At these revs the engine still has lots of power and shows no signs of overwork, so the limit seems conservative.

Watching the Revs

Indeed, as one of the testing staff remarked, one could enjoy the car much more if it had no rev counter, for when driving hard one has to keep a close watch on its reading. After the change up to top at 60 m.p.h. (64 m.p.h. indicated on this car) the acceleration thereafter in the high top gear is somewhat sluggish. It takes more than twice as long to reach 50 m.p.h. from 30 in top as it does in third, the respective figures being 16·6 and 8·1sec. From 40 to 60 m.p.h. the difference is between 16·5 and 9·6sec. And, having reached 60 from 40 in third in the latter figure, it then takes a further 24sec to reach 80 in top. It is thus a car for city traffic and the mountains in the indirects, and for cruising at very high speeds on motorways in top. One might suggest more practical maxima in the lower gears of 23 (unchanged), 45 and 70. Nevertheless, because of the lack of engine fuss, the mechanical refinement and the fine road-holding abilities of the car, one finds that surprisingly high averages can be maintained on cross-country routes for a whole day without tiring the driver or his passengers.

On the test car the steering column change was not up to the usual Lancia standard, except for upward and downward changes between third and top. With the transmission cold, moreover, it was often very difficult to engage second at all, and the downward change from this gear to first was always tricky despite synchromesh. The transmission was very quiet, and there was complete freedom from final drive whine in top gear. In this ratio the lowest practical speed, from the viewpoint of engine smoothness and acceleration, was around 20 m.p.h.

In almost all circumstances the driver would not be aware that the front wheels are driven, although the Flavia has one usual front-wheel-drive tendency—that is, slight understeer through corners with the throttle open changes when

Obstructed only by the wheel arches and spare wheel, the boot is huge and conveniently shaped. When opened at night it is lit automatically. Reflectors are buried in the stainless steel bumper

Flavia...

Resulting from the front-wheel drive, the car's under-surface is clean aerodynamically and allows plenty of ground clearance. A low waistline means deep windows

the throttle is closed, in this case to a neutral rather than an oversteer characteristic. The steering is geared at 4¾ turns of the wheel for a disappointing lock of around 36ft between kerbs, 39ft between walls. This gearing reduces inherent low-speed heaviness, yet one is not aware of particularly low gearing at normal touring speeds.

While the Flavia does not steer as beautifully as the larger Flaminia, its control is nevertheless well above average. The car remains directionally stable at speed in a cross wind, and no harsh reactions come back to the driver's hands. An unusual provision is a lever under the bonnet, by means of which the arc of movement of the steering idler arm may be reduced, to limit wheel lock when snow chains are fitted and avoid the tyres fouling the wheel arches.

Dunlop disc brakes of 11in. dia. on all wheels, assisted by a vacuum servo, assure the Flavia of repeated stopping power from the highest speeds it can reach, the moderate acceleration allowing them to cool thoroughly between applications. Only during a long Alpine descent could they be worked anywhere near their limit of endurance. Sixty pounds pressure on the pedal was sufficient for the quickest stop possible from 30 m.p.h., the limiting factor here being premature locking of the rear wheels with only two occupants aboard. On M.I.R.A.'s 1-in-3 test hill the handbrake would not hold the car, nor could it restart on this slope. On 1-in-4 it could be held and would restart, although the clutch seems on the borderline of efficiency, since it was also leisurely about taking up the drive between gear changes while the acceleration figures were being taken.

As recorded earlier, the Flavia excels in the matter of suspension. Except at very low speeds when the braced tread Michelin X tyres can be heard to thump slightly over cats' eyes and suchlike, practically no road noise comes up through the body structure. Moreover, the car seems, as it were, to turn a blind eye to rough sections of roadway in a manner which would suggest air springs, or at least something less conventional than laminated leaves. Thus at one end of the scale it can be driven, without discomfort or loss of control, at astonishing speeds over unmetalled tracks; and at the other, it remains extremely safe and stable when treated as a sports car, front and rear passengers enjoying an equally level and peaceful ride.

On Washboard or Pavé

Despite the two anti-roll bars the car is not roll-free, this being emphasized by the lack of lateral support in the seating. On M.I.R.A.'s washboard the vibrations began to smooth out at 50 m.p.h. and at 60 there was very little disturbance. On the rough pavé it rode particularly well, with no suspension bottoming, at 40-50 m.p.h. On the longwave pitching track—a series of 4in. waves of 40ft pitch—its behaviour was quite exceptional, for at low speed it did not leave the ground (whereas some current cars may leap a foot or so clear). By accelerating hard over the length of the run-in a true 75 m.p.h. could be reached, at which speed there was no indication within the car that the surface beneath was anything but level. An observer meanwhile watched the wheels rise and fall, still without leaving the ground. While we always try cars over these waves for background knowledge, we draw attention to them here because of the Lancia's exceptional behaviour.

In everyday use the Flavia should return about 27 m.p.g., and its good aerodynamic shape, suggested by the freedom from wind roar, is confirmed by its excellent figure of 29.2 m.p.g. at a maintained 70 m.p.h. The fuel tank thus gives a touring range of around 250 miles between brim-full and the 1½-gallon "reserve" lamp flashing.

Visibility is excellent all round due to the deep windows and low waistline, and in wet weather the single-speed wipers function efficiently on a screen much less curved than is usual nowadays. A screen-washing installation is included. The soft sun vizors are on truly flexible frames and—a small detail—the rear-view mirror, with dipping reflector, also holds the licence disc against the screen. With

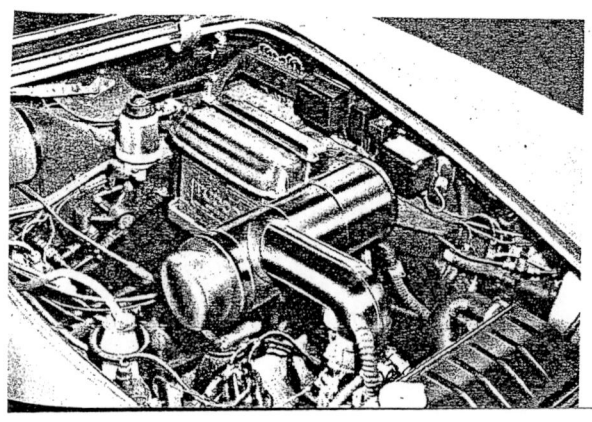
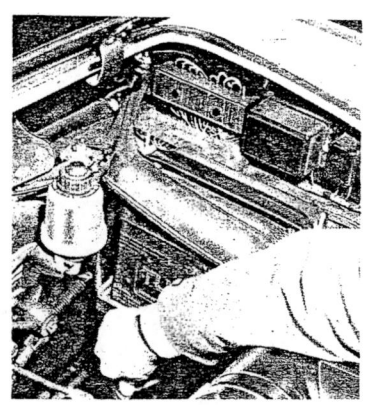

Left: Under the bonnet, supported by a stay, the first impression may be confusion. Plug changing presents no difficulties, but tappet adjustment entails unbolting plates in the wheel arches. Right: Just behind the transverse spring is this lever, by which the front wheel steering locks may be reduced when snow-chains are fitted

the four headlamps lit there is fine illumination, but the two "meeting" beams have a rather sharp cut-off.

Under the bonnet the "flat" engine is almost hidden beneath the radiator header tank and carburettor air cleaner. While the plugs can be reached from above, panels in the wheel arches must be removed to reach the valve gear. Most accessories, however, are very handy—ignition distributor, engine oil filter and dipstick, battery, generator and so on. The electrical installation is particularly neat and its components such as the cut-out and fuse box easy to reach.

As in all current Lancias there are independent brake pipe lines for front and rear wheels. An adequate set of hand tools is provided, one spanner serving the wheel hub caps, wheel nuts, sparking plugs and all oil drain plugs. Four grease nipples on the steering connections require attention every 2,000 miles, one on the steering idler arm shaft every 6,000 miles, and engine oil changes are recommended at 2,000-mile intervals.

Because of its price the Lancia Flavia is a somewhat exclusive one-and-a-half in this country—a car for the connoisseur. It sets a standard in certain important respects which is bound to give some other manufacturers food for thought, showing what can still be done with a four-cylinder engine and steel springs. The workmanship and detail finish suggest that it is intended as a lasting possession.

LANCIA FLAVIA

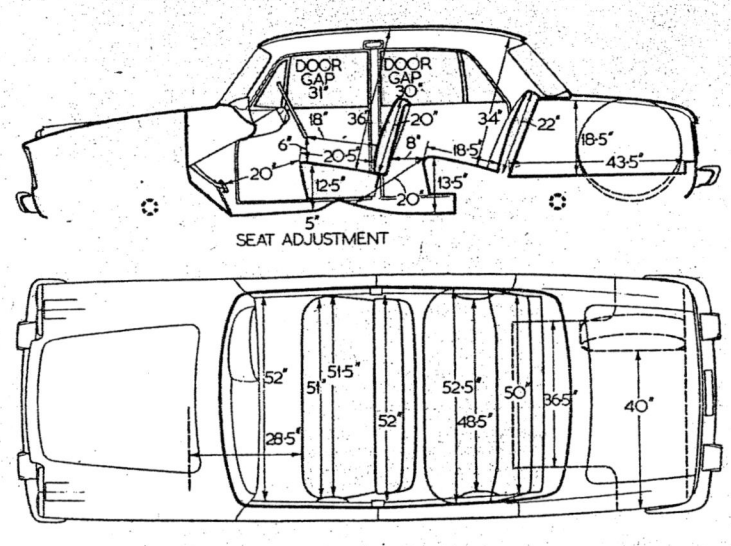

Scale ¼in. to 1ft. Driving seat in central position. Cushions uncompressed.

--- DATA ---

PRICE (basic), with saloon body, £1,499.
British purchase tax £688 12s.
Total (in Great Britain) £2,187 12s.
Extras (inc. p.t.): Leather upholstery £112 5s 10d. Whitewall tyres £13 2s 5d.

ENGINE: Capacity 1,500 c.c. (91·6 cu. in.).
Number of cylinders, 4 horizontally opposed.
Bore and stroke, 82 × 71mm (3·23 × 2·79in.).
Valve gear, overhead, pushrods and rockers, two camshafts.
Compression ratio, 8·3 to 1.
B.h.p. 78 net at 5,200 r.p.m. (b.h.p. per ton laden 59·3).
Torque, 82 lb. ft. at 3,500 r.p.m.
M.p.h. per 1,000 r.p.m. in top gear, 18·1.

WEIGHT (with 5 gal fuel): 23·3 cwt (2,615 lb).
Weight distribution (per cent): F, 61·1; R, 38·9.
Laden as tested, 26·3 cwt (2,915 lb).
Lb per c.c. (laden), 1·97.

BRAKES: Type, Dunlop discs.
Method of operation: hydraulic with servo
Disc diameter, F and R, 11in.
Total swept area, 496 sq. in. (377 sq. in. per ton laden).

TYRES: 165—15in. Michelin X.
Pressure (p.s.i.): F, 24; R, 24 (all conditions).

TANK CAPACITY: 10·5 Imperial gallons.
Oil sump, 10·5 pints.
Cooling system, 13·5 pints (including heater).

DIMENSIONS: Wheelbase, 8ft 8·3in.
Track: F, 4ft 3·2in.; R, 4ft 2·4in.
Length (overall), 15ft 0·2in.
Width, 5ft 3·2in.
Height, 4ft 11·1in.
Ground clearance, 5in.
Frontal area, 20 sq. ft. (approximately).

ELECTRICAL SYSTEM: 12-volt; 42 ampère-hour battery.
Headlamps, four-lamp system, 40-45 watt bulbs.

SUSPENSION: Front, double wishbones with transverse leaf spring and anti-roll bar. De Carbon telescopic dampers.
Rear, dead axle, half-elliptic leaf springs and anti-roll bar, De Carbon telescopic dampers.

--- PERFORMANCE ---

ACCELERATION TIMES (mean):

Speed range, Gear Ratios and Time in Sec.

M.p.h.	4·09 to 1	6·71 to 1	9·53 to 1	16·16 to 1
10—30	—	9·0	5·9	—
20—40	15·0	8·6	5·9	—
30—50	16·6	8·1	—	—
40—60	16·5	9·6	—	—
50—70	18·7	—	—	—
60—80	24·0	—	—	—

From rest through gears to:

30 m.p.h.	5·9 sec.
40 "	8·8 "
50 "	13·7 "
60 "	18·7 "
70 "	30·5 "
80 "	42·5 "

Standing quarter mile 22·0 sec.

MAXIMUM SPEEDS ON GEARS:

Gear		M.p.h.	K.p.h.
Top	(mean)	93·4	150·4
	(best)	96	154·6
3rd		60	96
2nd		42	68
1st		25	40

TRACTIVE EFFORT (by Tapley meter):

	Pull (lb per ton)	Equivalent gradient
Top	170	1 in 13·1
Third	295	1 in 7·5
Second	410	1 in 5·4

BRAKES (at 30 m.p.h. in neutral):

Pedal load in lb	Retardation	Equiv. stopping distance in ft
25	0·32g	94
50	0·70g	43
60	0·81g	37·3

FUEL CONSUMPTION (at steady speeds in top gear):

30 m.p.h.	43·5 m.p.g.
40 "	41·7 "
50 "	36·4 "
60 "	33·1 "
70 "	29·2 "
80 "	24·0 "
90 "	18·3 "

Overall fuel consumption for 1,207 miles, 25·4 m.p.g. (11·1 litres per 100 km.).
Approximate normal range 24-30 m.p.g. (11·8-9·4 litres per 100 km.).
Fuel: Premium grades.

TEST CONDITIONS: Weather: Dry, sunny, 0-12 m.p.h. wind.
Air temperature 58 deg. F.
Model described in *The Autocar* of 4 November, 1960.

STEERING: Turning circle:
Between kerbs: L, 36ft 5in.; R, 36ft 0in.
Between walls: L, 39ft 0in.; R, 38ft 7in.
Turns of steering wheel from lock to lock, 4·75.
With lock limiting device set:
Between kerbs: L, 41ft 3in.; R, 41ft 5in.
Between walls: L, 43ft 7in.; R, 43ft 8in.

SPEEDOMETER CORRECTION: m.p.h.

Car speedometer	10	20	30	40	50	60	70	80	90	100
True speed	9	20	29	38	46	56	65	75	84	93

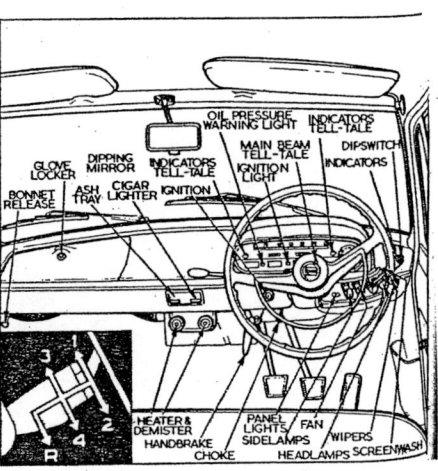

A New Car

LANCIA FLAVIA

by Gordon Wilkins

EVER since Vicenzo Lancia, the former Fiat Grand Prix driver, produced a car in the early nineteen twenties with unit body-chassis and independent front suspension, his name has been associated with advanced technical developments. The Aprilia had a V-4 engine and was one of the first successful efforts at independent rear suspension, and after the war came the Aurelia with V-6 engine at front and gearbox mounted at the rear in unit with the clutch and differential to make what the Americans now call a transaxle.

The model which has been most conspicuously missing from the post-war range has been a replacement for the Aprilia which in the immediate pre- and post-war period enjoyed a unique reputation for its excellent road holding, high performance, and effortless fast cruising combined with compactness and operating economy. Now comes the Flavia to fill the gap, but with a different character reflecting the views of Professor Fessia who is now Technical Director under the new management which is pursuing a vigorous expansionist policy.

FRONT WHEEL DRIVE

In its broad conception, flat-four engine and front-wheel drive, the Flavia continues the ideas employed by Fessia in the Cemsa Caproni prototype which he designed soon after the war, but in much more mature and developed form. The body is a four-door unit structure in steel, and to it is attached a sub frame by six flexible anti-vibration mountings. The frame is rectangular, in steel box sections, with two columns in cast aluminium supporting an upper cross member in steel. Engine, transmission, steering gear and front suspension are all mounted on the sub frame, so that noise and vibration are kept out of the body.

Suspension is to be leaf springs, which is unusual these days; one transverse leaf spring at the front and two semi-elliptics carrying a dead axle beam at the rear. There are anti-roll bars at front and rear, and dampers are telescopic de Carbons, which incorporate an air cushion. The independent front suspension uses double wishbones, with the leaf spring connected to the upper wishbone via a rubber cushion, so that it takes no part in locating the wheels or resisting brake torque.

A flat four engine is used in the Flavia.

Instruments and switches are grouped around the steering wheel of the Flavia.

No grease is required for front suspension pivots, or for the wheel bearings, which are sealed for life. Rear springs are mounted in rubber trunnions at their forward ends and in rubber-pivoted shackles at their rear ends, so no greasing is needed here either.

There are therefore only five points, on the three-element steering linkage, requiring periodical greasing. Leaf springs have plastic inserts between the leaves to reduce friction and maintain constant characteristics. Brakes are Dunlop discs on all four wheels with twin master cylinders for extra safety and a vacuum servo.

Steering gear is by Gemmer and has a flexible anti-vibration joint at the base of the column. Four and a half turns of the wheel give a 36 ft. 2 in. turning circle, which is very compact for a car with flat four engine and front drive. Naturally, if snow chains are fitted they go on the front wheels. To prevent them fouling the wing valances on full lock, there is a simple lever on the steering box which brings an auxiliary lock stop into action. The steering wheel movement is then reduced to three and a half turns, giving a 39 ft. 3 in. turning circle.

LIGHT ALLOY ENGINE

The engine is a flat four, water cooled, cast in light alloy. Dimensions are oversquare (82 x 71 mm.), 1498 cc. With a compression of 8.3 to 1 it uses normal fuel but runs up to well over 5000 rpm and gives 78 hp nett at 5200 rpm, with max torque of 81.5 lb. ft. at 3500 rpm. The torque reading is obtained at fairly high rpm, indicating that this is an engine of fairly sporting characteristics, although by no means highly tuned.

There are two main pressure die castin each consisting of two cylinders and half crankcase, which is split vertically on centre line. These castings, produced in laboration with Injecta SA, the S specialists, are highly complex and produ to very fine limits, the walls being in s parts only 0.118 in. thick. Cylinders h wet liners of centrifugally cast chromi iron. The two cylinder heads are of li alloy, with hemispherical combustion ch bers and inserted valve seats. Valves operated by pushrods and rockers from chain driven camshafts below the cranksh the chain having a hydraulic tensioner. forged steel crankshaft is carried in th main bearings. The carburetter is a tw choke downdraught, made by Weber Solex, and fuel is supplied by a Bendix e tric pump at the rear of the car. The ra tor has a thermostat and shutters adjust from the driving seat.

FOUR SPEED GEARBOX

Fichtel and Sachs supply the single-p clutch with a special Lancia-designed flex centre. There are four speeds, all sync mesh, in the gearbox, and unlike most this type of unit, it has a direct top g only the first three ratios being indirect constant mesh. This is obtained by mak input and output shafts concentric. The i from the clutch passes through the ce of the drive pinion and through to the of the gearbox and for top gear, po returns via the hollow shaft carrying the f drive hypoid pinion. The transmission its own oil pump.

Articulated drive shafts with Rzeppa

type constant velocity joints at each end are supplied by the British Birfield concern. To avoid the use of splines which might stick, variations in shaft length caused by suspension movement are accommodated by mounting the inner joints on ball bearings which permit the whole joint to slide endwise. All joints are covered with rubber seals.

The body is an interesting structure with four slim doors. Maximum interior width has been obtained by using curved side windows dropping in curved guides. Although much smaller (5½ in. narrower than the big Flaminia), the Flavia gives very nearly the same interior space. Generous legroom for rear passengers is a special feature for a car in the 1½-litre class.

ADJUSTABLE BACKREST

The front seat is a single bench and has a full reclining adjustable backrest. Red lamps set in the door edges light up to give a warning when a door is opened. Equipment includes a half horn ring, cigarette lighter, two map pockets at front, one in rear, windshield washer, parking brake warning lamp, choke reminder lamp, lockable glove box, two roof lamps, and lamps to illuminate engine and trunk. There are four headlamps. The main beams are automatically extinguished when the engine is switched off and only the dipped beam comes on when the engine is re-started, if the switches have not been altered meanwhile.

Professor Fessia told me that he had a specially difficult task in producing a front-drive car for Italy, as the Italian motorist expects very high standards of steering and road holding and would not tolerate heavy steering or a nose-heavy car. He has therefore managed to produce a front-wheel drive car capable of over 90 mph which is so light and responsive to handle that one could drive it for miles without ever imagining that it had power going through the front wheels. Sweeping round mountain hairpins, or parking in confined city spaces, there is never any snatch or vibration to indicate that the front wheels are doing the driving.

Driving position is admirable and the controls are very well arranged, with recessed finger-tip switches ranged round an unusual curved console under the steering wheel. The asymmetrical instrument panel contains a long ribbon-type speedometer and a circular tachometer, which frequently records over 5500 rpm when one is using full performance in the gears. But even at these revs the engine remains smooth and quiet. Interior door handles are neatly recessed to avoid catching clothes, and adjustable air vents demist side windows.

The steering column gear lever is particularly precise in action and the steering gear has good self centering action after corners. I saw indicated speeds of 27 mph in first gear, 48 in second, and about 68 in third. Lancia claim a top speed of 92 mph and average fuel consumption of 28 miles imp. gallons. Acceleration and hill climbing are very lively, without reaching the class of Grand Turismo versions, which are expected later.

GOOD SOUND PROOFING

The big saloon body with extensive sound proofing puts weight up to 2690 lb, but the 1½-litre engine handles it well and on winding roads or in the mountains, a driver who is willing to make full use of the excellent gearbox can put up some high averages. On the other hand, top gear flexibility is outstanding and snatch-free drive is obtained right down to a crawl, but a drop to a lower gear is needed for a quick getaway. Rough checks on first acquaintance showed 0-5 mph acceleration in about 14.2 sec. At 6 mph, top gear acceleration is still vigorous.

But above all, this is a family saloon with big interior and a large luggage trunk, which handles like a good sports car. To drive it is to become enthusiastic about its road qualities—and perhaps to speculate on how it would go with a 2-litre engine! It is a true Lancia; solid, beautifully built to last a long time, technically interesting and fascinating to drive. Silence, and freedom from vibration represent a big achievement and reflect the success of the extensive insulation measures employed. Brakes are of course equal to all demands, with a light pedal pressure.

SPECIFICATION

Engine: a water cooled flat four with bore of 82 mm and stroke of 71 mm capacity 1498 cc, compression ratio 8.3 to output of 78 hp at 5200 rpm and a maximum torque of 81.5 lbs ft at 3500 rpm.

Transmission: single plate clutch to a four speed all-synchromesh gearbox, and front wheel drive via hypoid final drive. Gearbox ratios are 3.94 to 1 for low, 2.33 for second 1.64 for third, 1 to 1 for top and 4.39 to for reverse in conjunction with a 4.1 to final drive.

Dimensions: wheelbase 104.3 in, track 51.1 in at the front and 50.3 in at the rear length 180.3 in, width 63.3 in, height 59 in, kerb weight 2689 lbs, fuel capacity 10 Imp gallons (12¾ U.S.).

The latest Lancia, the Flavia, is a spacious, well finished saloon with good road handling qualities.

THE AUTOCAR, LONDON

Fessia's Flavia

Lancia fondness for unorthodoxy in design is continued with the latest model. It is a front-wheel-drive sedan powered by a water-cooled flat four.

▶ Regardless of the fanfare and flag-waving with which warmed-over versions of last year's models are introduced, there *are* a few really new cars around. One of these is the Lancia Flavia, a front-wheel-drive, four-door sedan powered by a water-cooled, flat four. The new Flavia fills a breach in Lancia's line, coming between the Appia and Flaminia both in price and performance. Though its engine is not much larger than the former's 1100 cc, the interior space is startlingly generous, providing ample room for six passengers. Though acceleration isn't much, it can cruise fully loaded in the eighties to give an excellent combination of economy and performance. It caused a mild sensation when it was introduced at the Turin auto show in November.

Technically the Flavia strongly resembles the Cemsa Caproni, an 1100 cc four-seater offered in prototype chassis form by the well-known Italian airplane manufacturer at the Paris show in 1947. But this isn't so surprising, since Lancia's chief engineer is Antonio Fessia who, as a young engineer, designed the ill-starred Caproni automobile.

The engine block consists of two aluminum castings in which chrome-plated cast iron wet liners are fitted. Three bearings support the short crankshaft. There are three rings per piston, two compression (one of them chromed) and one oil-control. Two chain-driven cams are installed — one for each bank of cylinders — low in the block. They operate the valves by pushrods and rockers and the combustion chambers are hemispherically shaped. The pistons are cut away to provide valve clearance. Three rubber mounts tie the engine and transmission to a subframe which also carries the front suspension, steering and radiator. The subframe itself is connected to the unit body at six rubber-cushioned points. The transmission is four-speed, all synchromesh.

Lancia devotees the world over will lament the loss of the V4 to a boxer layout. Much the same chagrin was expressed when the well-known sliding-pillar independent front suspension, introduced in the Twenties, gave way to wishbone I.F.S. with the introduction of the Flaminia. The nostalgic will recall that two types "made" Lancia's name: the long, square Lambda, in its time a fast two-liter sports tourer with what may have been the first production use of unibody construction, and the beetlebacked, short-nosed and popular Aprilia which Vincenzo Lancia brought out in 1937. It was the first mass-produced sedan with inboard brakes at the rear, similar to those of the post-war Aurelia and Flaminia. Ugly, yet agile and charming, the Aprilia was long considered by Europe's automotive cognoscenti to be a yardstick for performance in the 1.5-liter category.

The Flavia, while bucking the norm in automotive design, is hardly as unorthodox or revolutionary as were the Lambda and Aprilia in their time. Its exterior, conservative and uncontroversial, is in no way exciting and its layout may suggest the Lloyd Arabella introduced last year. But looking at a car doesn't tell you much.

The Flavia has excellent roadholding, wholly up to Lancia standards. Its servo-operated four disc brakes, with separate circuits for front and rear systems, offer fantastic stopping power. And it's as comfortable and as silent as its big sister, the Flaminia. While recognizing the weight penalty of extravagant soundproofing, Lancia technicians spared no effort in making the Flavia absolutely silent. The factory maintains that the engine cannot be heard at an idle (they say, "an imperceptible whisper") and accelerating in neutral "the whisper becomes a hum, something like an electric motor." In their factory magazine, they recall the story about balancing the English penny on the radiator of a Rolls Royce; "we thought it must be a joke, but it must be the same with the Flavia." Incidentally, they describe the shifting as "swift and instinctive."

With a curb weight of 2700 pounds, the Flavia offers something less than sporting performance (0 to 50 mph in about 15 seconds). That's quite a load for a 1500 cc engine, even if it will develop 78 bhp at 5200 rpm. Still horsepower isn't everything and with the new Lancia you feel that torque *is*.

The front suspension is independent with a semi-elliptic transverse leaf spring. Attached to the subframe at the midpoint, it features bonded rubber links at each end between it and the parallel-wishbone suspensions. At the rear, a very orthodox solid axle/leaf spring arrangement is used. Telescopic shock absorbers are used front and rear and a torsion anti-roll bar is used front *and* rear.

Deliveries of the new Flavia, in Italy, are expected to begin next December. The price in Italy will be about $3000. Its interesting mechanical features, its first-class performance — in short, just the fact that it's a Lancia — augur well for its success. Perhaps the enthusiast's reservations about the new model will be dispelled in a few months when a G.T. version is expected to appear.

—SCI

New engine uses cast-iron wet liners supported by two aluminum castings. Two camshafts, one per bank, operate valves through pushrods and rockers.

With a transverse spring in front, plus anti-roll bars at both ends, the Flavia should carry on the Lancia tradition of excellent roadholding.

LANCIA FLAVIA

A front wheel drive design with all the virtues and none of the vice

RADICAL DEPARTURES from accepted practice are never looked upon with any great favor by the businessmen who head the world's great automobile manufacturing companies, and yet such departures actually have become the rule in recent years. The reason is clear: there is a growing sophistication on the part of the public that makes technical innovations seem more attractive than in the past and this has, in turn, influenced the manufacturers—who are, after all, acutely sensitive to buyer trends.

All of this must be very satisfying to Lancia & Company, a firm which has offered "radical" engineering features with each new model introduced during the 55 years that it has been in business. The very latest model in the Lancia line, and perhaps the most radical Lancia ever, is the Flavia. If this car were not already being produced in numbers, we would consider it a designer's technical exercise, a dream car, for it embodies almost every costly and/or intricate design detail that can be imagined.

The dream-car aspect does not, unfortunately, carry over into the Flavia's styling; in this respect it escapes being quite ordinary only because it is somewhat more homely than most. A high, ¾-front shot of the car looks quite good, but from most angles at eye-level, where most of us will have to examine the car, the body form is somewhat less than inspired.

On the other hand, the actual workmanship on the body is superb; the panels, even those hidden away under the hood and inside the trunk, are finished in a way that make claims of quality by others rather hollow. No clumsily camouflaged seams mar the appearance of panels, and the doors, hood and trunk-lid fill their respective openings a though they were custom-fitted. The paint and the variou pieces of trim all conform to the same high standard.

The Lancia policy of quality in every detail is even mor apparent in the interior, which is very subdued in deco but quite handsome nonetheless. The seats are of th bench-type and do not give the support possible with goo bucket-type seating—but they come very close and offe more flexibility in the number of passengers carried. Th seats contain none of the usual bundles of wire and wad of cotton; instead, molded blocks of foam rubber are use and are covered with either cloth or leather. Most of th seat's central area is quite soft but the forward edge much more firm and gives good support under the knee The front seat back is adjustable through a wide arc— from nearly vertical to horizontal—and the whole pack age is nearly perfect.

From the standpoint of driver comfort, the Flavia one of the best sedans we have ever seen. The steerin wheel is nicely raked and is positioned just right for bot comfort and convenience—and even very short people wi not have to look through the rim. The clutch and brak pedals, of the pendant type, fall handily to the foot, an

the shift lever, mounted on the steering column, is a very superior example of the type.

Instrumentation was very complete; there are real needle-type gauges to indicate the car's state of health and warning lights to call one's attention to the panel if anything should go amiss. In addition to a speedometer (of the creeping red-line variety, and scandalously inaccurate) there was a tachometer, an item not often seen in sedans.

Most of the miscellaneous small switches were arranged in a semi-circular console that sweeps around to the left of the steering wheel. These switches are, as is usually the case in Italian cars, innocent of any identifying marks and caused us some confusion until we learned to "play-by-touch." Two of the clever and attractive features that we found on the Flavia's dash were the butterfly valves (chromed) that controlled the direction of incoming fresh air, and the headlight-dimmer switch, a small button on the end of the turn-indicator lever.

As a mechanism the Flavia abounds with interesting features; not so much in its over-all concept, for there have been other sedans with front wheel drive—and powered by water-cooled, flat-4 engines as well. Where the Flavia is most interesting is in the many intriguing details, such as the exclusive use of Rzeppa-type U-joints and ball-bearing sliding splines on the driveshaft.

The engine is, as we have said, an opposed-4, and is water-cooled with almost everything cast of light alloy. The engine's lower end is a pretty straightforward piece of work, with a 4-throw, 3-main bearing crankshaft. The valve-gear, however, is more interesting; there are two camshafts, which reduces the necessary length (and weight) of the pushrods, and the valves, rather than being set in the heads in conventional fashion, follow the pattern Lancia set with its 2.5-liter V-6. In this arrangement the valves are inclined away from the bore-centerline in the same plane as the crankshaft axis. The layout has the surface virtue of permitting an inclined valve arrangement with the least possible complication in the valve gear—but it also severely limits the amount of incline, and thus the maximum valve size, and carries the further penalty of no less than 8 separate rocker-shafts.

The all-synchro transmission, which is in-unit with the differential and final-drive, resembles very closely the unit used by Chevrolet in their Corvair. Lancia elected to use the same type of high-offset hypoid gears and, as is the case in the Corvair, high gear is direct.

The rear suspension is nothing out of the ordinary, except for the use of semi-elliptical leaf springs, and rates comment only because it gives such very good results. The front suspension, consisting of tubular A-arms, is fastened to a large aluminum casting that is, in turn, part of a detachable sub-frame that carries the entire power and drive package. The rear axle is the least complicated part of the car, as it is nothing but a tubular steel beam, with a wheel fastened to each end. Coil springs and trailing links were considered, but made too much of an intrusion into the trunk space. And, speaking of trunk space, there is a lot of it in the Flavia: large, square-shaped and very usable.

The Flavia, like so many recently introduced automobiles, has disc brakes (Dunlop) but is somewhat different in having the discs on all 4 wheels. The braking system is further enhanced by the presence of two separate master cylinders (the car has independent front and rear braking systems) with power boosters for each . . . all in all, an efficient, safe and impressive arrangement.

Because we had some reservations about the Flavia's design, we were a bit apprehensive about driving it—but the driving proved to be a real pleasure. From the driver's seat it is quite impossible to tell that the car has front wheel drive, or that it has only 4 cyl. The Flavia's engine is absolutely smooth and silent, and as there is no discernible road-rumble and very little wind noise one travels in really remarkable silence. Had there been a clock, its ticking would surely have been audible.

Complementing this was the wealth of luxury detail,

such as the tricky combination ash-tray/cigarette-lighter, the interior lights that come on with the opening of any of the four doors, and the red warning lights set into the rear edge of each front door. These lights are switched on automatically as the door opens. Yet more lights are to be found in the trunk (two of them here) and under the hood; these, too, light when their respective lids are opened.

We had the car for only a very brief time, and are therefore not too well qualified to dwell on its handling and we were not able to get a fuel consumption check at all (we would guess the mileage range to be 25/30 mpg).

From our rather abbreviated experiences, however, we would say that the car was free of handling vices and showed better adhesion on the corners than we have come to expect from a sedan.

In terms of performance the Flavia was nothing to get excited about; it would go well enough in the lower gears but "died" after the shift into 4th. Even so, it pulled strongly enough to keep up with any normal traffic situation and showed a real capacity for fast cruising. It is, in fact, strongest in this last respect and we can think of few cars that would be as pleasant a companion on a long trip as Lancia's Flavia.

ROAD TEST
LANCIA FLAVIA

SCALE: 10" DIVISIONS

DIMENSIONS
Wheelbase, in.........104.3
Tread, f and r......51.2/50.4
Over-all length, in........180
    width..............63.2
    height.............59.1
    equivalent vol, cu ft....390
Frontal area, sq ft......20.8
Ground clearance, in......5.0
Steering ratio, o/a......18.2
    turns, lock to lock.......4.5
    turning circle, ft........36
Hip room, front...........54
Hip room, rear............53
Pedal to seat back, max...39
Floor to ground..........10.5

CALCULATED DATA
Lb/hp (test wt).........37.0
Cu ft/ton mile..........60.1
Mph/1000 rpm (4th)......18.3
Engine revs/mile........3280
Piston travel, ft/mile...1525
Rpm @ 2500 ft/min......5375
    equivalent mph........98.4
R&T wear index..........50.0

SPECIFICATIONS
List price............$3685
Curb weight, lb........2555
Test weight............2890
    distribution, %......61/39
Tire size.............165-15
Brake swept area........496
Engine type......flat-4, ohv
Bore & stroke....3.23 x 2.79
Displacement, cc.......1500
    cu in................91.5
Compression ratio........8.3
Bhp @ rpm......78 @ 5200
    equivalent mph........95.1
Torque, lb-ft....81.7 @ 3500
    equivalent mph........64.0

GEAR RATIOS
4th (1.00)..............4.10
3rd (1.64)..............6.72
2nd (2.33)..............9.55
1st (3.95).............16.2

SPEEDOMETER ERROR
30 mph........actual, 27.2
60 mph................53.8

PERFORMANCE
Top speed (mfg), mph......92
    best timed run........n.a.
    3rd (5500)............61.3
    2nd (5500)............43.2
    1st (5500)............25.5

FUEL CONSUMPTION
Normal range, mpg......n.a.

ACCELERATION
0-30 mph, sec...........5.7
0-40....................8.2
0-50...................13.1
0-60...................20.2
0-70...................30.4
0-80...................46.6
0-100..................
Standing ¼ mile........21.1
    speed at end...........61

TAPLEY DATA
4th, lb/ton @ mph. 140 @ 55
3rd................245 @ 48
2nd................325 @ 44
Total drag at 60 mph, lb..130

ENGINE SPEED IN GEARS — **ACCELERATION & COASTING**

33

LANCIA FLAVIA COUPÉ 2000
CAR TEST by STIRLING MOSS

If cars have sharply defined characters according to where they come from – and they do – then the Lancia must be the exception which proves the rule. Italian cars in general tend to be fragile, extrovert and often rather temperamental, at least in the higher-priced ranks – flamboyant in looks, noisy in behaviour and exciting in performance. But Lancias are cars of another breed indeed – they seem strangely non-Italian. They look neat, restrained and business-like rather than exotic or exciting. They perform adequately without boring you to tears or frightening you out of your wits. In a word they are careful cars – careful design, careful performance, careful handling, designed for the well-heeled owner who believes in keeping his car carefully.

The Flavia coupé is probably the most individual and the most up-to-date of the current crop of Lancias. For 1970 it has received what the makers refer to as an extensive re-designing, plus a new body – but those of us who knew the previous Flavia coupé will recognise it straight away. The changes are detail alterations rather than basic transformations. The classic Lancia flat-four engine still drives the front wheels, although it is now a full 1991 ccs, with thirty per cent more power than the one which drove the earlier coupé. Pininfarina's body shape for the car still owes a lot to his design for previous Flavia coupés, although the latest alterations increase the rear seat room in a car which was always essentially a two-plus-two. Now it just qualifies as a four-seater. Since there is only enough room for two at the most in the rear, seats are sensibly shaped to make them more comfortable and give more support than does the usual bench rear seat. The front seats too are very carefully shaped, giving plenty of location and good support in the lumbar region – the soft leather upholstery creates a genuine feeling of comfort.

Another typical touch of Lancia thoughtfulness is the generous amount of space for stowing things away. Apart from a fair-sized lockable cubbyhole in front of the passenger, there are shelves in front of both the driver and front passenger, plus pockets at the side of both footwells for handbooks or papers. The fuses are easily accessible, in a panel on the right of the dashboard cubbyhole, another little idea which could save trouble in any emergency.

Ventilation is well looked after – there are dashboard fresh-air vents, and extractor slits at the rear quarters, while both front and rear side windows have opening quarter lights, so you can virtually arrange the airstream inside the car. The two-speed booster fan is noisy but effective. Other extras such as the cigarette lighter and the clock are nicely finished and well placed.

The centrally mounted gear-lever is placed in just the right position for the driver's hand to drop on it automatically. The four-speed box has reasonably well-chosen ratios and an efficient change, but all the speeds are on the high side, so that you have to give the car plenty of revs in first to get it moving quickly. The engine is smooth and free from undue vibration, but you must be prepared to make it work hard for its keep. In spite of its two litres it doesn't pull well until it is turning over fairly quickly.

I've said that the driving position is comfortable, thanks to the seats and the ventilation. Another vital source of driver comfort is clear visibility, and in this respect too the Lancia scores good marks. The pedals are laid out so that one can heel and toe easily, another sign that the car has been designed for drivers enthusiastic enough to expect touches of refinement.

The ride is comfortable, although not completely silent, thanks to suspension thumps which may be due to the radial ply tyres fitted on the test car – the engine too tends to be noisy when it's revving hard. But the road-holding gives one a splendid feeling of confidence, amounting to a certainty that the car will go exactly where it is pointed. The steering is an important factor here – controlled by a neat, attractive two-spoke wheel set in the right position at the right angle and married to a sophisticated power-assisted system which remains so sensitive that only the freedom from effort reminds you that it isn't a manual system.

The lighting is well arranged. You turn the lights on with a small button mounted on the steering-column lights stalk, then you put the lever up to switch on the sidelights, you push it down to switch on dipped headlights and finally flick it towards you for main beams. It's a simple idea, and once you learn the movements, it's one which you can operate quickly with the same single control.

The horn, on the other hand, is sounded by a button in the centre of the steering wheel, a method which is rather old-fashioned but still tough to beat. I also give Lancia extra points for the beautiful noise of the hooter itself.

The keynote of a car like the Flavia coupé is that, in spite of its neat, sober appearance, it simply begs to be driven hard and promises to respond properly. There are times when things can get slightly out of hand – for example, too much throttle when you start off, and you can easily provoke a front wheel into spinning. In the same way, too eager a stamp on the brake pedal, would I felt, tend to lock up the back brakes. But if driven with a little finesse, it behaves impeccably, even giving plenty of warning in the shape of tyre squeal long before actually losing its grip on an overdone bend.

Certainly you *can* drive the Flavia hard in great comfort. Seating, ventilation, visibility, confidence, all conspire to make the keen driver enjoy himself immensely. It's quiet – apart from a fair amount of wind noise and a smooth hum from the engine – and there is enough room for three average-size passengers. But most of all, for an owner rather than a casual driver, comfort comes from the knowledge that the car's engineering is solid enough to be designed for this kind of use – so he can go on enjoying it for longer than he could in many faster, flashier competitors.

Lancia Flavia Coupé 2000:
Price: £2,288 (£2,989 including purchase tax)
Engine: 1991 cc
Maximum speed: 115 mph
Petrol consumption: 28·2 mpg
Length: 14 ft 11 in
Width: 5 ft 4 in
Height: 4 ft 5 in
Luggage: 16 cu ft

Road Research Report: LANCIA FLAVIA

▶ If Russia's Cosmonaut had a few moments to himself after being jolted into orbit, if he could switch off his headphones and savor the silence of space, he doubtless felt an eerie isolation and an astral quiet, only broken perhaps by the muffled hum of gyros deep within his capsule. A few days before this epochal achievement we had experienced a similarly eerie sensation of incredible solitude and silence in an earthbound man-carrying vehicle that might be termed the "Vostok of Turin": Lancia's new Flavia.

The above is a far-fetched analogy? Perhaps, but the Flavia deserves it completely. Unassuming on the outside, this masterfully-engineered, beautifully-made sedan makes available a new kind of touring travel. The three years expended in test-running this front-drive, flat-four chassis have obviously been well invested by Lancia, a firm that has never been associated with the orthodox and evidently does not intend to be today. Indeed, the Flavia is Italy's first large-production front-drive car.

STUDYING THE ORIGINS

With its front-wheel drive and four-cylinder, high-output, water-cooled engine placed ahead of the front wheels, the Flavia offers some clues as to the characteristics we might expect from the long-awaited small Ford Cardinal which, in one prototype version at least, is laid out in much the same way. The aluminum engine-gearbox assembly, and the fact that disc brakes are fitted, have stirred up a great deal of interest in the use of Flavia parts for a Formula Junior car. For these two reasons, in addition to the Flavia's own obvious merit as an automobile, CAR AND DRIVER now intends to discuss the technicalities of this new Lancia in considerable detail. If you're more interested in acceleration than in valve angles (and we don't blame you!) we suggest you jump to the rear of the R.R.R., but if machinery intrigues you stay tuned to this special report to C/D by Harry Mundy, Technical Editor of London's THE AUTOCAR. Harry's comments are based on inspection of the car at its Turin birthplace.

Design of the Flavia is the work of Professor Antonio Fessia, who joined Lancia during the period that the Flaminia was under development. He was responsible for the substitution of wishbone front suspension for the company's traditional sliding pillars on that car. Fessia was with Fiat pre-war and designed the famous Topolino. He left them and produced the Cemsa-Caproni, a front-wheel-drive car with an 1100 cc horizontally-opposed four-cylinder engine which appeared as a prototype in 1948. Its object was to utilize the surplus capacity of the Caproni aircraft factory during the post-war years, but the design didn't proceed beyond the prototype stage. Returning to Fiat, Fessia produced a similar layout for the Fiat 600, in parallel with Dr. Giacosa's rear-engined design which was finally adopted for production. It's logical that Professor Fessia should now propound and develop his ideas further for the Flavia.

BODY AND SUSPENSION DESIGN

The pressed-steel body shell follows normal practice for this integral type of construction. Beam strength is provided in two deep and wide sills at each side. They merge into the rear seat pan structure, the shallow channel-section floor tunnel which houses the exhaust piping, and the cowl assembly, which in turn merges into the fender valances from which a wheelbarrow box-section arm projects forward at each side. A removable front sub-frame is attached at six rubber mountings; this unit can be detached and wheeled away complete with the engine, transmission, suspension and steering linkage. Such construction allows unit subassembly during manufacture and aids service at major overhauls.

At each side of the welded sub-frame a substantial aluminum casting is bolted, to carry the wishbones, steering box and idler lever. These castings are braced with two steel channel-section box members across the upper and lower extremities of the aluminum castings. The upper one forms the saddle mounting for the transverse leaf spring, which at each outer end is attached to its upper wishbone by a substantial rubber bobbin. The use of a leaf spring is undoubtedly related to the front-wheel drive layout, for it is quite difficult to utilize coil springs and avoid the wheel drive shafts without having an offset load on the wishbones or a high reaction point for the springs, if mounted above them.

Each wishbone has tubular arms, copper-brazed to forged steel ends. Rubber bushings are used at the inboard attachments to the aluminum casting and they are noticeable for their very wide spacing. Ball pivots spaced at 10.25 inches are used top and bottom for the outer swivel joints. Each is sealed with a rubber gaiter and has a lubrication point. Typical of the attention to detail is the construction of the upper ball joint which, on the Flavia, takes the greatest load. It is formed in two halves, with a ball thrust race between them to lighten steering loads. A French-made de Carbon telescopic shock absorber is mounted to the rear of each lower wishbone.

EXPENSIVE DRIVE AND BRAKING

Expense has been subordinated to ideal design in the construction of the Hardy Spicer front-wheel drive shafts, which are often the Achilles heel of such a layout. A constant-velocity Rzeppa-type joint of approximately 3.25 inch diameter is used both inboard and outboard. The outer case of the inner one is formed with six equally spaced semicircular grooves, matching with similar ones in the surrounding pot joint. In each of these grooves five 0.375-inch balls are trapped in position. These accommodate endwise movement of the shaft arising from wheel movements, and virtually eliminate sliding friction. Each joint is gaitered and sealed with lubricant for life. An anti-roll bar, connected to the lower wishbones, passes beneath the side members of the sub-frame.

Several types of rear suspension, including independent, were tried on the prototype car before settling on a tubular steel beam attached to a semi-elliptic leaf spring at each side. It was considered by Professor Fessia that the best compromise of handling characteristics was obtained with this light beam. Coil springs and radius arms, in conjunction with the tubular beam, were also considered, but the leaf spring arrangement made the least intrusion on the luggage space.

Dunlop disc brakes — of the same size as used on the Mark II Jaguars — are fitted to all wheels. They are servo-assisted, with separate front and rear hydraulic circuits. This independence is achieved by the use of a tandem master cylinder, each half having its own circuit to the servo unit.

MASTERFUL FLAT-FOUR

There are many attractions in a horizontally-opposed four-cylinder layout; there are also some shortcomings if the main advantages are exploited to the full. It is almost certainly more expensive than an in-line arrangement; if its virtue of compactness is utilized, bearing sizes and crankcheek thicknesses can be marginal. Lancia seems to have avoided all the snags, and accepted the greater cost involved.

Most horizontal cylinder layouts use a single camshaft in the plane of the crankshaft, but this calls for long push rods with high reciprocating mass, and thus heavily-stressed valve gear at high speeds. The Flavia uses two camshafts to overcome this defect, so that its maximum power is produced at 5200 rpm, and the engine is capable of revving up to 6000 rpm. The two camshafts are driven by a duplex roller chain from the crankshaft, the chain incorporating a hydraulic tensioner. The push rods have a duralumin tubular center section to match the expansion rates of the aluminum crankcase and cylinder heads.

If the adjacent cylinders are spaced to use a minimum fire joint between the block and the head, crankshaft cheeks and bearings are often of meager proportions. In the Flavia the design seems to have been centered initially around the crankshaft and its bearings, for the cylinders are much wider than they need to be for gasket width or water space between the cylinders. This also leaves room for future bore increases. Another factor was undoubtedly the use of opposed valves in a hemispherical combustion chamber. They have an included angle of 39 degrees, which gives just sufficient clearance for the valve springs on the adjacent intake valves, as seen on the cross-section drawing.

This opposed valve arrangement is made possible by the use of individual transverse pivot shafts, as already applied to the Flaminia. Individual intake ports are uppermost on the cylinder heads, the exhaust ports projecting downwards to separate flanges on the underside of each head. Valve head diameters are 38 mm (1.496 inch) for the intake, and 33 mm (1.300 inch) for the exhaust; these are large by current standards, indicative of good breathing over a wide speed range. The valves seat on cast-in iron inserts.

HUSKY BOTTOM END

Crankshaft bearings are massive by any standards, the mains having a diameter of 2.375 inches, and widths of 1.06, 0.93, and 1.375 inches for the front, intermediate and rear respectively. Like the mains the big ends are Vandervell indium-infused lead-bronze type with a diameter of 1.937 inches and a width of 0.875 inch. Crankcheek thickness adjacent to each main bearing is 0.5 inch, the intermediate cheeks being 0.75-inch.

Bearing lubrication is from a Hobourn-Eaton internal-rotor oil pump with a gauze pick-up filter, and circuit through a full-flow filter before the oil is fed to a drilled gallery in the left crankcase half. Connecting rods have an angular serrated-face joint and 1-inch full-floating wrist pins. The German Mahle pistons, which have two compression rings and an oil control ring above the wrist pin, are noticeable for deep recesses in the crowns. These are not required for valve clearance at top dead center, but are undoubtedly provided for increasing compression ratio

Scissors jack is worked smoothly with ratchet that also doubles as lug and spark plug wrench.

Flavia doors open wide, permitting gracious entry into comfortable, bright interior. Ample headroom, chair-height seating, almost complete absence of noise make this one of the world's best tourers.

Sectioned Lancia Flavia seat shows foam rubber interior designed to reduce vibrations. Pirelli-developed seat definitely helps reduce driver fatigue.

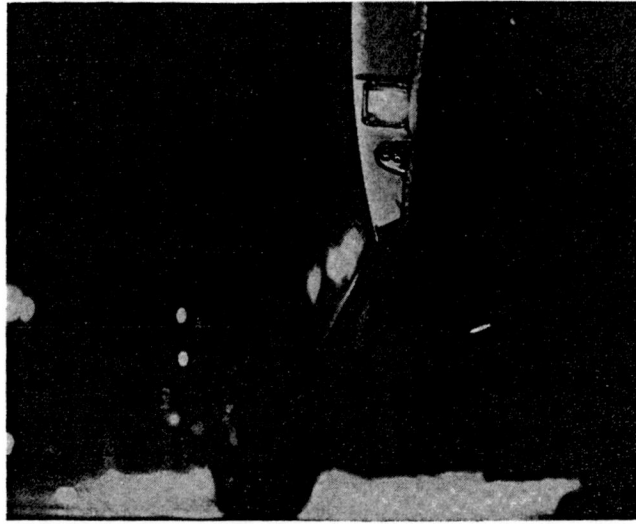
The Flavia is sprinkled with nice little touches such as this flush-mounted automatic door light that neatly defines the width of the door at night.

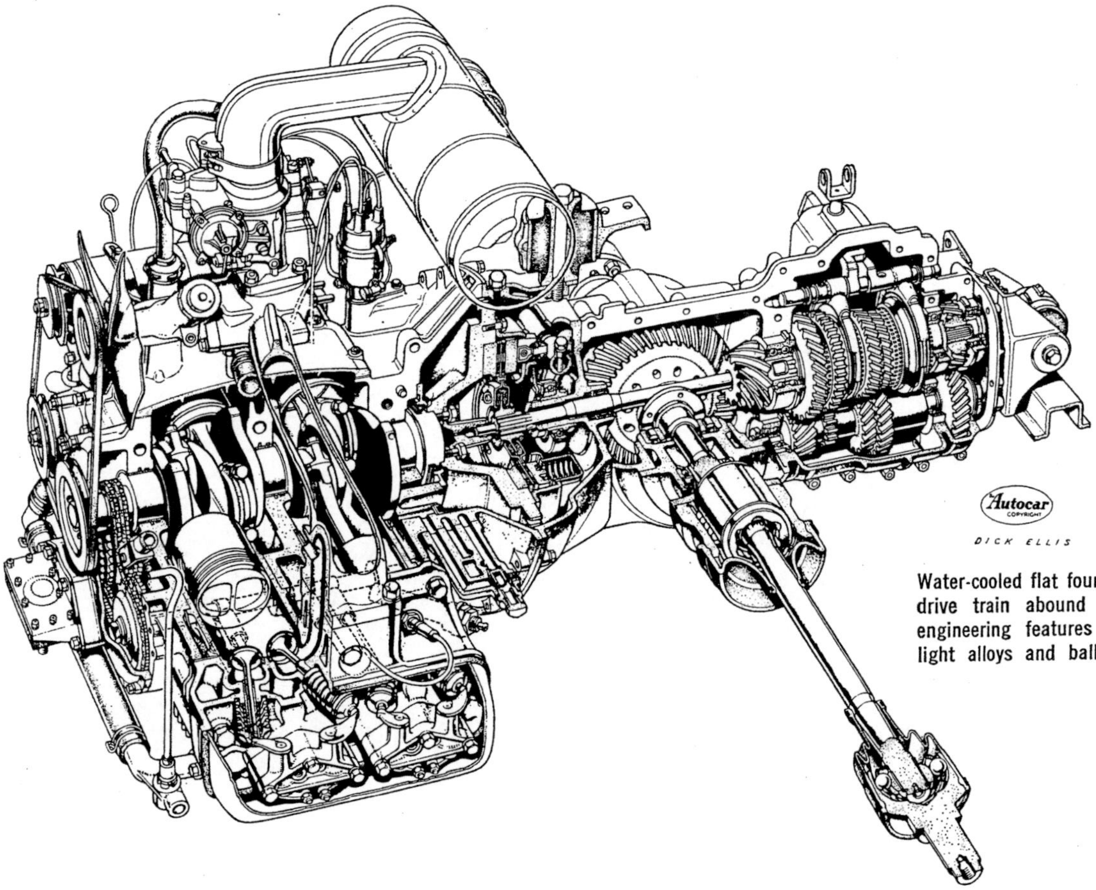

Water-cooled flat four with its gearbox and f.w.d. drive train abound with "cost is no object" engineering features such as extensive use of light alloys and ball-bearing-jointed half-shafts.

Road Research Report:
LANCIA FLAVIA

Importer:	Hoffman Motors Corp. 443 Park Avenue New York 22, N.Y.	9130 Wilshire Blvd. Beverly Hills, Calif.
Number of U.S. dealers:	198	
Planned annual production:	26,000	
Value of spare parts in U.S.:	$80,000.00	

PRICES:
- Basic Price .... $3695 POE New York
- Dealer preparation 75
- Options fitted:
  - Leather upholstery 175
  - Anti-freeze 3
- Total price as tested $3938

OPERATING SCHEDULE:
- Fuel recommended .... Regular (92 octane)
- Mileage .... 19-33 mpg
- Range on 12.7-gallon tank .... 240-420 miles
- Oil recommended .... SAE 10W-30
- Crankcase capacity .... 6 1/3 quarts
- Change at intervals of .... 2000 miles
- Number of grease fittings .... 4 (5 @ 6000 miles)
- Lubrication interval .... 2000 miles
- Most frequent maintenance: Clean or replace all filters, lube distributor, tune engine—4000 miles

ENGINE: (aluminum flat four with two cams in block)
- Displacement .... 91.53 cu in, 1500 cc
- Dimensions .... Four cyl, 3.23 in bore, 2.80 in stroke
- Valve gear: Two chain-driven camshafts in crankcase; pushrod-operated overhead valves inclined in horizontal plane.
- Compression ratio .... 8.3 to one
- Power (SAE) .... 90 bhp @ 5200 rpm
- Torque .... 94 lb-ft @ 3500 rpm
- Usable range of engine speeds .... 1300-5600 rpm
- Corrected piston speed @ 5200 rpm .... 2600 fpm

CHASSIS:
- Wheelbase .... 104.3 in
- Tread .... F 51.2, R 50.4 in
- Length .... 180.3 in
- Ground clearance .... 6.5 in
- Suspension: F, ind., transverse leaf spring, wishbones, anti-roll bar; R, rigid axle, longitudinal leaf springs, anti-roll bar.
- Turns, lock to lock .... 5.0 (4.2 "winter")
- Turning circle diameter between curbs: .... L 34 (40), R 35 (42) ft
- Tire and rim size .... "165" x 15, 15 x 4½J
- Pressures recommended .... 24 psi
- Brakes: type, swept area .... 11 in discs; 474 sq in
- Curb weight (full tank) .... 2540 lbs
- Percentage on driving wheels 60%

DRIVE TRAIN: (Front-wheel drive, engine ahead of gearbox)

Gear	Synchro?	Ratio	Step	Overall	Mph per 1000 rpm
Rev	No	4.40		18.04	—4.1
1st	Yes	3.95		16.20	4.6
			70%		
2nd	Yes	2.33		9.56	7.8
			42%		
3rd	Yes	1.64		6.74	11.1
			64%		
4th	Yes	1.00		4.10	18.2

Final Drive Ratio: 4.10 to one.

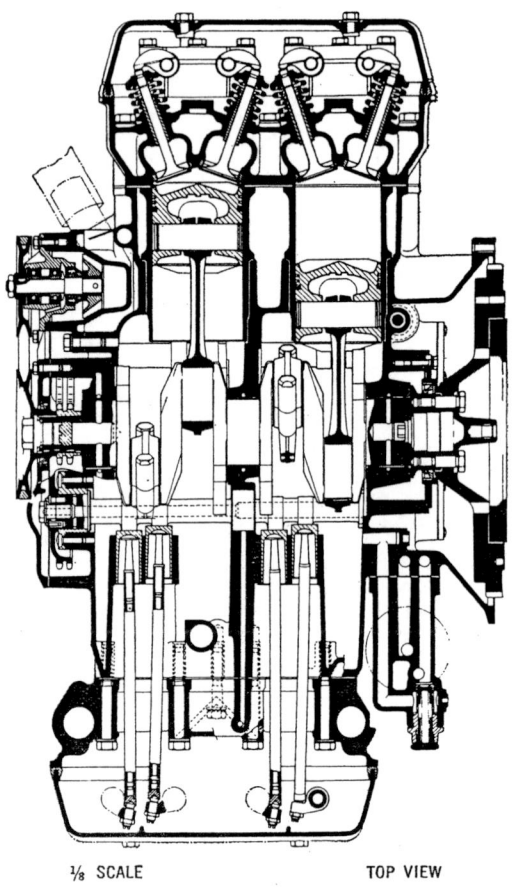

⅛ SCALE — TOP VIEW

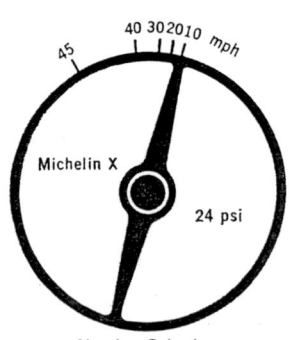

Steering Behavior
Wheel position to maintain 400-foot circle at speeds indicated.

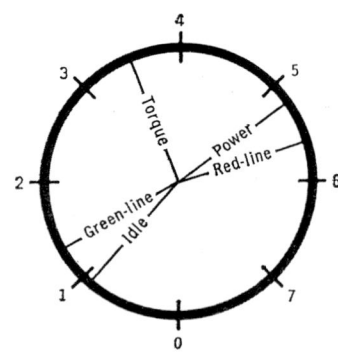

Engine Flexibility
RPM in thousands

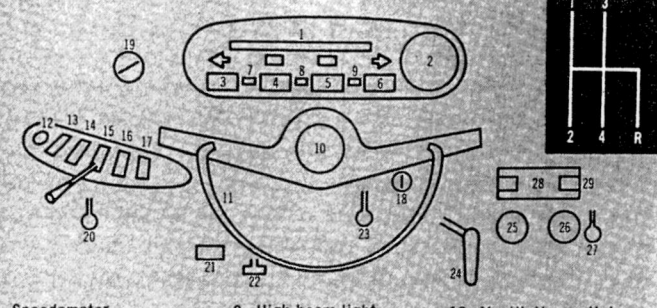

1 Speedometer
2 Tachometer
3 Fuel gauge, warning light
4 Water temperature
5 Oil pressure gauge, warning light
6 Ammeter, generator warning light
7 Lights-on light
8 Choke & hand brake light
9 High beam light
10 High beam flasher
11 Horn
12 Windshield washer
13 Windshield wiper
14 Headlights
15 Turn signals, dipswitch
16 Heater fan
17 Parking lights
18 Ignition (push to start)
19 Ventilation outlet
20 Hood release
21 Panel light rheostat
22 Odometer reset
23 Choke
24 Hand brake
25 Temperature control
26 Heater air control
27 Heater shutoff
28 Ashtray
29 Lighter

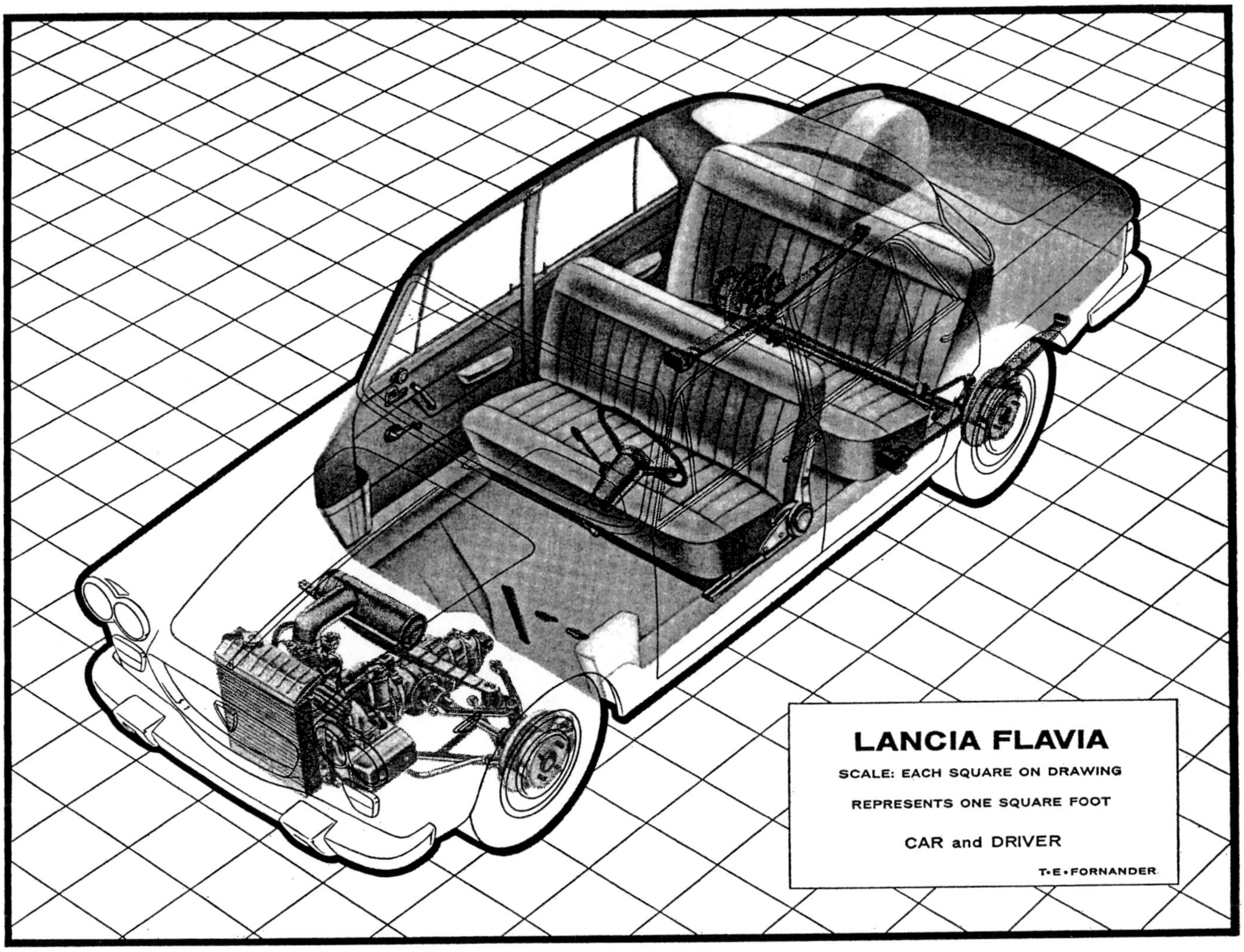

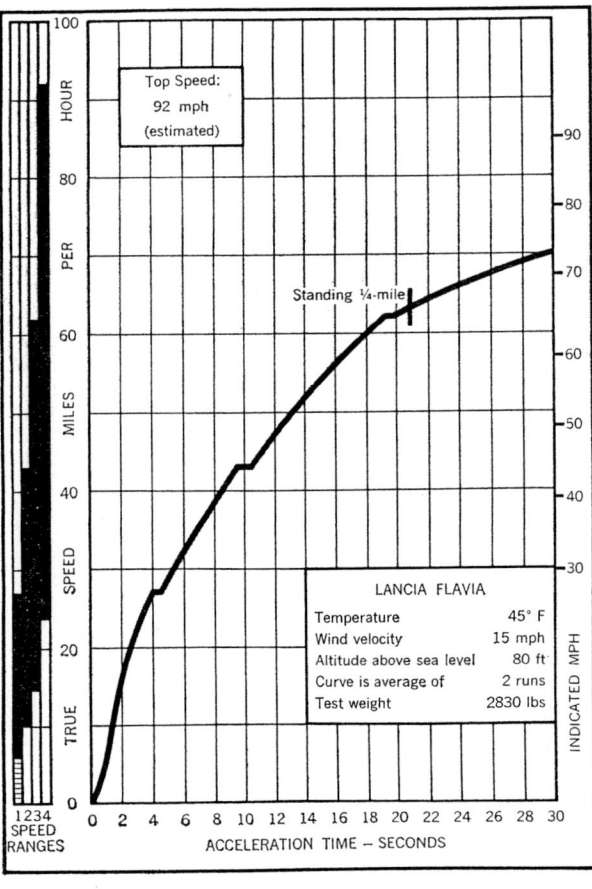

LANCIA FLAVIA
SCALE: EACH SQUARE ON DRAWING
REPRESENTS ONE SQUARE FOOT
CAR and DRIVER
T·E·FORNANDER

Top Speed:
92 mph
(estimated)
Standing ¼-mile
LANCIA FLAVIA
Temperature 45° F
Wind velocity 15 mph
Altitude above sea level 80 ft
Curve is average of 2 runs
Test weight 2830 lbs
TRUE SPEED MILES PER HOUR
INDICATED MPH
1234
SPEED
RANGES
ACCELERATION TIME – SECONDS

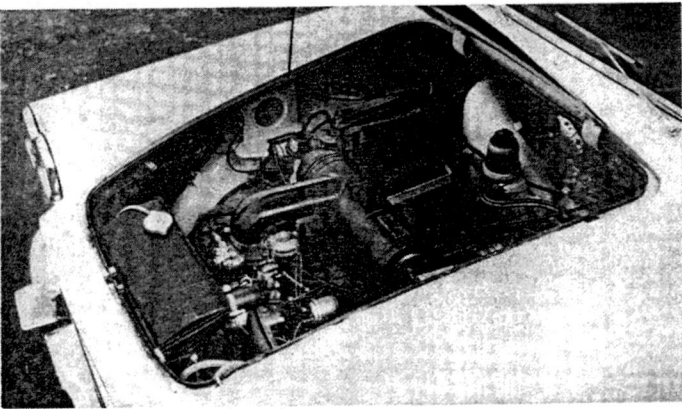

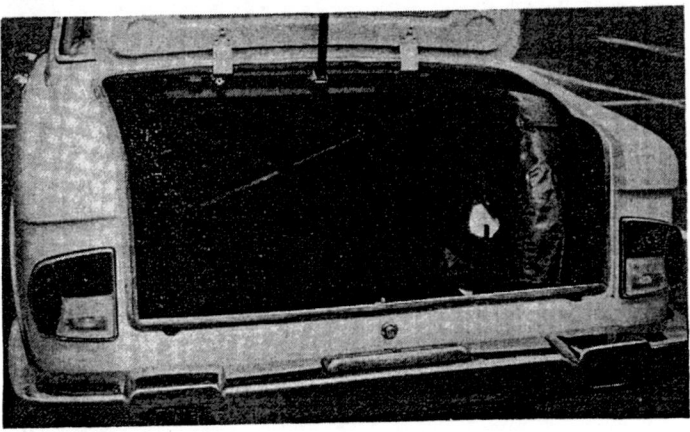

ROAD RESEARCH REPORT: LANCIA FLAVIA

at some future date.

The combined crankcase and cylinder block is split on its vertical center line like the transmission casing. A great deal of thought has been put into these components, and they are produced as aluminum die-castings with open sides so that loose segments in the internal dies are avoided throughout. The sump, with its cooling fins, is integral with each crankcase half, access to the oil pump and its pick-up filter being through a separate inspection cover. The halves are held together by set bolts on either side of each main bearing; Helicoil inserts are used in the female thread. There is, in addition, a series of bolts around the periphery of the joint face.

The wet cylinder liners are held in compression. The amount of clamping is controlled solely by the depth of the recess in the casing and the distance between the two flanges on the liner; in other words, no shims are used. A rubber ring, fitting into the chamber of the lower seating flange, forms the water seal. Between cylinder head, liner and crankcase there is a copper-asbestos gasket with a machined concentric V-section groove in the liner top face and around the combustion chamber in the cylinder head. A single water pump, with split outlet to each cylinder bank, is belt-driven from the crank in a four-point drive which includes the generator (hinged for adjustment) and a separate aluminum cooling fan.

INDUCTION AND DRIVE

Carburetion is by either a downdraft twin-throat Solex or Weber. The two throats lead into a common water-jacketed hot spot, from which individual pipes merge into separate intake ports on each cylinder head.

From the Fichtel and Sachs clutch, which incorporates a patented Lancia rubber-cushion disc, the drive is taken through the hollow hypoid pinion shaft to the rear of the main gearbox shaft. This allows a silent direct-drive top gear, as on the Corvair. All gears are in constant mesh with helical teeth, except for reverse; this is a separate train of straight spur gears placed between first and second. All forward ratios have synchromesh of blocker-ring type; selection is by a column-mounted lever through a complex but effective linkage.

What are the benefits of this elaborate engineering, so completely discussed by Mr. Mundy? Are all these features merely done for their own sake, to be in style or to create sales features? Our conclusion must be: not at all! The complex, imaginative design of the Flavia contributes specifically to product excellence and driver satisfaction.

LIGHTNESS YIELDS SILENCE

To begin with, Fessia's liberal use of aluminum and employment of integral construction reduces weight. This takes effect in two phases: overall weight and front-end weight. Let's look at overall weight first. When the Flavia was announced its curb weight was listed as 2689 pounds, properly judged by most observers as heavy for this class of car. With a full tank of gas, however, our leather-upholstered Flavia weighed in at only 2540 pounds — a pleasant, unusual surprise! Even more important, basic lightness has allowed Lancia to stay within this figure while applying lavish layers of soundproofing materials throughout the car, to reach its present silent state. For example, all the sheet metal surfaces under the hood are sprayed with a thick sound-deadening coating that's then painted. Under-floor matting is unusually generous.

The silence of this car is, as all of our Road Researchers commented, downright eerie. At around-town speeds the only sound from the engine is a breeze-like whisper, probably from the fan, and at cruising rates on the highway this is backed by a muffled hum that might be blamed on the camshaft drive. Other cars offer this kind of silence, but in addition the Flavia is virtually immune from wind noise. If all windows are shut (easy with the efficient ventilation system) and no crosswinds are blowing outside, you hear absolutely no wind! It's uncanny, especially in view of the squarish body shape. Finally the Flavia scores over most American cars — otherwise the world's standard of silence excepting Rolls — with its negligible road noise and utterly rattle-free body. Naturally, you feel it when the suspension moves and hear a distant rumble when the Michelin X tires traverse a rough surface, but otherwise, where sound is concerned, you might as well be riding in a vacuum, like Gagarin.

ROOMY, REFRESHING INTERIOR

Construction of the body yields other dividends as well. Though its overall dimensions are modest, its interior is expanded to maximum possible size by the smooth, flat sides of the body and the near-flush placement of the side windows, which are curved ever so subtly to provide even more elbow room. At a glance the Flavia looks like a high-built car, but as you become more familiar with it (and find that its height is practically identical with such competition as Mercedes and Peugeot) you realize that the illusion of height results from a fender line that's unusually low, thanks to the squat engine, leaving room for windows that are refreshingly high. This gives a wonderfully airy, clean-feeling interior and excellent visibility all around.

The second phase of the Lancia lightening campaign took effect over the front wheels. In a car of this engine size or larger, space within the wheelbase is best utilized by placing the engine out ahead of the front wheels — just as the powerplant is usually aft of the rear wheels in a rear-engined sedan. This biases the weight toward the front, which is necessary to get good traction but if overdone can result in unpleasantly heavy steering. In its search for silence Lancia couldn't accept the noise level of an air-cooled engine, which might offer lightness, so water cooling had to be used. Moreover the heavy water-filled radiator was placed out ahead of the engine, to prevent carburetor icing, instead of behind the engine as in many other front-driven cars. In spite of all these measures the front wheels carry no more than 60 percent of the curb weight, a mean rather than an extreme for front-driven cars. To achieve this the dry engine weight was held to 258 pounds, an impressively low figure.

SUPERB STEERING

Even more impressive is the effect of this lightness, and of the expensive half-shaft design, on the Flavia's steering. When parking it's admittedly heavy, but no worse than other front-engined sedans in this class and better than many. The instant the car moves away the steering lightens substantially to become as smooth and easy as anything on the road. Through its entire lock-to-lock range, with power on or off, there's not a sign of front-wheel-drive syndrome: the vibration in the steering wheel that confirms the front wheels are both steering and driving.

Steering lock is always a problem with front drive, especially with a wide, opposed engine tending to get in the way. This is aggravated by the need to leave room to fit chains to the front wheels in winter. Rather than sacrifice the all-year turning circle to the needs of winter, Lancia chose to install an auxiliary steering movement limit stop on the linkage idler arm. The normal range of 5.0 turns lock-to-lock is limited to 4.2 turns with the limit stop engaged, and the turning circle is increased 6 or 7 feet accordingly. Lancia attention to detail was never better illustrated.

STABLE HANDLING

Though it's not a sports car, and not intended to be, the Flavia's handling is stable and responsive. When you swing it into a corner it takes a four-square stance and shifts willingly into the new line, the rear end obediently trailing the front. The higher roll stiffness of the rear suspension effectively counterbalances the extra weight at the front, giving the Flavia remarkably mild understeer as the Steering Behavior graph shows. At very high cornering speeds the inside rear wheel lifts (as on many front-drivers) and understeer increases, bringing both ends of the car near break-away simultaneously. No violent reaction results if you back off on the throttle during such maneuvers; in fact we've experienced far more dangerous "whiplash oversteer" on rear-drive sedans in this situation.

Cornering is accomplished, like everything else, in silence in the Flavia, by virtue of Michelin X (on our car) or Pirelli Cinturato tires. Good handling is designed in as an enhancement of safety, for the Flavia in its native land is not even intended to be a sports sedan, but rather a smooth, sound tourer for upper-middle Milanese — and now for Americans of the same class. This is symbolized by the bench seats front and rear, without even pull-down arm rests to simulate buckets. Foam rubber cushioning by Pirelli is comfortable and has the controlled firmness that's not designed for showroom selling but markedly reduces fatigue on long trips. A central lever controls a long fore-aft adjustment and a Reutter mechanism allows multiple back inclinations, all the way down to a flat bed position. The optional leather upholstery on C/D's Flavia was a pleasure to the eye and fingertip.

LANCIA FLAMINIA AND FLAVIA

RACING RECORD

DATE	EVENT	DRIVERS	CAR	RESULT
4TH September 1960	Monza Coppa Inter-Europa	G. Rota, Elio Zagato	Lancia Flamina Zagato	15th Place
Car ran as number 43 and completed 79 laps			
10th September 1961	Monza Coppa Inter-Europa	Elio Zagato	Lancia Flamina Zagato	8th Place
Car ran as number 59 and completed 84 laps			
10th September 1961	Monza Coppa Inter-Europa	P. Frescobaldi	Lancia Flamina	9th Place
Car ran as number 56 and completed 82 laps			
10th September 1961	Monza Coppa Inter-Europa	Giorgio Bassi	Lancia Flaminia	12th Place
Car ran as number 57 and completed 75 laps			
6th May 1962	Targa Florio	Guiseppe Ramirez, L. Ramirez	Lancia Flavia	20th Place
Car ran as number 64 and completed 10 laps			
6th May 1962	Targa Florio	Cesare Fiorio, Kynder	Lancia Flaminia Special	Not running at finish
Car ran as number 140 and completed 7 laps			
6th May 1962	Targa Florio	C.D'Angelo, A.Federico	Lancia Flaminia Zagato	Did not finish
Car ran as number 76 and completed 2 laps.			
5th May 1963	Targa Florio	Leo Cella, Franco Patria	Lancia Flaminia Zagato	11th Place
Car ran as number 94 and completed 9 laps			
5th May 1963	Targa Florio	B.Donato, Vittoria Mascari	Lancia Flaminia Zagato	18th Place
Car ran as number 92 and completed 9 Laps			
5th May 1963	Targa Florio	Luigi Cabella, Luciani Massoni	Lancia Flaminia Zagato	22nd Place
Car ran as number 86 and completed 8 laps			
5th May 1963	Targa Florio	A.Arutunoff, B. Pryor	Lancia Flaminia Zagato	26th Place
Car ran as number 98 and completed 8 laps			

LANCIA FLAMINIA AND FLAVIA

RACING RECORD

DATE	EVENT	DRIVERS	CAR	RESULT
12th May 1963	Spa-Franco Champs 500Kms	A. Arutunoff	Lancia Flaminia Zagato	23rd Place
	Car completed 27 laps in 2500 Class			
19th May 1963	Nürburgring 1000Kms	Tom Davis, Bill Pryor	Lancia Flaminia Zagato	33rd Place
	Car ran as number 41 and completed 33 laps			
2nd June 1963	Consuma Hillclimb	Franco Patria	Lancia Flavia	15th Place
	Car ran as number 204 in the Touring Group			
2nd June 1963	Consuma Hillclimb	Leo Cella	Lancia Flavia	19th Place
	Car ran as number 206 in the Touring Group			
2nd June 1963	Consuma Hillclimb	Luciano Massoni	Lancia Flaminia	26th Place
	Car ran as number 64 in the Grand Touring Group			
2nd June 1963	Consuma Hillclimb	Luigi Cabella	Lancia Flaminia	29th Place
	Car ran as number 182 in the Touring Group			
25th August 1963	Swiss Mountain G.P	Carlo Facetti	Lancia Flaminia Zagato	44th Place
	Car ran as number 155 in the Prototype GT Group			
8th September 1963	Monza Coppa Inter-Europa	Leo Cella	Lancia Flaminia Zagato	10th Place
	Car ran as number 34 and completed 81 laps			
8th September 1963	Monza Coppa Inter-Europa	Giorgio Pianta	Lancia Flaminia Zagato	13th Place
	Car ran as number 36 and completed 75 laps			
8th September 1963	Monza Coppa Inter-Europa	Giiovanni Rota Elio Zagato	Lancia Flaminia S	14th Place
	Car ran as number 30 and completed 75 laps			
24th April 1964	Traga Florio	Francesco Santoro Mario Raimondo	Lancia Flaminia	23rd Place
	Car ran as number 104 and completed 9 laps			
24th April 1964	Targa Florio	Leo Cella Rene Trautmann	Lancia Flavia Zagato	Did not finish
	Car ran as number 182 and completed 4 laps			
24th May 1964	Consuma Hillclimb	Luciano Massoni	Lancia Flaminia	28th Place
	Car ran as number 262 in the Touring Group			

LANCIA FLAMINIA AND FLAVIA

RACING RECORD

DATE	EVENT	DRIVERS	CAR	RESULT
24th May 1964	Consuma Hillclimb	Alessandro Ferretti	Lancia Flavia	29th Place
Car ran as number 257 in the Touring Group				
24th May 1964	Consuma Hillclimb	Piero Corbellini	Lancia Flavia	30th Place
Car ran as number 253 in the Touring Group				
24th May 1964	Consuma Hillclimb	Claudio Castellano	Lancia Flavia	42nd Place
Car ran as number 260 in the Touring Group				
24th May 1964	Consuma Hillclimb	Romano Ferretti	Lancia Flavia	63rd Place
Car ran as number 254 in the Touring Group				
24th May 1964	Consuma Hillclimb	Mr. Brandy	Lancia Flavia	91st Place
Car ran as number 256 in the Touring Group				
24th May 1964	Consuma Hillclimb	Luigi Petri	Lancia Flavia	97th Place
Car ran as number 261 in the Touring Group				
24th May 1964	Consuma Hillclimb	Paolo Renier	Lancia Flavia	121st Place
Car ran as number 255 in the Touring Group				
28th February 1965	Daytona 2000 Kms	Dick Irish Bill Pryor	Lancia Flaminia Zagato	Not running at finish
Car ran as number 21 in the Touring Group				

Lancia Flaminia 2,458 c.c.

LOOKING through the specifications of current Italian cars, it comes as something of a surprise to discover that, if one discounts a couple of Ghia projects based on American Chrysler models, the Lancia Flaminia four-door saloon is the largest Italian car. It is longer, wider and heavier than any other, and has by far the widest seating. Considering that its 60 deg vee-6 engine is probably the most compact 2½-litre in production, and that the clutch and gearbox are in unit with the final drive, it is perhaps even more surprising that this car also has the longest wheelbase.

Although the Flaminia saloon was introduced six years ago, its appearance is still so striking that few cars arouse such obvious interest and admiration. When parked, it would often attract a small cluster of inquisitive viewers, and on the move it clearly caught the eye of many a fellow motorist. This could have been due in part to the traditional Lancia deep blue in which the test car was painted, which helped to give it a rich air of quality.

This quality, in design, material and workmanship, permeates the Flaminia. The light alloy engine is a high efficiency one—as it needs to be to pull a car, which may weigh nearly two tons when fully laden, at 100 m.p.h.—developed progressively from the original Aurelia unit of 1950. Its transmission has synchromesh for all four speeds, and unsprung weight at the back is kept low by mounting the rear wheels on a light de Dion tube, the Dunlop disc brakes being inboard. An interesting point is that the outer universals of the drive shafts are exposed to view when the wheel hub-plates are removed; by installing the longest possible drive shafts in this manner, their angular movements and hence the work done by the universals, are reduced to the minimum.

Apart from balancing the fore-and-aft weight distribution, mounting the transmission at the rear results in freedom from a gearbox hump on the front floor as well as a very shallow propeller shaft tunnel. With the car ready for the road and its 12.7-gallon fuel tank half full, the Flaminia is slightly tail-heavy. Suspension arrangements are quite orthodox, with wishbones and coil springs at the front and half-elliptics at the rear, all controlled by Lancia-made telescopic dampers. Compared with the traditional Lancia

PRICES			
Four-door sedan (cloth or Vynide) ..	£2,469		
Purchase tax	£926	17s	9d
Total (in G.B.)	£3,395	17s	9d
Extra			
Leather trim	£154		

44

Autocar road test · No. 1882

Make · LANCIA   Type · Flaminia Sedan 2,458 c.c.

Manufacturer: Lancia & C., via V. Lancia 27, Turin, Italy.
Concessionaires: Lancia Concessionaires Ltd., Lancia Works, Alperton, Middlesex.

Test Conditions
Weather ...... Dry and sunny with 0-8 m.p.h. wind
Temperature .... 70 deg. F. (21 deg. C.)
Barometer .... 30·3in. Hg.
Dry concrete and tarmac surfaces.

Weight
Kerb weight (with oil, water and half-full fuel tank)
    31·1cwt (3,486lb–1,581kg)
Front-rear distribution, per cent F, 47·8; R, 52·2
Laden as tested ...... 34·1cwt (3,822lb–1,734kg)

Turning Circles
Between kerbs .... L, 38ft 11in.; R, 37ft. 10in.
Between walls .... L, 40ft. 11in.; R, 39ft. 11in.
Turns of steering wheel lock to lock .... 4·25.

Performance Data
Top gear m.p.h. per 1,000 r.p.m. .... 20·0
Mean piston speed at max. power ... 2,780ft/min.
Engine revs. at mean max. speed ..... 5,205 r.p.m.
B.h.p. per ton laden .... 64·5

FUEL AND OIL CONSUMPTION

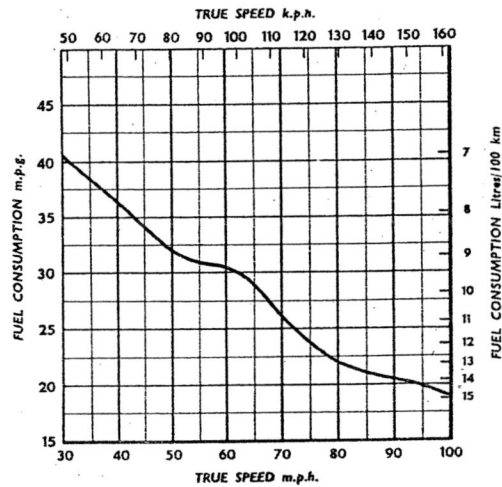

FUEL .... Premium grade
    (97 octane RM)
Test Distance .... 1,081 miles
Overall Consumption .... 20·2 m.p.g.
    (14·0 litres/100 km.)
Normal Range .... 19–25 m.p.g.
    (14·9–11·3 litres/100 km.)
OIL: SAE 20 ...... Consumption 1,500 m.p.g.

HILL CLIMBING AT STEADY SPEEDS

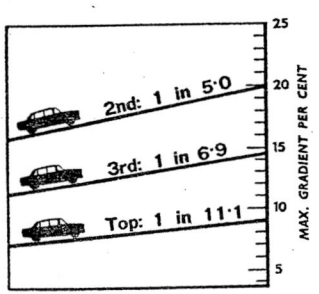

2nd: 1 in 5·0
3rd: 1 in 6·9
Top: 1 in 11·1

GEAR	Top	3rd	2nd
PULL (lb per ton)	200	320	440
Speed Range (m.p.h.)	42–52	40–48	38–42

MAXIMUM SPEEDS AND ACCELERATION (mean) TIMES

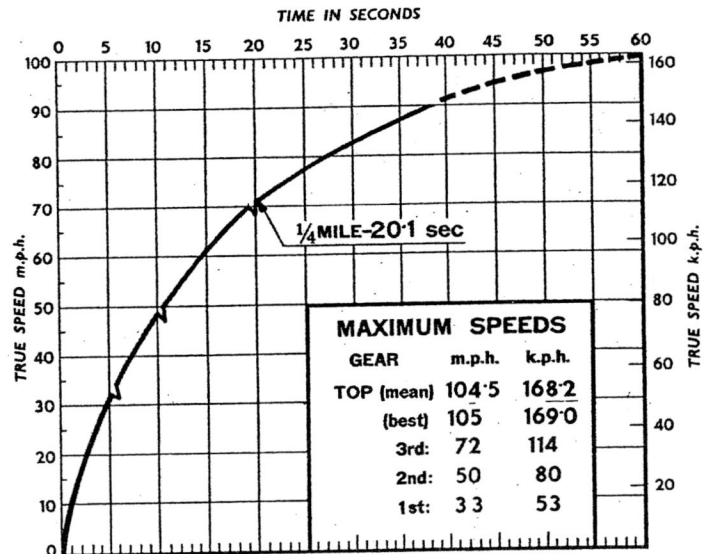

¼ MILE – 20·1 sec

MAXIMUM SPEEDS

GEAR	m.p.h.	k.p.h.
TOP (mean)	104·5	168·2
(best)	105	169·0
3rd:	72	114
2nd:	50	80
1st:	33	53

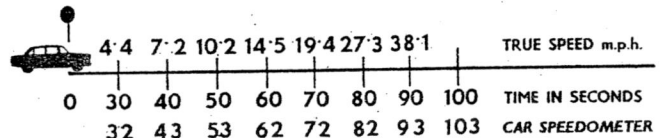

TRUE SPEED m.p.h.	4·4	7·2	10·2	14·5	19·4	27·3	38·1
TIME IN SECONDS	0	30	40	50	60	70	80	90	100
CAR SPEEDOMETER		32	43	53	62	72	82	93	103

Speed range and time in seconds

m.p.h.	Top	3rd	2nd	1st
10–30 ...	—	7·5	4·7	3·9
20–40 ...	11·4	7·2	4·6	—
30–50 ...	10·0	6·4	5·6	—
40–60 ...	11·0	7·6	—	—
50–70 ...	12·0	9·0	—	—
60–80 ...	14·1	—	—	—
70–90 ...	18·7	—	—	—

BRAKES (from 30 m.p.h. in neutral)	Pedal Load	Retardation	Equiv. distance
	25lb	0·11g	275ft
	50lb	0·55g	55ft
	75lb	0·80g	38ft
	100lb	0·90g	33·6ft
Handbrake		0·08g	375ft

CLUTCH   Pedal load and travel—40lb and 5·5in.

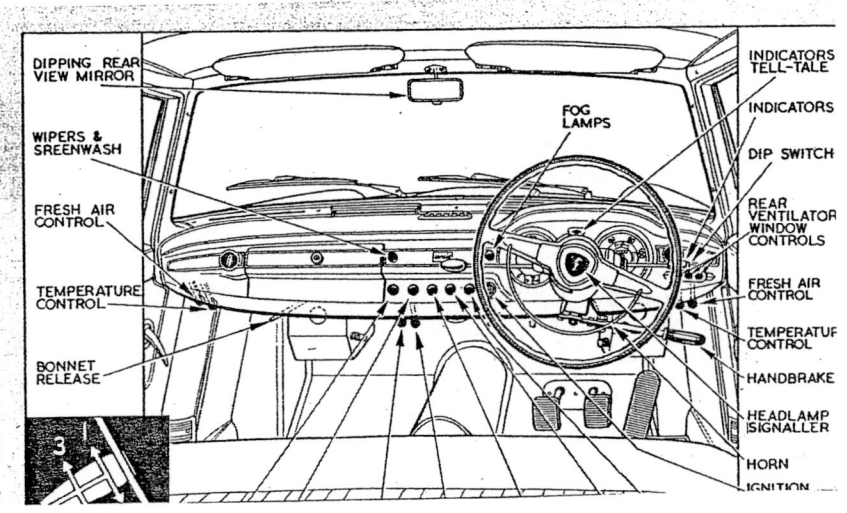

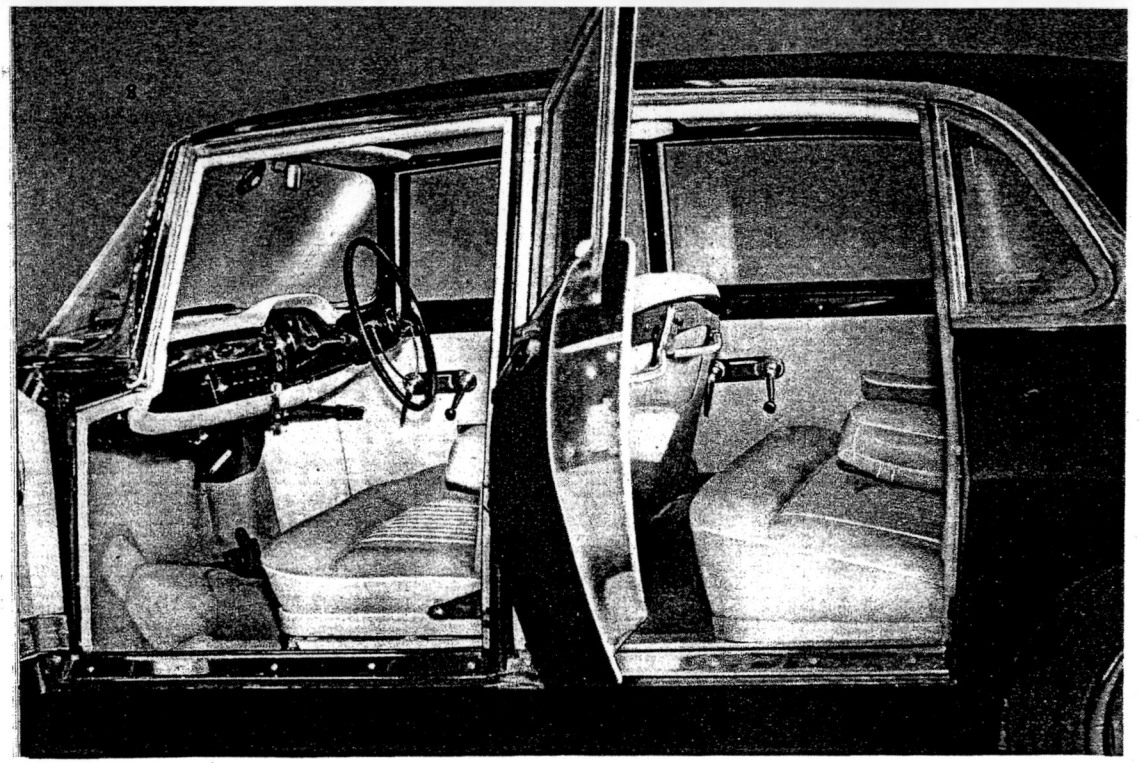

Front and rear floors, covered with light-coloured rubber mouldings, are deep and the propeller shaft tunnel is very small. Leather-trimmed padding surrounds the facia, the sun vizors are resilient, and a framed mirror with dipping reflector is fitted

front suspension (vertical pillars with enclosed coils), the Flaminia type has the disadvantage of requiring considerable routine attention from the grease gun.

Stepping into the car through the wide and heavy doors, one senses at once the rich aroma of leather, which covers not only the seats but also the door panels and padded coaming below the windscreen. There is no woodwork, the screen and door fillets being metal pressings brightly cellulosed in the same colour as the body exterior. Although neatly trimmed, the seats are not quite so comfortable as they appear. The front seat cushion is almost horizontal, and its most resilient section too far ahead of the backrest, so that one tends to slide forward and slouch. To counter this, it was found best to set the adjustable backrest more upright than one might otherwise have chosen. Although there is a centre folding armrest, this is too narrow to support one against cornering forces. With leather trim more resilience in the backrests would help; alternatively, the standard cloth trim would afford more grip on one's clothes.

There are fixed armrests on all four doors. Despite the compact engine and long wheelbase (9ft 5in.), there is no length to spare in the passenger compartment. Drivers of above-average height could do with more seat adjustment than is provided, yet as things are those behind have no more than adequate leg room.

As befits a costly car of this quality, the interior is equipped suitably for long-distance touring. There are map pockets in the front doors, and a facia locker; two pockets, as well as leather hand-pulls, are provided behind the front seat. A unique feature is that the rear quarter-lights can be opened and closed by the driver by means of a group of three press-buttons, the power coming from inlet manifold depression supplemented by a reservoir.

Individual levers below the facia allow the driver and front passenger to control a powerful fresh air supply, and to set its degree of warmth. The heater unit is a rather unsightly black box above the driver's feet. On the test car the heating and ventilation controls were obviously not all correctly adjusted, so that a full assessment was not possible. There are no direct heater ducts to the rear compartment. The four wiper blades—two outside, two inside—which enabled owners of earlier Flaminias to keep the rear window clean have been discontinued.

Driving Controls

On taking his place behind the wheel, the driver finds everything where it should be, although a row of similar control knobs need identification symbols. The wheel itself has a serrated top surface which provides an excellent grip, even in "sticky" weather. There is a half-ring for the horn and the centre boss is pressed to signal-flash the dipped headlamp beams. The gear lever extends from the left of the column, and to the right is a lever which combines the functions of the turn-indicators and headlamp dipping. An engine revolution counter is included among the instruments, and a red warning lamp supplements the oil pressure gauge. Although there is no oil temperature gauge, the Flaminia is unusual in having an oil cooler.

It is also rare these days to find brake and clutch pedals which are not of the pendant type. A well-engineered parking-lever moves in a near-horizontal arc beneath the facia, but the mechanism was not quite powerful enough to hold the car on a 1-in-4 slope. Particularly in dull weather, the driver is all too aware of reflections in the screen; matt black would be a more appropriate finish for the coaming above the facia.

Although rather "tappety" when cold, the Flaminia engine was an instant starter, hot or cold, the mixture control lever allowing progressive settings until normal running temperature has been reached. It promotes mixed

The vee-6 engine is remarkably compact. There is an engine oil cooler beside the radiator, the latter having thermostatic shutters. Electrical circuits are protected by 12 fuses

46

One of Pininfarina's finest pieces, the big Flaminia is without ornament below the waistline. All the rear lamps can be seen from the sides, and reversing lamps are included. Reflectors are recessed in the bumper

feelings, one's less favourable reactions being greatly outweighed by an overall impression of fine quality and potential endurance. On paper its output has been increased by almost 10 per cent since our last test of this version (a left-hand drive car tried in Italy in December 1958), one contribution to this being a rise in compression ratio from 7·8 : 1 to 8·4.

This has resulted in a distinct but relatively small step-up in performance. For instance, the mean maximum has risen from 102·3 m.p.h. to 104·5, and the elapsed time from zero to 70 m.p.h. is reduced from 22·1sec to 19·4sec. Yet the standing-start quarter mile was covered in only 0·1sec less, the new figure being 20·1sec. Undoubtedly the 0-70 m.p.h. figure was the better for the fact that one can now safely take the car to 70 m.p.h. in third gear (although the makers conservatively recommend 68 m.p.h., at 5,200 r.p.m., as the normal limit), since tyres of larger section have raised the overall gearing slightly. During the performance testing about 5,500 r.p.m. were used as the engine speed limit, this being exceeded fractionally to reach 50 m.p.h. in second.

On the debit side, one must criticize the low-speed carburation, which at times is somewhat hesitant and may be a factor in disappointing torque below about 35 m.p.h. in top gear; at high speed there is considerable roar from the cooling fan, and the engine loses some of its refinement as 5,000 r.p.m. are approached. Nevertheless, its natural stride on motorways is around 85-90 m.p.h. true speed, at which it provides extraordinarily quiet and easy running. Considering the usual somewhat demanding circumstances of road-testing, coupled with the weight, size and performance of this car, an overall fuel consumption of 20·2 m.p.g. seems very reasonable; its top-gear cruising figures of, for instance, 27 m.p.g. at a maintained 70 m.p.h. and 21 m.p.g. at 90 m.p.h. add emphasis to its worth as a fine car for the motorway or *autostrada*. Technicians raising an eyebrow at the curious contours of the consumption graph will be interested to learn that comparative figures for the 1958 version would form a curve of practically identical shape, but just below that of the present car.

In the previous test the steering-column change drew high praise indeed; thus we might assume that the linkage on the car just tried was not so carefully adjusted. Apart from the considerable difficulty encountered in engaging first while at rest and in changing up to second until the gearbox had warmed through, believed to be inherent in this box, all the movements except the upward change for third to top required more effort than expected. However, there was never any question of the efficiency of the synchromesh.

The indirect gears are quiet running, and the hypoid final drive likewise. While the clutch was generally smooth— although not always entirely so—it proved quite unable to move the car away from a standstill on a 1-in-3 test gradient.

Regular *Autocar* readers will know that the staff sometimes quote the Flaminia as a prime example of how a car should steer. Perhaps for this reason as much as any other it is always stimulating to renew acquaintance with it. The mechanism is exceptionally light, and so quick in its responses due to lack of springiness or play that one is surprised to discover when parking that over four turns of the wheel are needed between the limits of quite reasonable locks—a mean of 38ft 4in. between kerbs. Moreover the car has inherent directional stability at any speed.

Well-balanced Suspension

In the matter of suspension, an excellent compromise has been achieved between the low-rate softness expected of a quality saloon and the freedom from sloppiness or roll which is, of course, a Lancia tradition. The even distribution of weight and well-phased damping assure an equally comfortable ride in front or rear seats. Only at low speeds did it become apparent that the car was shod with Michelin X tyres, with the usual slight harshness associated with them—a small penalty to pay for their freedom from squeal, their long life and a tenacious grip of the road. Otherwise the car picks up very little road noise and, provided the main windows are kept closed, it passes quietly through the air at high speed, all making for restful travel.

On certain stretches where a smooth surface was evidently laid over an indifferent foundation the passengers would ride less comfortably than expected, yet over really bad sections, including some specially laid *pavé*, the behaviour was exceptionally good, providing a near-level ride without loss of controllability. On really rough going the front suspension would occasionally compress to its bump stops. Over such special surfaces the structure of the car feels immensely strong and rigid. While the slippery nature of the seat trim may discourage the driver from habitually making the best of the Flaminia's road-holding abilities, it is comforting to know that its behaviour is safe and predictable and its normal reactions are neutral; when the limit of tyre adhesion is exceeded it is, in fact, the tail which finally slides.

Since the beginning of 1960, Flaminias have had Dunlop disc brakes all round, boosted by a Lockheed servo, and for many years all Lancias have had separate hydraulic circuits for front and rear wheels. The superb behaviour of these

Lancia Flaminia . . .

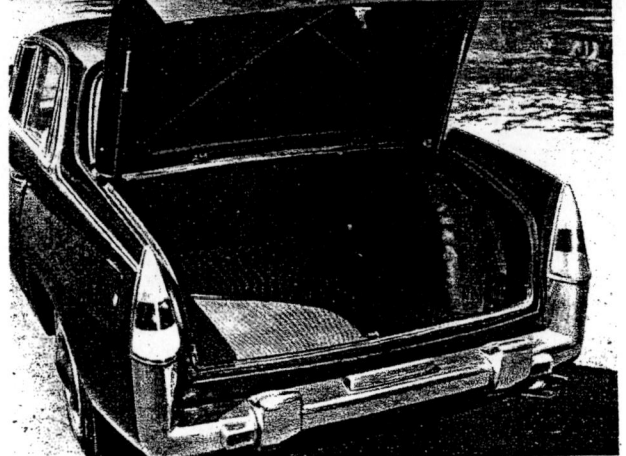

Spring-loaded stays prop the boot lid, and luggage is well-protected against damage. A good quality jack and a proper set of tools are provided. A key must be used to open the fuel filler door

screen washers and wiper blades are brought into action together for a set period. Very powerful and melodious wind horns are welcomed. The overall lighting arrangements are comprehensive, including two built-in fog lamps which also do duty as parking lamps and signal flashers, supplementary amber flashers on the car's flanks just behind the headlamps, powerful twin reversing lamps and even red ones in the trailing edges of each front door, which light up automatically when the door is opened.

In addition there are two fixed inspection lamps beneath the bonnet and another inside the boot. The headlamps are powerful, and have asymmetric dipped beams which feed extra illumination along the roadside to pick out cyclists and pedestrians. A finger-tip repeater button, in the extremity of the indicators lever, seems as practical and instant a dip-switch as we can recall.

One might be excused by Crewe for referring to the Flaminia as Italy's little Rolls-Royce. It is, after all, that country's most costly and best-equipped family saloon, and the standard of engineering is very high indeed. Although not devoid of shortcomings, it is a splendid car which anyone would be proud to own.

brakes is now general knowledge, and those on the Flaminia are in keeping with the usual standard.

Although they operate efficiently, the two-speed wipers leave the sharply curved corners of the screen uncleaned. A commendable feature is that, at the touch of a button, the

Specification

ENGINE
- Cylinders ... 6 in 60 deg. vee
- Bore ... 80·0mm (3·15in.)
- Stroke ... 81·5mm (3·21in.)
- Displacement ... 2,458 c.c. (150 cu. in.)
- Valve gear ... Overhead, pushrods and rockers
- Compression ratio 8·4 to 1
- Carburettor ... Solex C40PAAI downdraught twin-choke
- Fuel pump ... Bendix electric
- Oil filter ... Carello-Fram with disposable element. Gauze strainer in sump
- Oil cooler ... Radiator, with thermostatic valve in filter
- Max. power ... 110 b.h.p. (gross) at 5,200 r.p.m.
- Max. torque ... 139 lb. ft. at 3,000 r.p.m.

TRANSMISSION
- Clutch ... Fichtel and Sachs single dry plate, 9in. dia.
- Gearbox ... Four-speed, all-synchromesh
- Overall ratios ... Top 3·91, Third 5·91, Second 8·60, First 12·94, Reverse 14·08
- Final drive ... Hypoid bevel, 3·91 to 1

CHASSIS
- Construction ... Semi-integral structure with steel body, separate sub-frame carrying engine, front suspension and steering unit

SUSPENSION
- Front ... Unequal length wishbones with coil springs, Lancia telescopic dampers, anti-roll bar
- Rear ... De Dion axle tube carried on half-elliptic leaf springs, Lancia telescopic dampers, Panhard rod
- Steering ... Lancia worm and roller. Wheel dia., 16·75in.

BRAKES
- Type ... Dunlop discs F. and R., Lockheed vacuum servo, Lancia master cylinder with independent circuits F. and R.
- Dimensions ... F. 11·5in. dia. R. 12in. dia.
- Swept area ... F. 200 sq. in.; R. 236 sq. in. Total: 436 sq. in. (278 sq. in. per ton laden)

WHEELS
- Type ... Steel disc, 4 studs 4·7in wide rim.
- Tyres ... 175-400 Michelin X.

EQUIPMENT
- Battery ... 12-volt 42-amp. hr.
- Headlamps ... Carello 45-40 watt
- Reversing lamp ... Two standard
- Electric fuses ... 12
- Screen wipers ... Two-speed, self-parking
- Screen washer ... Electric, automatic interconnection with wiper motor
- Interior heater ... Standard fresh air, with single-speed booster
- Safety belts ... No anchorages provided
- Interior trim ... Leather seat, door and facia trim, p.v.c. roof lining
- Floor covering ... Moulded rubber mats
- Starting handle ... None
- Jack ... Vertical pillar with winding handle
- Jacking points ... Two each side under body sills
- Other bodies ... Medium chassis Farina coupé, short chassis G.T. Touring convertible, short chassis Zagato Sport coupé

MAINTENANCE
- Fuel tank ... 12·7 Imp. gallons (inc. 1·75 reserve with warning lamp)
- Cooling system ... 18 pints (including heater)
- Engine sump ... 10·5 pints SAE 10W20 or 20W30. Change oil every 2,000 miles; change filter element every 4,000 miles
- Gearbox and final drive ... 7·3 pints SAE 90. Change oil every 6,000 miles
- Grease ... 14 points every 2,000 miles (front suspension and rear outer universals), 1 point every 4,000 miles (pedal cross-shaft), 1 point every 6,000 miles (steering idler-shaft)
- Tyre pressures ... F. 26; R. 31 p.s.i. (all conditions)

Scale: 0·3in. to 1ft.

Cushions uncompressed.

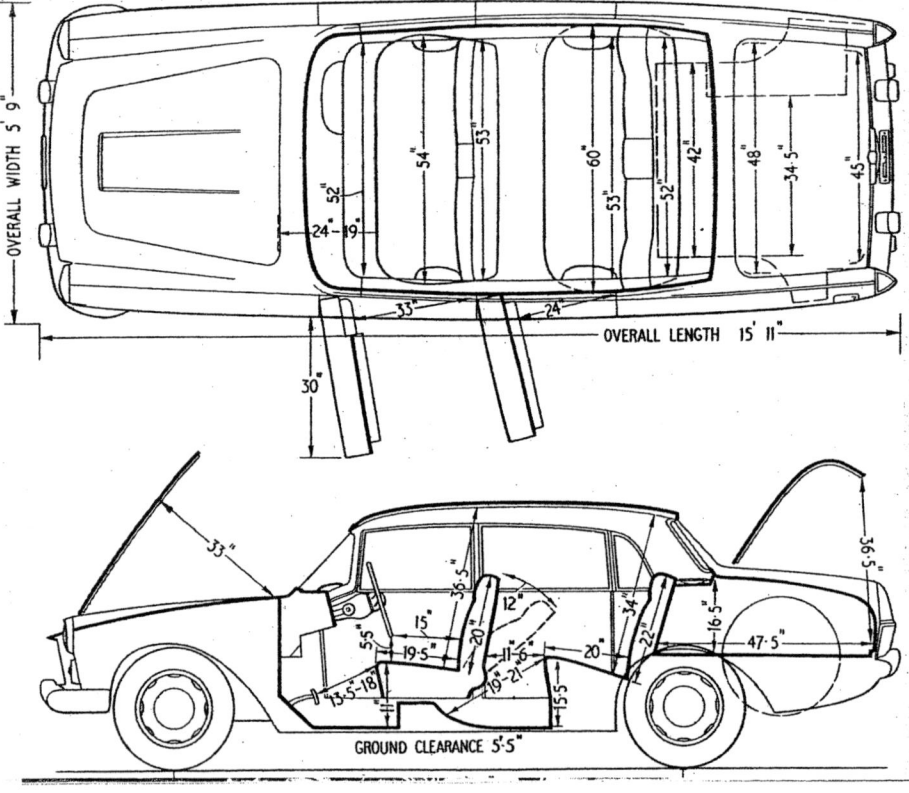

Larger-Engined Lancias

THE FLAVIA 1·8 AND FLAMINIA 2·8

SIGNIFICANT mechanical revision of the flat-four, front-wheel-drive Lancia Flavia and the vee-6 Flaminia came into effect yesterday. Both models have larger engines and new gear ratios to suit; but in the case of the Flavia the new 1·8-litre car supplements the 1·5, which continues in production virtually without change.

Dealing first with the new-type Flavia, its cylinder capacity has been raised from 1,500 to 1,800 c.c. by an increase in both bore and stroke. The dimensions are 88 × 74mm (3·46 × 2·91in.) in place of 82 × 71mm (3·23 × 2·79in.), and the net power is up to 92 b.h.p. for all versions of this car, the compression ratio being 9·0 to 1. By comparison the 1·5-litre saloon's engine develops 78 b.h.p., and hitherto there has been a 90 b.h.p. variant for the sporting coupé and convertible. Claimed top speeds are 100

A steering lock is now featured on the Flavia

Flavia body styling is unchanged

m.p.h. for the 1·8 saloon and 107 m.p.h. for the others, which have higher final drive gearing.

Whereas maximum power is still delivered at 5,200 r.p.m. (as on the standard 1·5-litre engine), the point of maximum torque—now up from 82 to 105 lb. ft.—has been lowered from 3,500 to 3,000 r.p.m. Widespread criticism of the 1·5 saloon's low indirect gear ratios, and especially of the very wide spacing between top and third, has obviously reached a sympathetic ear in Turin's via Vincenzo Lancia, for all the indirects have been raised appreciably. In fact, they are higher than those of the superseded 1·5-litre coupé and convertible. Final drive gearing of the saloon is unchanged at 4·1 to 1, but for the other types it is henceforth 3·9 to 1.

Overall ratios are now as follows, with the previous figures in brackets:—

	Saloon	Coupé and Convertible
Top	4·10 (4·10)	3·91 (4·10)
3rd	5·70 (6·71)	5·42 (5·82)
2nd	8·08 (9·53)	7·68 (8·94)
1st	13·65 (16·16)	12·99 (15·13)

These changes should add greatly to the Flavia's versatility off *autostrada* and motorways, and will be especially welcomed by potential buyers in this country. A new mechanical feature is that a cooler is now incorporated in the engine lubrication system, the unit being mounted vertically beside the water radiator. The body designs are unchanged except that the four-door saloon now has a folding armrest to divide the back seat, and a steering lock is incorporated.

In the case of the Flaminia 2·8 the engine capacity is up from 2,458 to 2,775 c.c., the bore having been opened up from 80 to 85mm while the stroke remains unchanged at 81·5mm. In inches, the new bore and stroke measurements are 3·35 × 3·21.

The new net power outputs, with superseded figures in brackets, are: long-wheelbase four-door saloon, 129 b.h.p. at 5,000 r.p.m. (110 at 5,200); medium wheelbase coupé, 140 b.h.p. at 5,400 r.p.m. (127 at 5,600); short wheelbase convertible, G.T. and G.T.L., 150 b.h.p. at 5,600 r.p.m. (140 at 5,600). In each case the compression ratio is standardized at 9·0 to 1. Claimed maximum speeds for the three types are 106, 112 and 118-120 m.p.h. respectively. These are only fractionally faster than the superseded 2·5-litre cars could manage, but the gains in engine torque, together with revised gear ratios, are of much greater practical importance.

Maximum torque figures for the three stages of engine tune are now: 169lb. ft. at 2,500 r.p.m. (was 139 at 3,000); 163 at 3,000 (was 135 at 3,500); and 165 at 3,500 (was 150 at 3,600). Whereas the standard saloon's final drive ratio is practically unchanged at 3·92 to 1, the medium-wheelbase coupé has been raised from that figure to 3·77, and the other three from 3·62 to 3·54.

New overall gear ratios, with the former figures bracketed, are:—

	Saloon	Coupé	Convertible, G.T. and G.T.L.
Top	3·92 (3·91)	3·77 (3·91)	3·54 (3·62)
3rd	5·57 (5·91)	5·35 (5·91)	4·53 (5·10)
2nd	8·03 (8·60)	7·73 (8·60)	6·58 (7·52)
1st	12·11 (12·94)	11·65 (12·94)	10·94 (11·80)

There are no changes to the Flaminia coachwork, and at the moment of writing there is no news of any changes to the little vee-four Fulvia introduced at Geneva last spring.

Prices in this country of the Flavia 1·8 and Flaminia 2·8 have not yet been fixed. The Flavia 1·5 saloon remains unchanged at £1,456 (£1,760 including purchase tax), but the Fulvia price has been substantially reduced from £1,195 (£1,445 with tax) to £1,149 (£1,389 with tax).

AUSTIN HIRE CAR

AUSTIN'S FL2 Hire Car, derived from the FX4 Metropolitan Taxi model, is now being offered with an alternative seating layout in the rear compartment to suit the requirements of hire car operators. The new layout incorporates two forward facing folding seats, which can form a single bench seat.

Lancia Flavia Coupé 1,800 c.c.

ONE-MAKE enthusiasts have a tendency to be blind, and to see no wrong in the beast they worship. Their eulogies can be boring to the uninitiated, who become sceptical in defence, and judge the car when they see one with unaccustomed severity. To withstand such a stringent ordeal the car not only must be good, but pleasing in the little things as much as the big ones; and to say that the Lancia Flavia coupé offers few disappointments is tantamount to praise of a very high order.

Well over two years have elapsed since we last tested a Flavia (10 November, 1961) so it will help to run over briefly the interesting mechanical specification. Motive power stems from a flat four-cylinder engine ahead of the front wheels and driving them through a four-speed, all-synchromesh gearbox. Front suspension consists of double wishbones and a transverse leaf spring, while at the back there is a lightweight beam axle located transversely by a Panhard rod and sprung with conventional half-elliptic leaf springs. Anti-roll bars are fitted fore and aft, and there are de Carbon telescopic dampers all round.

In our previous test of the saloon version with 1,500 c.c. engine we commented that the car "would benefit greatly from an increase in engine capacity and hence torque," so it was in a way satisfying when the 1·8-litre power unit came on the scene last September—as an option on the saloon and standard on the coupé and convertible. Until then these more sporting variations had been fitted with a tuned version of the 1·5-litre engine with separate twin-choke Solex carburettors for each cylinder bank, developing 90 b.h.p. at 5,800 r.p.m. The larger engine has reverted to a single progressive-choke Solex mounted centrally with long induction pipes, so that although the peak power is only marginally increased to 92 b.h.p. at 5,200 r.p.m., the peak of the torque curve (if one can pin-point it, so flat

PRICES	£	s	d
Pininfarina Coupé	2,066	0	0
Purchase tax		430	19	7
Total (in G.B.)	2,496	19	7

How the Lancia Flavia Coupé compares:

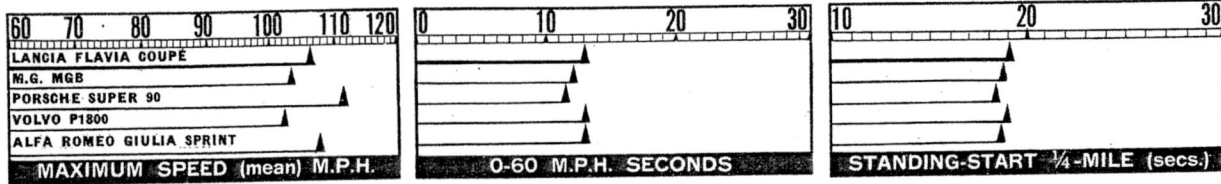

Autocar road test • No. 1957

Make · LANCIA Type · Flavia Coupé (1,800 c.c.)
(Front engine, front-wheel drive)

Manufacturer: Lancia & C., via Vincenzo Lancia 27, Turin, Italy
U.K. Importers: Lancia (England) Ltd., Ealing Road, Alperton, Wembley, Middlesex

Test Conditions
Weather........Dry and cloudy with 5 m.p.h. wind
Temperature.....................4 deg. C. (40 deg. F.)
Barometer..29·5in. Hg.
Dry concrete and tarmac surfaces

Weight
Kerb weight (with oil, water and half-full fuel tank)
  22·3 cwt (2,494lb-1,131kg)
Front-rear distribution, per cent F. 61·5; R. 38·5
Laden as tested............25·5 cwt (2,830lb-1,329kg)

Turning Circles
Between kerbs............L. 34ft 5in.; R, 33ft 7in.
Between walls............L, 36ft 11in.; R, 36ft 1in.
Turns of steering wheel lock to lock .... 4·6

FUEL AND OIL CONSUMPTION

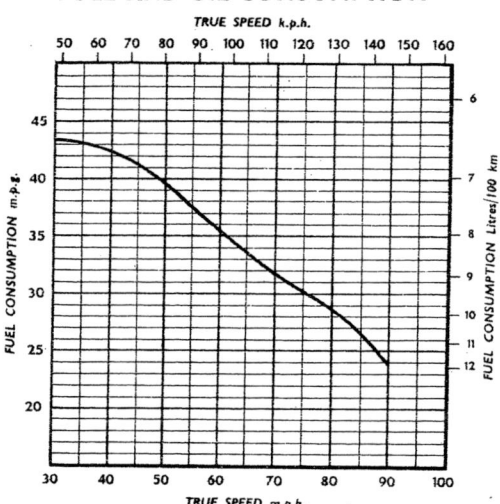

FUEL...........................Premium grade
  (95–97 octane RM)
Test Distance.........................1,043 miles
Overall Consumption............22·9 m.p.g.
  (12·3 litres/100 km.)
Estimated Consumption (DIN) 28·6 m.p.g.
  (9·9 litres/100 km.)
OIL: S.A.E. 20W......Consumption negligible

HILL CLIMBING AT STEADY SPEEDS

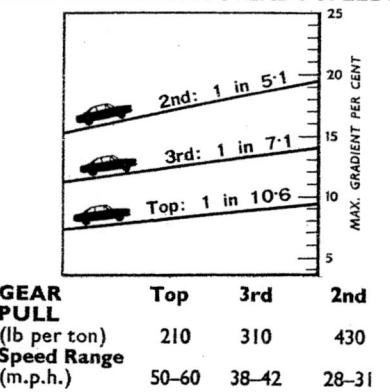

GEAR PULL	Top	3rd	2nd
(lb per ton)	210	310	430
Speed Range (m.p.h.)	50–60	38–42	28–31

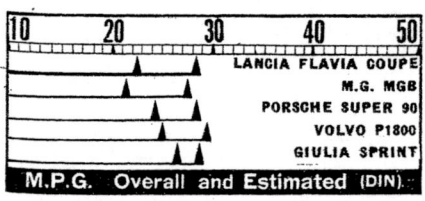

M.P.G. Overall and Estimated (DIN)
LANCIA FLAVIA COUPE
M.G. MGB
PORSCHE SUPER 90
VOLVO P1800
GIULIA SPRINT

MAXIMUM SPEEDS AND ACCELERATION TIMES

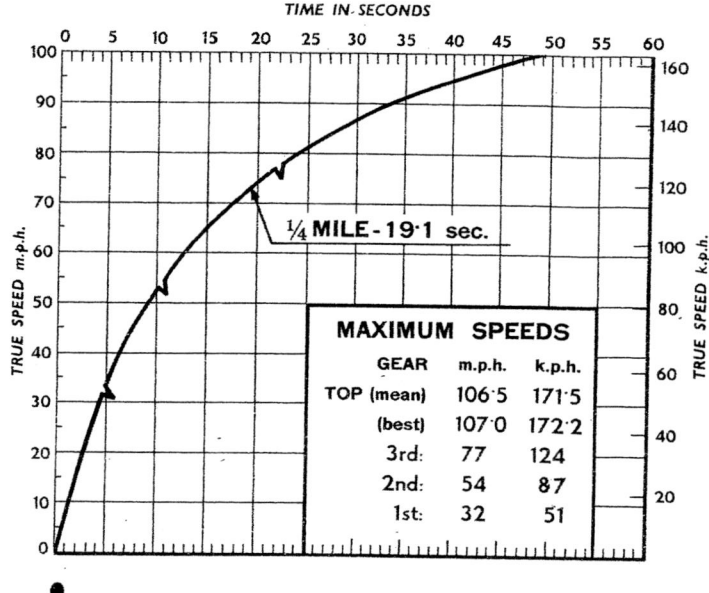

¼ MILE - 19·1 sec.

MAXIMUM SPEEDS
GEAR	m.p.h.	k.p.h.
TOP (mean)	106·5	171·5
(best)	107·0	172·2
3rd:	77	124
2nd:	54	87
1st:	32	51

TIME IN SECONDS	4·4	6·7	9·4	13·2	17·5	23·8	34·3	49·1
TRUE SPEED m.p.h.	30	40	50	60	70	80	90	100
CAR SPEEDOMETER	31	41	51	61	71	81	91	101

Speed range, gear ratios and time in seconds

m.p.h.	Top (3·91)	3rd (5·42)	2nd (7·68)	1st (12·99)
10—30	—	7·3	5·0	3·4
20—40	10·2	7·3	5·2	—
30—50	10·6	7·0	5·2	—
40—60	10·4	7·3	—	—
50—70	11·9	8·0	—	—
60—80	13·5	—	—	—
70—90	17·0	—	—	—
80—100	23·8	—	—	—

BRAKES (from 30 m.p.h. in neutral)	Pedal Load	Retardation	Equiv. distance
	25lb	0·42g	72ft
	50lb	0·80g	38ft
	75lb	0·97g	31·0ft
Handbrake		0·30g	100ft

CLUTCH   Pedal load and travel—45lb and 5in.

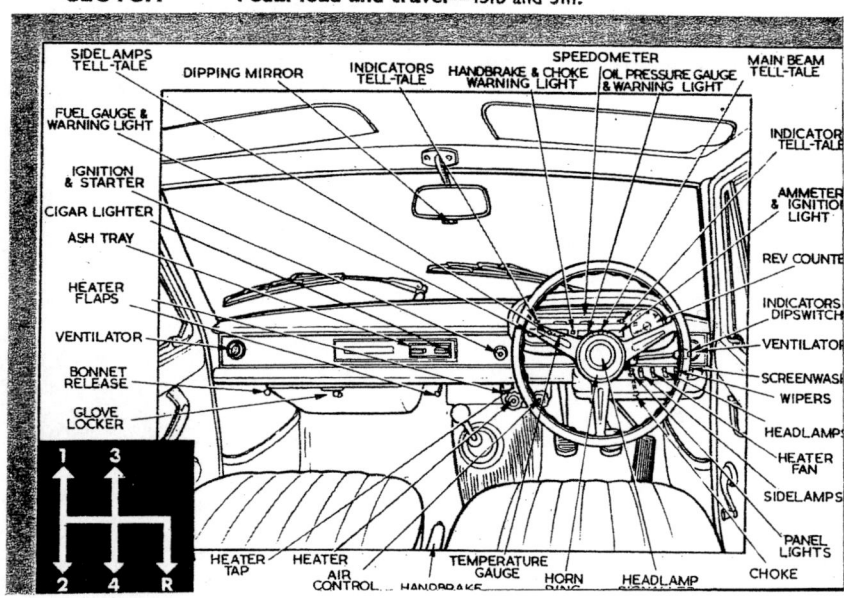

51

Left: Mahogany rimmed steering wheel almost matches the mock wood facia panel which has swivelling vents at each extremity. The gear lever is robust and very businesslike in appearance. There are pockets each side of the foot wells. Right: On releasing the catches each side the seat backs spring forward to make it easier to climb into the back. Unless the front seats are right forward knee-room is restricted

Lancia Flavia Coupé . . .

is the shape) comes 500 r.p.m. lower at 3,000 and its value is greatly improved from 85 to 108 lb. ft.

Another point of criticism has always been the low indirect gear ratios, particularly in the saloon, which seemed to be out of character with the car. With the extra torque of the larger engine it has been possible to raise these on all models, and on the coupé and convertible to fit a higher final drive ratio as well, to take full advantage of the lower drag shape of the body. This results in the very even spacing of 32, 54, and 77 m.p.h. that we recorded as the maxima in the indirect gears. These road speeds correspond to the manufacturer's recommended engine limit of 5,650 r.p.m. which is denoted by a tiny red blob on the rev. counter. As the scale extends to 6,500 r.p.m. and there is no emphatic warning in the handbook, we tried going beyond this limit to about 6,000 r.p.m. during our performance measurements. The engine remained perfectly smooth with no signs of distress at all, and there were some slight gains in the acceleration times from a standing start, but later in the day a rocker arm fractured (due to a material fault) so perhaps owners would be advised not to exceed the suggested limit.

One of the most remarkable things about the Lancia was the consistent way in which it reproduced its performance even in opposite directions. Not only did each run often produce an identical time, but reference to the table for 20 m.p.h. speed ranges in individual ratios shows that the torque curve must indeed be flat, so close are the figures in each gear.

Even in top gear the same was true. On four runs in opposite directions the rev. counter went straight to the red mark (106·5 m.p.h.) and stayed there for mile after mile. The ribbon-type speedometer proved very misleading at all times, for it suffered from a combination of overdamping and friction that made it extremely slow to react. Sometimes it took as long as two or three minutes to reach the steady speed we were holding.

Because the pull is so uniform, one gets no great impression of power when accelerating, yet from rest to 100 m.p.h. in 49·1 sec is decidedly brisk. When on the road, the engine always responds sweetly and without fuss except for one major fault—fan noise. Part of the cooling system is controlled by shutters in front of the radiator block which open automatically when the engine temperature rises. During our December weather not only did the shutters never open, but the temperature gauge never moved off its bottom stop; the noise of the air trying to suck its way past the obstructive shutters was very irritating and gave the impression at high revs that the engine was being flogged. A high-temperature thermostat, or better still a thermostatically controlled fan would be very desirable.

With some 61·5 per cent of the weight on the front, and the drive at that end, one might expect the Lancia to feel rather different from a conventional rear-drive car. This is not the case at all, and very few drivers would be able to detect anything unusual in the handling. With the throttle open through a corner there is slight understeer which gives excellent stability once the car has been set up for the corner. Lifting off half way round causes the nose to dive in a little, but this seems to check itself once the transition is over. At the standard tyre pressures of 27 p.s.i. back and front we found this tendency to swing rather alarming, especially on downhill bends, and felt much happier with an extra 3 p.s.i. in the back.

During fast cornering there is very noticeable body lean,

Much deeper than it looks here, the boot is amply large enough to carry all the luggage four people would take away on holiday. A plastic tool case is lashed down behind the spare wheel

Pininfarina's close-coupled coupé looks particularly pretty on the Lancia chassis. The test car was very well finished in a subtle dark (but not traditional) Lancia blue

but all the wheels stay firmly on the ground and the Michelin X tyres howl a protest only when the road surface is particularly polished. With far the greater proportion of the weight over the wheels doing the driving it is very hard to provoke wheelspin, even in the wet.

On rough surfaces the ride of the Flavia is quite outstanding, and all the more impressive because it is so quiet. Some harshness from the braced-tread tyres can sometimes be felt as a thumping, but most of the time one is continually surprised at the way irregularities and badly repaired road works can be stormed across without a murmur and hardly a tremor. Compared with the saloon we tested before, the coupé even falls a little short in this respect and it may be that the suspension has been stiffened slightly in the interests of cornering power.

As with all front-wheel-drive cars, the directional stability is unimpaired by the violent lurching on a *pavé* surface. There were no rattles anywhere and the whole car felt taut and firm even at 50 m.p.h. Closely spaced undulations could be taken as fast, but not quite with the same abandon, as in the saloon, probably on account of the 6·7in. shorter wheelbase.

With 11in. dia. Dunlop discs on all four wheels, and a vacuum-servo to lighten the pedal loads, the brakes were well able to cope with all the demands we made on them. There was never any hint of fade—in fact they became more sensitive the hotter they were. We took our measurements with them in this warm state and reached an ultimate figure of 0·97g at only 75 lb load when all four wheels were just on the point of locking together. The handbrake did not have enough bite to lock the back wheels, however hard the driver pulled, but nevertheless it produced 0·3g retardation. It also held the car firmly on 1-in-3 facing up or down.

Getting away again on a 1-in-4 produced some clutch slip and smells of hot linings, but there was no permanent damage, and once it had cooled down again all the former efficiency was restored. There was just enough grip to spin the wheels momentarily during a sprint getaway, but ultra-fast gear changes caused a brief period of clutch slip before the drive took up fully.

A particularly enjoyable feature of the Flavia is the really superb driving position. One sits fairly high with a commanding view over the bonnet and square-topped wings, and the relationship between the wood-rimmed steering wheel and the pedals is so arranged that one can settle into the classical arms-stretched posture very naturally. The backrests can be adjusted for rake, and they are all well rounded to hold one in place during fast cornering.

Tall drivers found the headroom rather restricted, but this could be overcome by leaning back at a greater angle. From the bulkhead between the seats a truly massive gear lever protrudes and works in a more or less vertical "gate", heavily spring-loaded towards third and top. There is very powerful synchromesh on all the ratios, but this makes first gear selection on the move quite stiff unless one double-declutches to reduce the drag. The clutch and brake pedals have hard synthetic rubber pads that produced slip with certain types of shoe soles.

To the right of the driver is a small shelf containing four piano-key switches for the accessories. There is no identification and in the dark this system can be very

The flat-four engine is hardly visible beneath all the accessories. There is a rubber cover on the battery, and a block of 12 (no less) fuses alongside. An automatic inspection lamp comes on with the ignition switch when the bonnet is up

confusing; it would be better if they were grouped in two pairs. The choke is tucked away under the dashboard and switches on a bright red light when in use. This same light comes on with the handbrake.

Standard Italian practice is to fit a warning lamp to show when the sidelamps are lit, and this gives a dull green light. In addition to the gauges there are tell-tale lamps to attract the driver's attention when there is low oil pressure or lack of dynamo charge. When three gallons are left in the 10·5-gallon tank, enough for about 75 miles, the fuel warning lamp starts to flash on left-hand corners, and it glows continuously after another gallon has been consumed.

The headlamp switch works through a relay so that the dipped pair of outer lamps only can be turned on first. Main beams of all four lamps are then selected with the button on the tip of the indicator lever. These give a tremendous blaze of light, which makes the dipped cut-off seem all the more abrupt. Dipped beams can be flashed at any time with the outer ring of the steering wheel boss. The inner button sounds strident FIAMM air horns.

Temperature control for the heater is on the air-mixing system so that it is instantly adjustable by means of a small handwheel. For summer use the hot water supply can be turned off separately, and there are individual trap doors to direct the air supply to either driver or passenger.

Although the coupé is close-coupled, strictly speaking, with only two-plus-two accommodation, the back seats are not unduly cramped, and with the front ones slid well forward there is adequate leg-room. The sloping roof line does not restrict headroom as much as one has come to expect from this styling, probably because the seat cushions are near the floor.

The standard upholstery material is cloth, which has a very luxurious feel and look about it, and which we know from our experience with much older Lancias wears very well indeed. Being light coloured on the test car, it tended to show grubby marks a bit, but cleaning with spirit was no problem. Leather upholstery is a very expensive extra (£111) and a hard one to justify.

In front of the passenger there is a large drawer with its own lock, and the two keys (one for this and the boot, and the other for the doors and ignition) have black and white plastic handles to identify them. The interior door handles are particularly well designed to operate as a natural part of the action of swinging the door open, and on the passenger's door there is a stout grab handle. Only the front quarterlights are clumsy to manipulate, but this can be forgiven as they create no wind roar or draught even at maximum speed.

We called the Flavia saloon a "car for the connoisseur" when we summed it up two years ago. This is even more true of the Flavia coupé, for its price is heavily inflated by duty and tax. Nonetheless, it is a very desirable car that would be a continual source of pleasure and satisfaction to its owner. The Pininfarina styling of the coupé is elegant from any angle, and the standards of construction and finish live up to the looks, even under the closest scrutiny. There are many cars for the individualist, but few like the Flavia that immediately class him as a knowledgeable enthusiast who appreciates the finer points of motoring enough to invest in a thoroughbred of engineering.

Specification: Lancia Flavia Coupé

PERFORMANCE DATA
Top gear m.p.h. per 1,000 r.p.m. ... 18·9
Mean piston speed at max. power ... 2,520 ft/min.
Engine revs. at mean max. speed ... 5,640 r.p.m.
B.h.p. per ton laden ... 72·0

Scale; 0·3in. to 1ft. Cushions uncompressed.

ENGINE
Cylinders ... 4, horizontally opposed
Bore ... 88mm (3·46in.)
Stroke ... 74mm (2·91in.)
Displacement ... 1,800 c.c. (110 cu. in.)
Valve gear ... Overhead, pushrods and rockers
Compression ratio ... 9-to-1
Carburettor ... Solex progressive choke
Fuel pump ... Bendix electric
Oil filter ... Fram full flow
Max. power ... 92 b.h.p. (net) at 5,200 r.p.m.
Max. torque ... 108 lb. ft. at 3,000 r.p.m.

TRANSMISSION
Clutch ... Fichtel and Sachs s.d.p., 8·0in. dia.
Gearbox ... Four-speed, all-synchromesh
Overall ratios ... Top 3·91, third 5·42, second 7·68, first 12·99, Reverse 14·48
Final drive ... Hypoid bevel, 3·91 to 1

CHASSIS
Construction ... Integral with steel body

SUSPENSION
Front ... Double wishbones, transverse leaf spring, de Carbon telescopic dampers, anti-roll bar
Rear ... Beam axle, half-elliptic leaf springs, de Carbon telescopic dampers, anti-roll bar
Steering ... Gemmer worm and roller. Wheel dia. 15·9in.

BRAKES
Type ... Dunlop disc front and rear with Lancia vacuum-servo
Dimensions ... F, and R, 11in. dia. discs
Swept area ... F, and R, 232 sq. in. Total: 464 sq. in. (364 sq. in. per ton laden)

WHEELS
Type ... Pressed steel, four studs, 4·5in. wide rim
Tyres ... 165-15in. Michelin X or Pirelli Cinturato with tubes

EQUIPMENT
Battery ... 12-volt 42-amp. hr.
Headlamps ... Carello dual system—45-40 watt
Reversing lamps ... Two
Electric fuses ... 12
Screen wipers ... Single speed, self-parking
Screen washer ... Standard, vacuum operated
Interior heater ... Standard, fresh-air type
Safety belts ... Extra, anchorages provided
Interior trim ... Cloth, p.v.c. headlining
Floor covering ... Moulded rubber
Starting handle ... No provision
Jack ... Scissor type
Jacking points ... Two each side
Other bodies ... Saloon and convertible

MAINTENANCE
Fuel tank ... 10·5 Imp. gallons (no reserve)
Cooling system ... 14 pints (including heater)
Engine sump ... 10 pints SAE 20W. Change oil every 2,000 miles; Change filter element every 4,000 miles
Gearbox and final drive ... 4 pints SAE 90. Change oil every 6,000 miles
Grease ... 11 points every 2,000 miles
Tyre pressures ... F and R, 27 p.s.i. (normal driving); F, 27; R, 30 p.s.i. (fast driving). See text

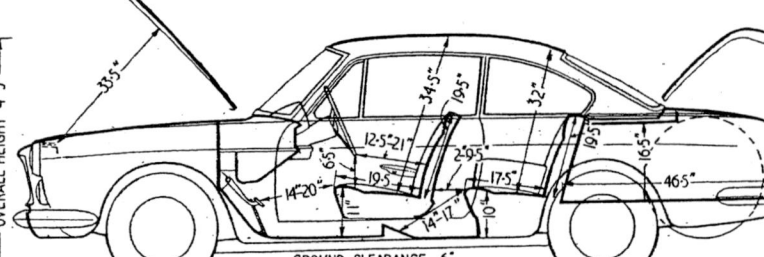

C ARS ON TEST

LANCIA FLAVIA 1.8 COUPÉ

The neat lines of the Pininfarina-styled body look equally pleasing from front or rear, and the dual headlight arrangement marries in well with the body contours.

JUST ONCE, EVERY SO OFTEN, there comes into our hands for road test a car which stands head and shoulders above the rest in a great many ways. The Lancia Flavia coupé, with its supremely elegant Pininfarina bodywork and the recently-introduced 1,800 c.c. power unit, is one of these rare machines, whose superiority is evident but curiously intangible. Its performance is not measurably superior to many of its competitors in the capacity class, and there are cars of similar engine size which will cruise comfortably at higher speeds. None of them, however, demonstrates quite such flawless engineering or such a feeling that the whole car is absolutely "right". Since the November, 1963 issue, *Cars Illustrated* has published road-tests on 58 different cars, as well as driving many more for the purposes of gaining full road impressions although without the opportunity to carry out our full test routine: only the Lancia stands so far above the rest. For British motorists, of course, it is an expensive luxury at only slightly less than £2,500 but to the driver who can indulge himself in a machine which has been designed to be appreciated by true connoisseurs, we feel, on reflection, that it is probably worth it.

The Flavia coupé is based mechanically on the flat-four front-wheel-drive Flavia saloon, originally introduced with an engine capacity of 1,500 c.c. An increase in bore and stroke, announced at the end of 1963, to new outstanding over-square dimensions of 88 mm. × 74 mm. give a capacity increase to 1,800 c.c. and, with a compression ratio of 9 to 1, a maximum (net) power output of 92 b.h.p. at 5,200 r.p.m. Increased torque—108 lb/ft. compared with 85 lb/ft.—reaches its maximum value at 3,000 r.p.m., 500 r.p.m. lower in crankshaft speed. The cylinders are arranged in "flat four" configuration, with push-rod operated overhead valves and a single progressive-choke Solex carburettor, mounted centrally on the power unit. Water-cooling is employed, and the engine is

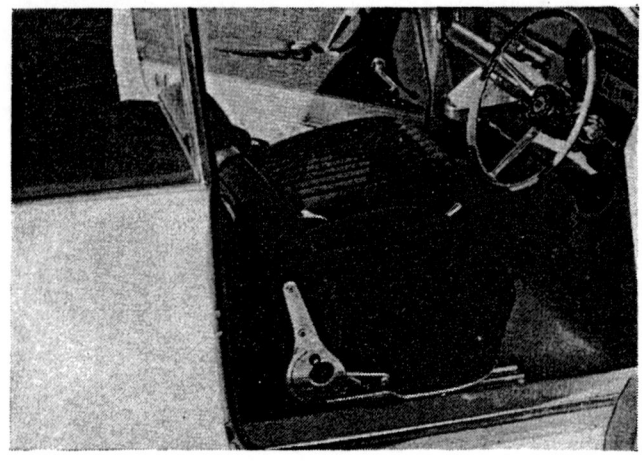

mounted fairly and squarely over the front wheels, which it drives through an all-synchromesh gearbox. The power unit is almost unbelievably smooth and silent, while the torque curve is extremely flat to endow the car—which is no lightweight for a car of under 2-litres, weighing as it does well over a ton—with outstanding flexibility and tractability. The silence with which it operates is by no means simply a matter of effective insulation, a point which is demonstrated by the fact that, at low speeds, the S.U. electric fuel pump can be plainly heard: it is simply that there is virtually a total absence of mechanical noise. Only at high speed does any sound penetrate the interior from the engine compartment, and that is a shrill whine from the cooling fan. Throughout the test period the engine was an instantaneous starter, with no necessity for the choke to be employed in the warm August weather.

The warm-up period is short, with thermostatically-controlled shutters to help, and the engine idles reliably and smoothly even when cold.

The engine, which, as we have said, drives the front wheels, does so through a single dry-plate clutch and a four-speed and reverse gearbox which has synchromesh on all four forward ratios. With the introduction of the larger engine, higher ratios have been fitted to the box and, in the case of the well-shaped coupé, a higher final drive ratio. The result is a set of ratios which can scarcely be improved on with maximum speeds of 30, 54 and 76 m.p.h. The synchromesh is completely effective except on second gear, where a clumsy hand on the gear lever results occasionally in a faint crunch, while first gear was sometimes difficult to engage as a result of the baulking effect of the synchromesh. In operation, the complete transmission train is silent, and lever movement is short and light, with a very short travel across the "gate". The clutch is light to operate, and grips progressively and, under normal conditions, completely effectively: during acceleration testing, very fast up-changes produced a small amount of slip which only manifested itself, however, under these extreme conditions.

Front suspension consists of double wishbones with a transverse leaf-spring, while at the rear the wheels are mounted on a light beam axle, located transversely with a Panhard rod and suspended, conventionally, on semi-elliptic leaf springs mounted longitudinally. Anti-roll bars and de Carbon shock absorbers are fitted front and rear. The ride is soft and smooth, and there is perceptible body-roll under conditions of fast cornering, but wheel-movement is well-controlled and the road-holding is truly excellent. Equally outstanding is the car's ability to deal with rough surfaces; extremely uneven roads can be traversed without reduction in road speed, and the bumps are ridden in an impressively smooth, shock-free manner. The front-wheel-drive arrangements are almost undetectable, although the car possesses some of the inherent characteristics of this layout when being cornered hard.

Under power, there is understeer to give admirable stability, but lifting the foot does not immediately induce oversteer as in some other f.w.d. machines. The only result is that the nose swings in slightly, despite the considerable proportion of the weight which is on the driven front wheels. Michelin "X" tyres are fitted to all four wheels, and the front tyres squeal somewhat readily on dry surfaces. Directional stability is unimpaired either by strong winds or uneven surfaces.

The Lancia's ability to stop is equally impressive. All four wheels are fitted with 11 in. Dunlop disc brakes, and a vacuum servo unit operates on front and rear brakes through separate circuits, so that the car has stopping power to spare. Throughout the test there was never any hint of fade or uneven pulling, although repeated applications produced a strong "hot" smell. The handbrake, which is fully effective, is operated by a sturdy lever, mounted on the floor between the front seats, where it is easily accessible.

As might be expected from a thoroughbred car such as this, the driving position is truly excellent. The seat-cushion is fairly high, giving a commanding field of view over the bonnet and front wings, and the relationship between pedals, steering wheel and adjustable back-rest is such that a driver of almost any height or build can settle immediately into the classical driving position. The seats themselves are extremely well designed, and offer lateral support, as well as a high degree of comfort, which is seldom equalled on a passenger car. On the test car they were upholstered, in common with

the interior trim and rear seat, in dark blue cloth. This is a finish which for some obscure reason is unpopular in this country, but which is, in our opinion, by far the most practical, being warm in winter, cool in summer, kind to the material of which clothes are made and, moreover, extremely hard-wearing. The dark-blue colour of the test car upholstery, however, proved to be a disadvantage when dogs are carried!
The interior of the car is extremely roomy for two adults: tall drivers complained of a lack of headroom, but in every other respect there were no complaints. In the continental fashion, no carpets are fitted, which looks a trifle austere on a car of this class and quality but which is undeniably a practical feature. The steering, with its wood-rimmed wheel, is light, extremely precise and offers a good feel of the road, although we found it rather low-geared and, at parking speeds, rather heavy. There is, however, an unusually good lock for a front-wheel-drive car. Visibility all round is good in dry weather: in the rain the wiper blades tended to lift clear of the screen at high speeds. The pedals are well-arranged for heel-and-toe operation, and the gear-lever is well-placed, but minor hand controls for lighting, screen-wipers, etc. are less well-arranged. They are grouped in a rather illogical order on a sort of piano keyboard on the right-hand end of the facia, and at night are too close together for easy identification. Concentric buttons on the steering wheel boss are arranged as headlamp flashers and as the "trigger" for really strident Fiamm air horns. For night driving, the full beam of all four headlamps gives a tremendous blaze of light which, almost literally, turns night into day: by contrast, the dipped beam is short, in the continental fashion, and after some miles of driving behind the main beams the sudden necessity to change to dipped headlamps results in an embarrassing decrease in the range of visibility.

No rattles emerged from the sleek, elegant and wind-cheating Pininfarina coupé body, but a long trip in heavy rain produced some water leaks, rather surprisingly.

In terms of performance, the Lancia's great virtue is less in what it actually does than in the splendidly sophisticated manner in which it does it. It is certainly one of the least tiring cars to drive fast for long distances that we have encountered, and an effortless 95–100 m.p.h. can be maintained, by virtue of a silent power unit, excellent road-holding and first-class

The flat-four water-cooled engine is mounted well forward in the chassis and almost directly over the front wheels, which it drives through a four-speed gearbox with synchromesh on all forward speeds. Its most striking attribute is its remarkable mechanical silence.

brakes, almost indefinitely. The very flat torque curve of the power unit provides good top-gear performance, and only the joy of using it causes one to recourse to the gearbox. With just over 90 b.h.p. and a total weight of more than 2,500 lb., the car's acceleration can, not surprisingly, be improved on by some cars of similar engine capacity, but few owners would quarrel with an ability to reach 60 m.p.h. from a standstill in just over 13 seconds, nor with the manner in which 80 m.p.h. comes up in 23.8 seconds. A maximum speed of 105 m.p.h.—in one direction the car exceeded 108 m.p.h.—provides a very high cruising speed, while the fuel consumption, at 23 m.p.g. driven hard, provides a satisfactory cruising range from the 10½-gallon fuel tank. More gentle driving allowed the consumption figure to improve to 26 m.p.g.

If we were allowed to choose the car in which we were required to travel from, say, London to the Mediterranean, our choice of the 1,800 c.c. Flavia coupé would be without hesitation.

Cars on Test

LANCIA FLAVIA COUPÉ 1.8

Engine: horizontally-opposed four-cylinder, 88 mm. × 74 mm. (1,800 c.c.); compression ratio 9 to 1; pushrod-operated overhead valves; single Solex carburettor; 92 b.h.p. (DIN) at 5,200 r.p.m.
Transmission: Single dry-plate clutch; four speed and reverse gearbox with synchromesh on all four forward speeds and floor-mounted central gear lever.
Suspension: Front, independent with wishbones and transverse leaf-springs; rear, rigid axle with longitudinal semi-elliptic leaf-springs; de Carbon oleo-pneumatic shock absorbers front and rear. Tyres: 165 × 15x.
Brakes: Hydraulic disc brakes on all four wheels with servo assistance and independent circuits for front and rear.
Dimensions: Overall length, 14 ft. 8½ ins.; overall width, 5 ft. 3½ ins.; overall height, 4 ft. 5 ins.; ground clearance, 6 ins.; turning circle, 34 ft. 5 ins.; kerb weight, 22½ cwt.

PERFORMANCE

	m.p.h.			secs.
MAXIMUM SPEED	—108.3	ACCELERATION	0–30 —	5.0
(mean of 2 ways)	—105.2		0–40 —	7.2
			0–50 —	10.0
Speed in gears First	— 30		0–60 —	13.7
			0–70 —	17.5
Second	— 54		0–80 —	23.8
			0–90 —	34.7
Third	— 76	Standing quarter mile	—	19.5

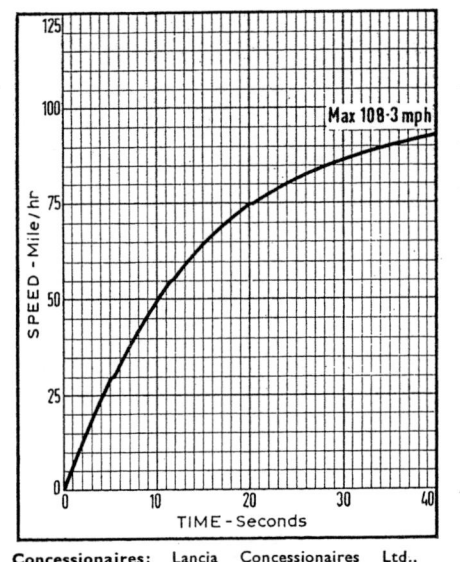

Concessionaires: Lancia Concessionaires Ltd., Lancia Works, Alperton, Wembley.
Price in U.K.: £2,497 19s. 7d., including purchase tax.

Lancia Flaminia Coupé 3B 2,775 c.c.

Autocar Road Test

NUMBER 2030

MANUFACTURER:
Lancia et Cie, Via Vincenzo Lancia 27, Turin, Italy.

U.K. Concessionaires: Lancia Concessionaires Ltd., Lancia Works, Ealing Road, Alperton, Middlesex.

PRICES

Basic	...	...	£2,803	0s	0d
Purchase Tax	...	...	£585	10s	5d
Total (in G.B.)	...	...	£3,388	10s	5d

PERFORMANCE SUMMARY

Mean maximum speed	...	111·5 m.p.h.
Standing start ¼-mile	...	18·7 sec
0-60 m.p.h.	...	12·7 sec
30-70 m.p.h. in 3rd gear	...	14·5 sec
Overall fuel consumption		16·2 m.p.g.
Miles per tankful	...	200

AT A GLANCE: Coachbuilt Italian coupé by Pininfarina with larger, 2.8-litre vee-6 engine; outstanding rough-surface ride; heavy but fade-free brakes; superb roadholding; steering heavy at low speeds; well-chosen gear ratios but poor gear-change in right-hand-drive form.

THE Italian tradition of two-door coupés based on more sedate four-door saloons has now become well established and one of the earliest manufacturers to start this trend was Lancia. Their Flaminia coupé, with coachwork styled by Pininfarina, is now entering its sixth year of production and during this time has changed very little. An expensive car—it costs £3,389 in Britain—the latest model, with 2·8-litre 60 deg vee-6 engine, arouses mixed feeling even among hardened Lancia enthusiasts.

Virtually the only change over the years has been to increase the engine capacity and power. The car started with an engine size of 2,458 c.c., ar this has been expanded to 2,775 c. with a net output of 140 b.h.p. 5,400 r.p.m., compared with 119 b.h. from the 2·5-litre.

Never very smooth at low revs, t vee-6 engine proved an easy start provided the choke was kept out un the whole unit had warmed throug There was a tendency to spit ba through the big triple-barrel Sol carburettor, and for a plug or two "wet" if the car was pottered abo too much when still cold. T accelerator pump on the carburett seemed to be set rather too rich; t had the effect of producing a doub jerk when the throttle was open suddenly.

Not much torque is produc below 2,000 r.p.m. or so, and t

Autocar Road Test 2030

MAKE: **Lancia**

TYPE: **Flaminia Coupé 3B**

Maximum speeds and acceleration mean times
Speed range and time in seconds

m.p.h.	Top (3.77)	Third (5.35)	Second (7.76)	First (11.65)
10— 30	—	7.1	4.6	3.5
20— 40	9.9	6.7	4.8	—
30— 50	10.1	6.5	5.4	—
40— 60	11.2	7.2	—	—
50— 70	11.7	8.0	—	—
60— 80	12.3	9.7	—	—
70— 90	17.4	—	—	—
80—100	22.2	—	—	—

TEST CONDITIONS
Weather ... Overcast, with 8-10 m.p.h. wind
Temperature ... ... 16 deg. C (63 deg. F)
Barometer, 29.4in. Hg. Damp concrete and tarmac surfaces

WEIGHT
Kerb weight (with oil, water and half-full fuel tank): 29.5cwt (3,304lb-1,499kg)
Front-rear distribution, per cent ... F 49, R 51
Laden as tested ... 32.5cwt (3,640lb-1,651kg)

TURNING CIRCLES
Between kerbs ... L, 36ft 11in.; R 35ft 3in.
Between walls ... L, 39ft 2in.; R, 37ft 5in.
Steering wheel turns lock to lock 5.0

PERFORMANCE DATA
Top gear m.p.h. per 1,000 r.p.m. ... 20.6
Mean piston speed at max. power ... 2,895ft/min.
Engine revs at mean max. speed ... 5,420 r.p.m.
B.h.p. per ton laden 86.2

OIL CONSUMPTION
SAE20W30 ... ... 4,000 m.p.g.

FUEL CONSUMPTION
At constant speeds
30 m.p.h. 35.7 m.p.g.   70 m.p.h. 22.2 m.p.g.
40 " 31.5 "   80 " 20.4 "
50 " 28.1 "   90 " 18.2 "
60 " 25.0 "   100 " 16.5 "
Overall m.p.g. ... 16.2 (17.5 litres/100km)
Normal range m.p.g. 15-20 (14.1-18.8 litres/100km)
Test distance ... ... 1,089 miles
Estimated (DIN) m.p.g. 20.2 (14.0 litres/100km)
Grade ... ... Premium (96-98RM)

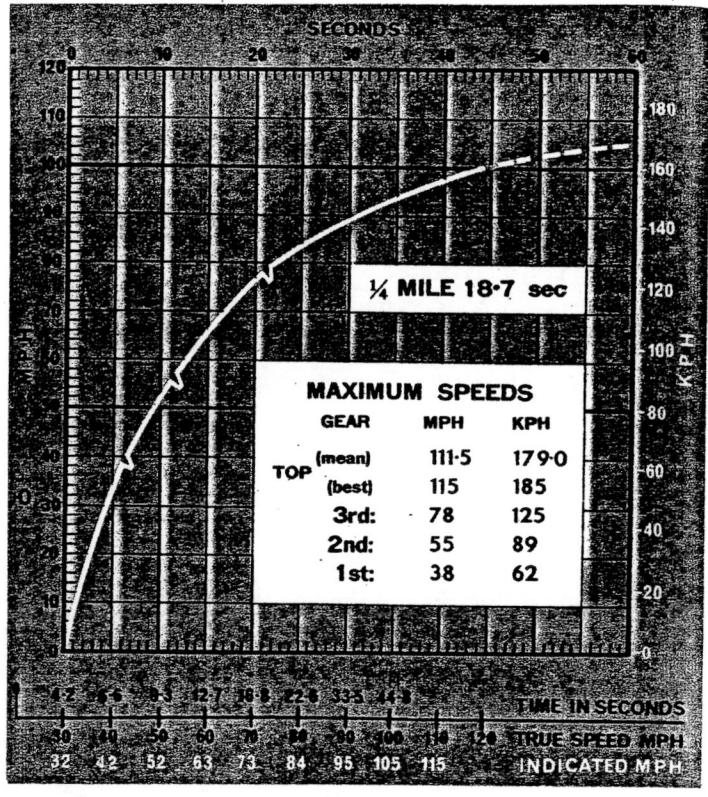

MAXIMUM SPEEDS

GEAR	MPH	KPH
TOP (mean)	111.5	179.0
TOP (best)	115	185
3rd:	78	125
2nd:	55	89
1st:	38	62

¼ MILE 18.7 sec

BRAKES (from 30 m.p.h. in neutral)	Pedal load	Retardation	Equiv. distance
	25lb	0.15g	200ft
	50lb	0.45g	67ft
	75lb	0.65g	46ft
	100lb	0.80g	38ft
	125lb	0.90g	33.4ft
Handbrake		0.30g	100ft

CLUTCH: Pedal load and travel—40lb and 6in.

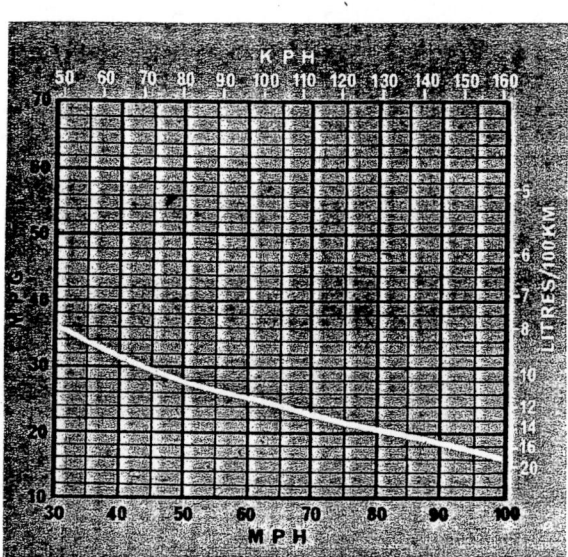

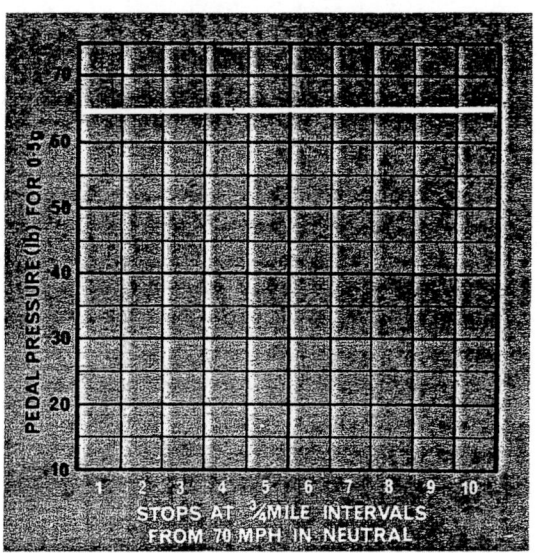

STOPS AT ¼ MILE INTERVALS FROM 70 MPH IN NEUTRAL

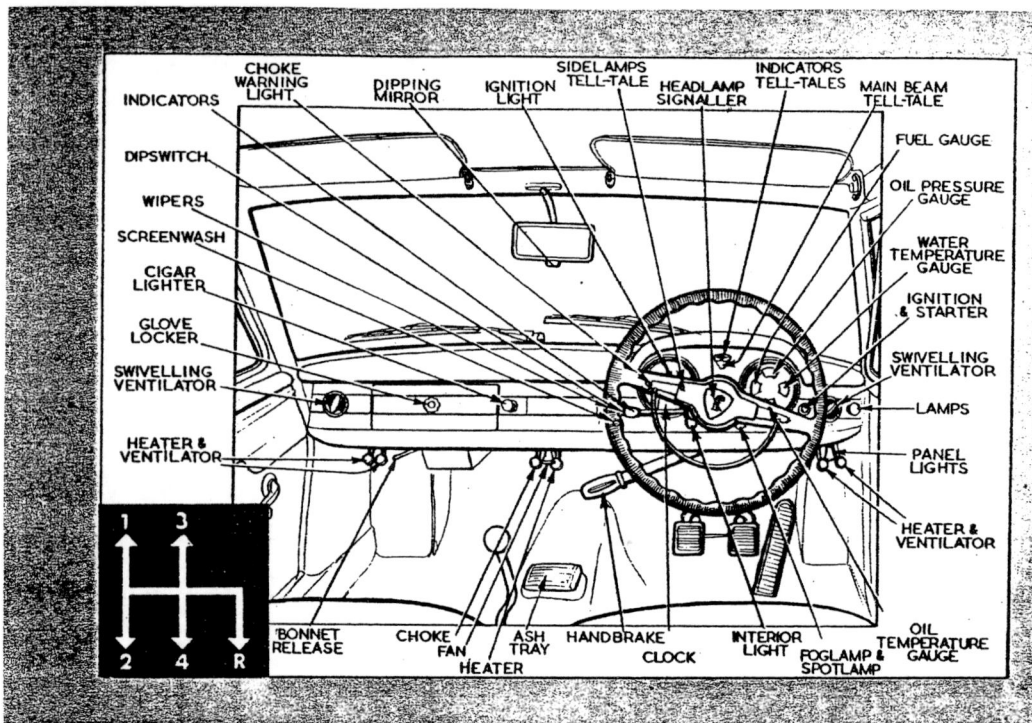

ngine runs out of breath at around ,500 r.p.m., which is the recommended limit. As there is no red line n the rev counter—which reads up o 6,500 r.p.m.—one has to keep a watchful eye on the needle, there being little indication from the engine when the limit is exceeded. One annoying and restraining feature was the siren-like howl which came from the fan drawing air through the radiator shutters which never seemed to open.

Gearchange

In order to keep the weight distribution as even as possible between the front and rear wheels, the Flaminia range all have clutch and four-speed gearbox in unit with the final drive, a divided propeller shaft being coupled direct to the flywheel and thus turning at engine speed. The rear suspension is by half-elliptic springs, with a De Dion tube and Panhard rod. Dunlop brake discs are mounted inboard, next to the differential, to keep the unsprung weight as low as possible. The location of the gearbox entails a long front-to-rear linkage, and the change is not a good feature of the Flaminia coupé in its right-hand drive form. The movements are rather heavy, with little lateral movement between the planes; second gear was especially difficult to obtain when the box was cold. However, the gear stick being located to the left of the shallow transmission tunnel, it would obviously provide a much better leverage and more natural action for the left-hand drive operator.

On the road, the Lancia is reasonably brisk for its size, reaching 60 m.p.h. in 12·7sec and 100 m.p.h. in 44·8sec. At the mean maximum speed of 111·5 m.p.h., the engine is turning almost exactly at the peak of its power curve—5,400 r.p.m. Overdrive or a fifth gear would help here as the character of the car encourages fast cruising.

Although the all-disc braking system has a servo fitted, pedal pressures needed even for quite gentle stops are high. On the credit side there is great resistance to fade—even after 10 stops at 0·5g from 70 m.p.h., the pedal pressure remained constant at 65 lb. Several runs through a shallow ford did not affect the brakes, although the ignition system got a little wet, producing temporary misfiring. The handbrake is placed almost horizontally beneath the facia, where it is rather difficult to reach and awkward to pull on hard. It would not hold the car on a 1-in-4 test

The test car was running on standard Michelin X tyres, although either Pirelli Cinturatos or the Michelin XA2 covers are available. At low speeds the steering is heavy and the steering-wheel is rather high on the facia in relation to the seat, so that even a well-built has some difficulty in moving the out of parking places. In town, almost complete lack of self-centring makes "back double" driving tiring.

On The Road

However, once the Flaminia is the open road, with speed limits behind, it seems to get up on its and really starts to enjoy life. All heaviness goes from the steering

There is plenty of space under the bonnet to get at the engine; the oil cooler can just be seen on the far side of the radiator. Padding under the bonnet lid helps reduce the noise level

Left: The doors open wide and entry and exit is easy. The awkward position of the handbrake can be seen. The facia top is covered in padded black leathercloth. Right: Rear seat passengers have a limited amount of leg room. The front seats slide forward as the squabs are released to allow passengers in or out

Lancia Flaminia Coupé 3B . . .

the car can be driven very fast indeed. The grip from the tyres on dry roads is excellent, with just a deep roar on corners indicating that they are doing their job. Handling is practically neutral, although wet roads betray a very slight, and not at all disconcerting, degree of oversteer. The steel braced tyres do thump and bang more than usual over drain covers and potholes, but one soon becomes accustomed to the noise.

Ride Comfort

Rough road motoring is a revelation in the Flaminia coupé, and one can race over *pavé* and washboard tracks with only an occasional shudder from the bodywork and the thunder of the tyres indicating what is going on underneath. Once, on a double-track level-crossing where the rails were well proud of the road, the suspension got caught out and the car hopped about. Roll is very limited, the car setting itself up in a corner and not wallowing at all.

Although this Flaminia is capable of over 110 m.p.h., and will cruise at 100 m.p.h. for as long as the road will permit, it does become rather fussy at over 85 m.p.h., with a lot of engine noise and wind roar. There is a typical "vee" beat to the exhaust note, which is strong but not objectionable. The well-planned ventilation system is such that the car can be driven in hot weather with just the rear quarter-lights open; with the main windows wound down there is a lot of buffeting and wind shriek.

Several arguments can be put up against cloth upholstery, but a long drive on a hot day should convince almost anybody that it is the coolest and most comfortable material to sit on. The seats in the test car were covered in a dark blue wool cloth material, which stopped people sliding about on corners—but showed every spot of dust, cigarette ash or grit. Leather upholstery is an alternative for £119 12s 6d extra. The front seat cushions are rather too horizontal, so that one's thighs are unsupported, and the seats cannot be moved far enough for taller drivers. Spring catches allow the back rests to be let down, but they will not lie flush with the rear seats. In the back, leg room is very limited, despite cut-outs in the front seats. The car cannot be called a full four-seater, although adults can be carried for short distances in reasonable comfort provided those in the front are prepared to compromise.

Pedals

At the front the floor is almost flat, broken only by the very shallow transmission tunnel. The pedals are bottom hinged—a more expensive and complicated arrangement than pendant ones, but they have the advantage of following the natural movements of foot and ankle. The synthetic rubber pads on the clutch and brake pedals are hard and slippery.

Lancia have laid out the facia of the coupé with more thought for looks than for ergonomics and a more hap-

A good deal of luggage can be stowed in the shallow but long boot. There are two reversing lamps in the lower section of the tail lamp clusters

A locking flap is fitted over the fuel filler. Bright side indicators are just to the rear of each front wheel arch

hazard arrangement would be hard to find. On the painted metal dashboard to the right of the steering wheel are the combined ignition-starter switch, and the driving lamps control. Flanking the column itself are switches for the fog lamps and interior lamp, while over to the left is the two-speed wiper switch, with the vacuum-operated screen washer button just below.

All the other controls are hidden under the facia, and the driver has to risk taking his eyes off the road for a moment to find them. By his right knee is the panel lamp control —wired separately from the driving lamps—and two heater quadrants, which control distribution and air flow on that side of the car. They are matched with an identical pair on the other side of the car. On the individual heater boxes are pull-out tubes, which look like those old-fashioned car ashtrays. These can be rotated to vary the direction of air flow. On the facia ends are cold air outlets, the angle of the air stream being controlled by butterfly flaps. Two more controls under the centre of the facia control the temperature and the single-speed booster fan.

Instrument Layout

All the instruments are contained in two big dials, the left-hand one being the rev counter on its own, and the right-hand one the speedometer, with smaller quadrant dials in the face indicating fuel tank contents, water temperature, oil pressure and oil temperature—although a huge oil cooler is standard equipment. There are the usual array of warning lamps including driving lamps on, choke in use and low fuel level.

An obscure electrical fault in one of the headlamp circuits reduced its light output to a glimmer halfway through the test, but it was reassuring to know that the electrics have no fewer than 12 fuses to protect them. A relay ensures that when the head-lamps are switched on, they come up on dipped beams first. The lamps are brought on to main beams by pressing a button on the end of the indicator arm. During daylight, the headlamps can be flashed by pressing the centre boss of the steering wheel. The range and spread of the head-lamps is very good, with the typical sharp Continental cut-off when dipped. Fog lamps, built into the sidelamps, have a wide and not too bright spread of light.

A half-ring on the steering column controls a pair of very echoing air horns; the spring pressure on the horn ring is a little too weak, so that what is meant to be a polite toot often turns into an angry blast.

Storage space inside the car is rather limited; a small lockable

HOW THE LANCIA FLAMINIA COUPÉ 3B COMPARES:

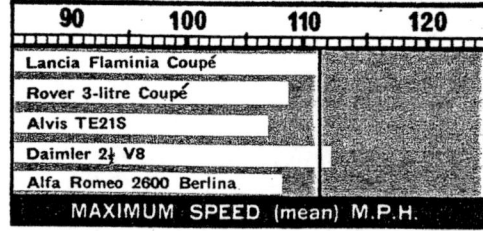

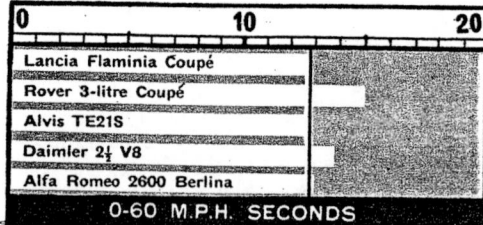

cubbyhole on the facia is useful only for minor objects, while the pockets on the doors have their lips tight under the armrests, so that getting things out can be quite a struggle. A single ashtray is provided at the front, on the transmission tunnel, where the heater air blows the contents all over the floor.

It seems to have become a regrettable trend in "coachbuilt" cars to prove their handiwork by having more exposed screwheads than mass-produced models and the Flaminia coupé abounds in them. At the front there are sensible rubber mats on the floor, and in the back is fitted carpet.

Boot space is generous, and its interior is fully trimmed. A puncture proved to us that the jacking system is very simple and easy. The spare tyre sits in a well on the right of the boot, protected by a plastic cover. There is also a very good tool kit, which contains an excellent wheelbrace.

Under the bonnet the layout is well arranged, with the twin rocker box covers finished in smart crackle black. The fuses and relays are easily reached on the left-hand wheel arch, and oil fillers on each rocker box are connected to the carburettor air cleaner by rubber breather tubes.

Although the Lancia is a quality car, it does require an abnormal amount of service by present day standards. There are 19 grease points needing attention every 2,500 miles, and the engine oil has to be changed at the same intervals.

As a prestige vehicle the Lancia Flaminia is certainly a handsome and fast means of transport. Its price in Britain is high, but it retains that certain air of quality that only a firm like Lancia can manage to put into their cars.

SPECIFICATION: LANCIA FLAMINIA COUPE 3B FRONT ENGINE, REAR-WHEEL DRIVE

ENGINE
- Cylinders ... 6, in 60 deg. vee
- Cooling system ... Water; pump, fan and thermostat
- Bore ... 85·0mm (3·35in.)
- Stroke ... 81·5mm (3·21in.)
- Displacement ... 2,775 c.c. (169 cu. in.)
- Valve gear ... Overhead, pushrods and rockers
- Compression ratio 9·0-to-1
- Carburettor ... Solex C35P3
- Fuel pump ... Bendix electric
- Oil filter ... Fram, full-flow, renewable element
- Max. power ... 140 b.h.p. (net) at 5,400 r.p.m.
- Max. torque ... 163 lb. ft (net) at 3,000 r.p.m.

TRANSMISSION
- Clutch ... Fitchel and Sachs, single dry plate
- Gearbox ... 4-speed, all-synchromesh, central control
- Gear ratios ... Top 1·00; Third 1·42; Second 2·05; First 3·09; Reverse 3·35
- Final drive ... Hypoid bevel, 3·77

CHASSIS and BODY
- Construction ... Integral, with steel body

SUSPENSION
- Front ... Independent, wishbones, coil springs and telescopic dampers
- Rear ... De Dion tube, with half-elliptic springs, Panhard rod, and telescopic dampers
- Steering ... Lancia worm and roller Wheel dia. 16·5in.

BRAKES
- Make and type ... Dunlop discs, with vacuum servo
- Dimensions ... F 11·5in.; R 12·0in.
- Swept area ... F 200 sq. in.; R 236 sq. in. Total 436 sq. in (268 sq. in. per ton laden)

WHEELS
- Type ... Pressed steel disc, 4·5in. wide rim
- Tyres ... Michelin X tubed, 175—400mm

EQUIPMENT
- Battery ... 12-volt 45-amp. hr.
- Generator ... Marelli, 300 watt
- Headlamps ... Carrello 45-40-watt
- Reversing lamp ... 2, standard
- Electric fuses ... 12
- Screen wipers ... 2 speed self-parking
- Screen washer ... Standard, vacuum operated
- Interior heater ... Standard, fresh air, single speed fan
- Safety belts ... Extra, anchorages provided
- Interior trim ... Wool cloth seats, p.v.c. headlining
- Floor covering ... Rubber mats front, carpet rear
- Starting handle ... No provision
- Jack ... Screw pillar
- Jacking points ... 2 each side
- Other bodies ... 4-door saloon

MAINTENANCE
- Fuel tank ... 12·7 Imp. galls. (low-level warning lamp) (58 litres)
- Cooling system ... 17·6 pints (including heater) (10 litres)
- Engine sump ... 10·75 pints (6 litres) SAE20W30. Change oil every 2,500 miles. Change filter element every 5,000 miles
- Gearbox and final drive ... 7·3 pints SAE90. Change oil every 7,500 miles
- Grease ... 19 points every 2,500 miles
- Tyre pressures ... F, 27; R, 34 p.s.i. (normal driving)

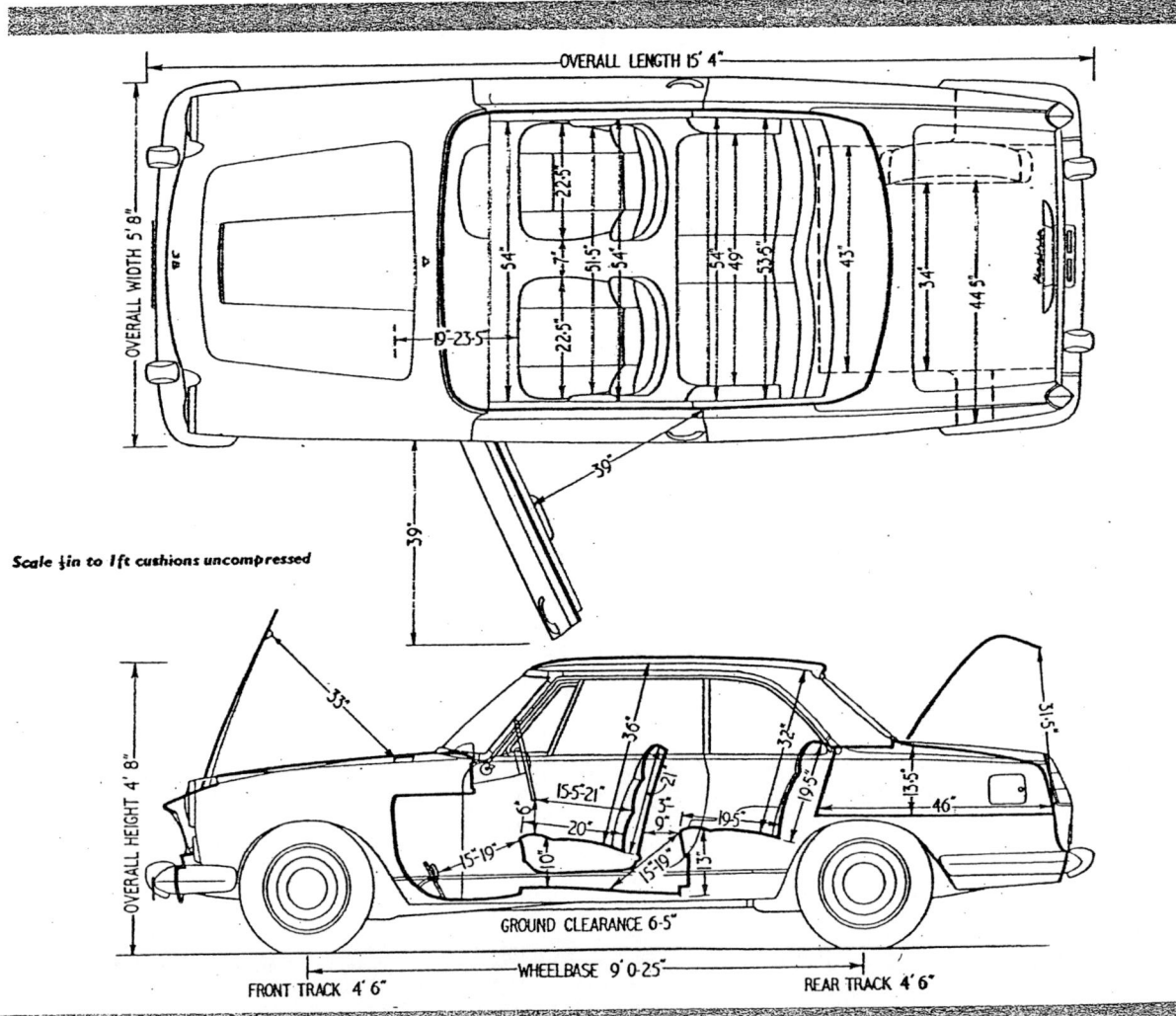

Lancia Flavia Zagato Sport 1,800 c.c.

BY including in their standard catalogue ranges a few individualistic creations by the specialist coachbuilders, the major car manufacturers of Italy broaden their own commercial scope while lending support to an important local industry. Being made in relatively small numbers, these are inevitably rather more expensive than the standard lines.

Zagato is still a quite small family business with a factory near Milan, backed by a long tradition of never-to-be-forgotten designs for sports cars. Their open "spider" 2-seaters for Alfa Romeo in the 30's were absolute classics. Lancia provide special short-wheelbase variations of their vee-6 Flaminia and flat-4 Flavia to carry the coachbuilt bodies, and in the case of the streamlined Zagato coupés tune the engines above their regular outputs.

Beauty being in the eye of the beholder, and the Zagato style for the Flavia being aggressively off-beat and controversial, it certainly does not please all the people all the time. Yet most of us liked the look of the car better and better as we grew accustomed to it, and as a provocative eye-catcher it would be hard to rival. While the æsthetics of a body have no real part in a road test, its functional efficiency certainly has. The special merits of this one lie, first, in its aerodynamic form and tidy detail on the exterior, enabling it to penetrate the air at the car's maximum speed (110-115 m.p.h., depending on conditions) with scarcely a whisper of turbulence; and, secondly, in a novel and remarkably effective system of ventilation.

But one must complain of a very restricted view of what goes on behind the car. The concave rear window is shallow, amplifies reflections, and is poorly served by the internal mirror. A dark, non-reflective trim for the shelf behind the back seat would help. Moreover, the blind rear quarters supporting the roof are wide; although external mirrors above the wings are provided, the driver's view in the one nearest him is distorted by the curved screen. Nowadays one is the more aware of restricted vision of this sort because the average standard has become so high. The view forward and to the sides is excellent.

Hinged along its top, the back window can be opened

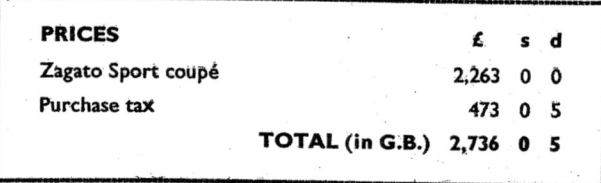

PRICES	£	s	d
Zagato Sport coupé	2,263	0	0
Purchase tax	473	0	5
TOTAL (in G.B.)	2,736	0	5

How the Lancia Flavia Zagato Sport compares:

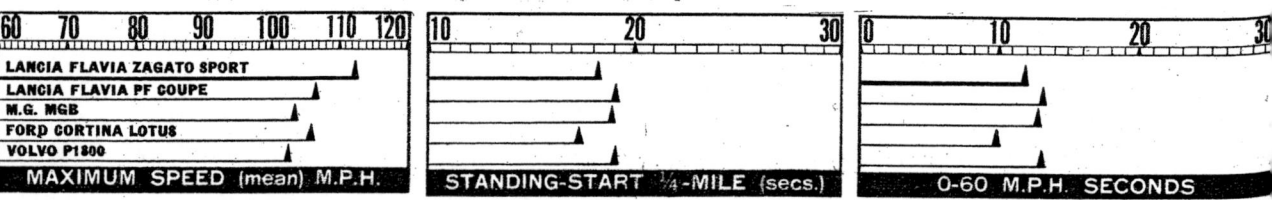

Make · LANCIA   Type · Flavia Zagato Sport
(Front engine, front-wheel drive)

Manufacturer: Lancia & C., Via Vincenzo Lancia 27, Turin, Italy.
U.K. Concessionaires: Lancia Concessionaires Ltd., 16 Albemarle Street, London, W.1.

Test Conditions
Weather .... Fine, with nil wind
Temperature .... 5 deg. C. (41 deg. F.)
Barometer .... 29·44in. Hg.
Dry concrete and tarmac surfaces.

Weight
Kerb weight (with oil, water and half-full fuel tank)
    20·6cwt (2,310lb-1,050kg)
Front-rear distribution, per cent F. 63; R. 37
Laden as tested .... 23·6cwt (2,646lb-1,205kg)

Turning Circles
Between kerbs .... L. 40ft 2in.; R. 37ft 1in.
Between walls .... L. 42ft 3in.; R. 39ft 3in.
Turns of steering wheel lock to lock .... 3·8

FUEL CONSUMPTION

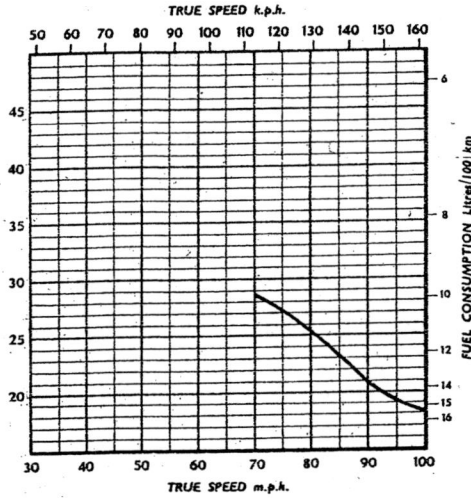

At Steady Speeds in Top
30 m.p.h. .... Due to suspected inconsistencies in our fuel meter readings, the lower speed figures will be published in a later issue.
40 "
50 "
60 "
70 " .... 28·5 m.p.g.
80 " .... 25·3 "
90 " .... 21·7 "
100 " .... 18·0 "

Test Distance .... 1,013 miles
Overall .... 20·5 m.p.g.
    (13·8 litres/100 km.)
Estimated (DIN) .... 28·5 m.p.g.
    (9·9 litres/100 km.)
Normal range .... 18–24 m.p.g.
    (15·7–11·8 litres/100 km.)
Grade .... Premium
    (96–98 octane RM)

OIL CONSUMPTION (SAE 10W30)
    2,700 m.p.g.

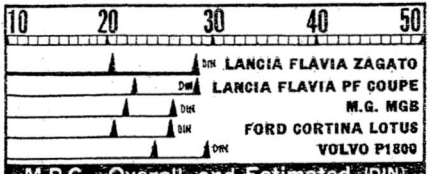

MAXIMUM SPEEDS AND ACCELERATION MEAN TIMES

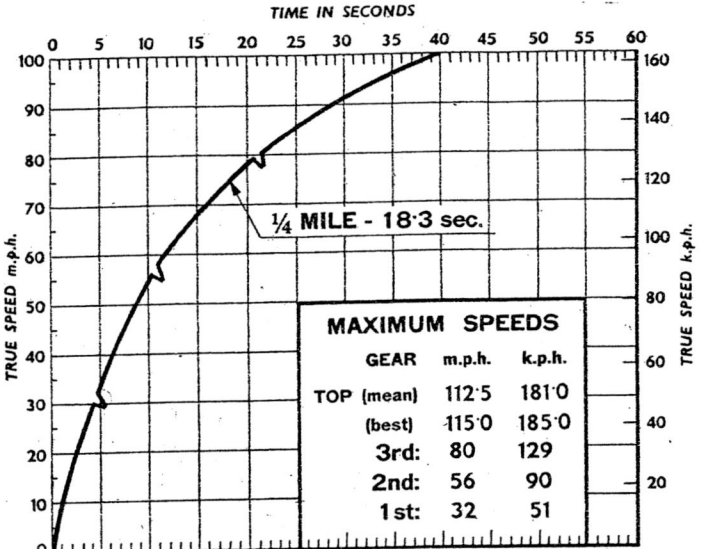

¼ MILE – 18·3 sec.

MAXIMUM SPEEDS

GEAR	m.p.h.	k.p.h.
TOP (mean)	112·5	181·0
(best)	115·0	185·0
3rd:	80	129
2nd:	56	90
1st:	32	51

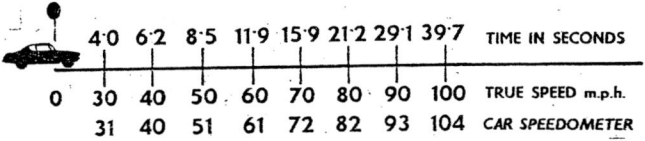

	4·0	6·2	8·5	11·9	15·9	21·2	29·1	39·7	TIME IN SECONDS
	0	30	40	50	60	70	80	90	100	TRUE SPEED m.p.h.
		31	40	51	61	72	82	93	104	CAR SPEEDOMETER

Speed range, gear ratios and time in seconds

m.p.h.	Top (3·82)	Third (5·3)	Second (7·12)	First (12·7)
10—30	—	—	—	3·3
20—40	—	7·2	4·7	—
30—50	10·7	6·2	4·8	—
40—60	9·9	6·6	—	—
50—70	10·1	7·5	—	—
60—80	11·5	9·6	—	—
70—90	14·2	—	—	—
80—100	18·5	—	—	—

BRAKES	Pedal load	Retardation	Equiv. distance
(from 30 m.p.h.	25lb	0·25g	120ft
in neutral)	50lb	0·60g	50ft
	75lb	0·75g	40ft
	85lb	0·84g	36ft
	160lb	0·91g	33·1ft
Hand brake		0·29g	104ft

CLUTCH Pedal load and travel—40lb and 5·5in.

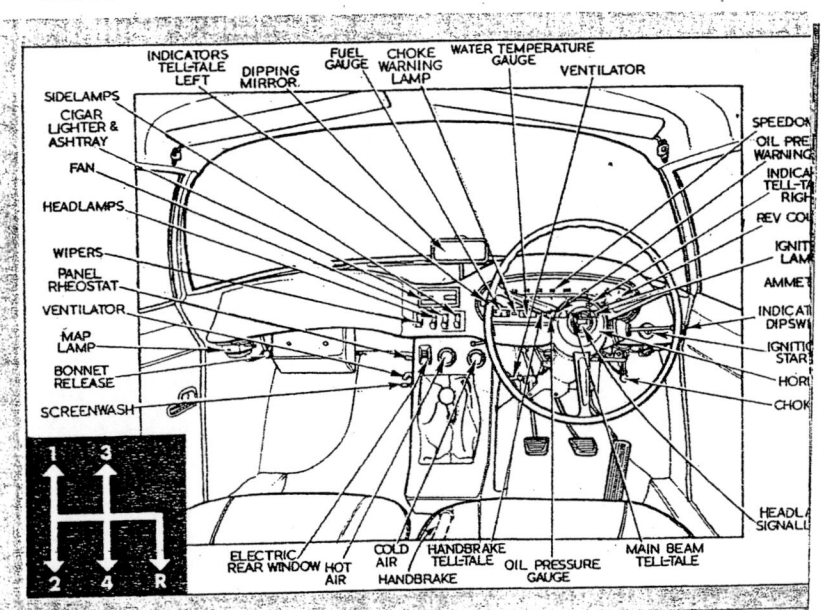

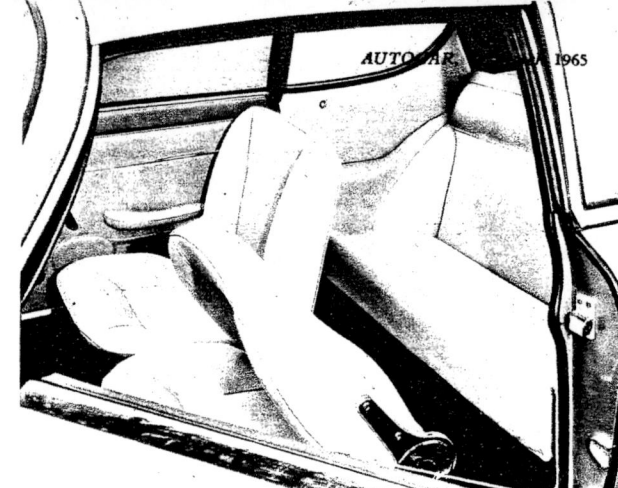

Left: Trimmed in pale plastic, the front seats have adjustable backrests and deep cushions. Door windows are unframed. The wood-rimmed steering-wheel is set rather high, and the central gear lever's arc of movement is nearly vertical.

Right: In the back is a simple but reasonably practical seat, although there is barely enough room for heads and legs

Lancia Flavia Zagato Sport . . .

two or three inches at the base, an electric motor with two-way switch within the driver's reach enabling him to adjust it while the car is moving. This aperture being in a low-pressure area, one has only to open the forward fresh air intake, directing the air current to pass through or miss the heater as required, for a consistent and unobtrusive flow to be induced. So long as the side windows are kept shut, the car's interior is maintained at a very even temperature without draught, wind road, or "mugginess," and without needing the booster fan except in crawling traffic; non-smokers in particular appreciate the manner in which tobacco fumes are carried away. Provided that the front ventilator is even partially open, the flow continues; shutting it while the back window is open immediately brings cold draughts down one's neck.

Whereas the other Flavia models (standard saloon, Pininfarina coupé and Vignale convertible) share a common engine type with single, twin-choke carburettor, the Zagato Sport version has two compound carburettors with an individual choke for each cylinder; its net output of 100 b.h.p. at 5,200 r.p.m. is 8 b.h.p. higher, and its 120 lb. ft. maximum torque compares very favourably with the single-carburettor type's 108.

Slightly higher final drive gearing (3·82 to 1, in place of 3·91) complements the extra power, light weight and low drag of the body. Unfortunately our test car arrived with only 850 miles behind it, and although the figure had reached 1,450 before performance figures were taken, Lancias need much more than this before they "free."

Nevertheless their claim of 112-113 m.p.h. top speed was reached and supported by excellent acceleration figures. Inevitably one compares the Zagato Sport with the heavier, less powerful Pininfarina coupé we tested last winter (17 January 1964); mean top speed for that car was 106·5 m.p.h. The Zagato covered the standing-start quarter-mile in 18·3sec (PF coupé 19·1) and reached 60 m.p.h. from rest in 11·9sec (13·2) 80 m.p.h. in 21·1sec (23·8) and 100 m.p.h. in 39·7 (49·1). In the indirect gears we restricted ourselves to the manufacturer's rather conservative maxima of 32, 56 and 80 m.p.h. respectively, all of which are below the recommended limit of 5,800 r.p.m. But to reach a true 115 m.p.h. in top took the revs rather higher, to about 5,900 r.p.m. in theory, although the rev counter showed about 6,200 r.p.m. Perhaps this exaggeration is a deliberate safety valve.

In the ample boot tools are stored behind a panel on the left, the spare wheel with plastic cover on the right. Powerful reversing lamps are included in the rear lamp groups

With a choke to each cylinder and air cleaners that do not silence much, there is a rather insistent induction "beat" when the car is accelerated hard, sounding very like a familiar sports coupé with air-cooled flat-four engine at the back. Recalling the exceptional quietness and refinement of the standard Flavia saloon, it comes as a surprise to find this one so noisy under the bonnet—but, of course, some sporting drivers prefer it that way. On the overrun back-pressure in the exhaust produces an intermittent, gravelly resonance, but with the throttles just cracked open to maintain a moderate speed the car wafts along extremely quietly. Incidentally, the Lancia's running gear is unusually free from restraining frictions, for when brought to a stop on the slightest "invisible" slope it will often start rolling.

On cold mornings the engine starts easily, sounds a bit rattly until warmed to proper running clearances, but pulls away strongly almost at once. It is docile and tractable down to low crankshaft speeds, and the transmission allows it to do this without jerking and snatching. There are no vibration periods right up to maximum revs, nor sympathetic resonances in the body roof or floor. Moreover, on motorways it rolls along extraordinarily easily and quietly for mile after mile at 105-110 m.p.h. with no real fuss or apparent strain. A refined instrument, the gearbox is very quiet-running and has unbeatable synchromesh for all forward speeds. The lever moves easily, is lightly spring-loaded across a narrow gate, and a pleasure to use. Its arc of

Side windows that extend into the roof panel, and a concave rear window hinged for ventilation, give the Zagato body individuality—if a bit bizarre

travel is near-vertical, which soon seems natural enough.

While the parking brake could not quite hold the car pointing either way on our 1-in-3 test hill, there was sufficient power and clutch "bite" to take it away from here forwards or backwards. The clutch, which functions smoothly and progressively, also stood up well to the usual energetic acceleration testing.

If our test car was typical, as we understand, the balance of braking between front and rear wheels needs urgent attention. As it is, the back wheels lock and slide far too easily, whereupon the car's directional stability is usually lost, even when the roads are dry.

While taking brake test figures, about $0.8g$ was the limit before the rear wheels locked; doubling pressure on the pedal (at 160lb) to get the best possible g figure still did not lock the front ones. With four people on board, putting more weight on the back wheels, one can do much better of course. Rumour has it that competition drivers halve the pad area in contact with the rear wheel discs to correct the balance. Apart from this the brakes are all one would wish—powerful, progressive, and with no fade problem.

Our drivers found the front-wheel-drive Flavia Sport exceptionally sensitive to tyre pressures, and were unhappy with it on the recommended 28.5 p.s.i. all round. After trying various combinations, we sided with a private owner who recommended 27 p.s.i. in the front ones, 30 p.s.i. in the back. While the car's cornering power is obviously very high indeed, one has to "live" with it for a time to gain full confidence and get the best out of it safely. Fast drivers, accustomed to the fine directional control and stabilizing effects that power applied to the rear wheels can give them, inevitably have to learn a new technique for this one, remembering for instance that it is not so easy to recover if one steps beyond the limit of front-tyre adhesion. The plus qualities of Michelin X covers are well enough known, but their final breakaway is rather rapid. They are also harsh when the car is moving slowly, thumping hard over cat's eyes and minor blemishes in the road surface, but roll very quietly at higher speeds, when the car's directional stability is sure and relaxed.

Front-wheel drive plays no tricks with Flavia's steering mechanism as such, for it does not tug or jerk on sharp lock, nor become particularly heavy at low speeds. Although the gearing is fairly low with nearly four turns of the wheel lock-to-lock (for wide turning circles that would make Vincenzo Lancia turn in his grave), the response is quicker than this might suggest. Self-centring action, weak when the car is moving slowly, becomes quite adequate at normal touring speeds. The steering-wheel is placed rather high and offset considerably to the right. With the driving seat well back it is a bit remote. Its wooden rim looks well, gives a sure grip and never feels icy cold.

Virtually roll-free cornering and a quite soft and comfortable ride, with damping that is positive without being suggestive, result from the Flavia suspension arrangement, which has a transverse leaf and double wishbones at the front, a lightweight "dead" axle on half-elliptic springs behind, and anti-roll bars at each end. Over certain indifferent surfaces the seat springs seem to get into phase with the road springs, and become somewhat bouncy, but generally are comfortable and give good, well-defined support. The car rode very well over the special *pavé* and washboard surfaces with no chronic body creaks or rattles and the structure gives an impression of great strength.

A good pedal layout allows heel-and-toe operation of accelerator and brake, and leaves plenty of space for the left foot beside the clutch, the pendant levers for this and the brakes being long and moving through logical arcs. The centre boss of the steering-wheel flashes the headlamp dipped beams, an arrangement less useful at night than in daylight, as one cannot signal except when driving on sidelamps only. Around the boss is a small annular ring for sounding powerful twin air horns.

A row of four identical black and white rocking switches control screenwipers, headlamp low beams, heater fan and parking lamps—in that order. They have no means of identification, and it is all too easy to lose the headlamps, for instance, when intending to switch off the wipers. One separate lighting switch remote from the rest would be a safer arrangement. Main or low beams are selected by pressing a repeater button in the end of the indicator stalk, a familiar Lancia feature and perhaps the best arrangement of all. While four main beams give a splendid range and spread of illumination, the two dipped ones are restricted by British standards, putting one at a disadvantage on busy roads.

Inside the body there are lamps beneath each extremity of the facia panel, and beneath the bonnet are two festoon bulbs. Single-speed wipers begin to lift from 80 m.p.h. upwards, and the press-button for the vacuum-operated

Two oval air filters indicate where the carburettors are— and hence the horizontally-opposed cylinders below them. Other items in this view include the radiator shutters, and dual-circuit brake master cylinders beside their vacuum servo

sprays is somewhat remote, to the left of the substantial structure beneath the facia from which the gearlever sprouts. Beside it is a rheostat switch for the instrument panel lamps, which are not strong enough. A ribbon-type speedometer, although giving fairly accurate readings while the car was accelerating, was sluggish and inaccurate while speed was dropping. Beneath it are gauges for fuel contents (with low-level warning lamp), water temperature, oil pressure and dynamo charge. Despite the thermostatically controlled radiator shutters, we never saw the thermometer needle move far from the low-temperature end of the scale. Details of the heating and ventilation arrangements include rotary handwheels for temperature control and for regulating fresh-air intake but to direct full blast to the screen one must close small flaps either side of the centre structure—remote and difficult to find in a hurry, and crude by today's standards. One cannot have cool air coming up while warm air is being fed downwards. However, as we commented earlier, the overall efficiency of the system is extremely high. One would welcome more stowage space for travelling odds and ends inside the car, there being no glove locker in the facia, but merely small and inadequate pockets in the doors.

Like all current Lancias, the Zagato coupé has automatic red lamps in the door trailing edges. Trim of this car was in a pale plastic which quickly became grubby, but was easily cleaned off with a damp leather. Above the waistline the interior, including padded roof trim and all paintwork, was in black, which looked well and practical. There is nothing fancy or decorative about the neatly finished interior.

While headroom in the front is adequate except for the very tall, in the back there is none to spare, hinged sun visors for the curved side windows getting in the way unless dropped down. The passenger compartment as a whole is free from dangerous projections, and the door catches are recessed; there is ample resilient padding below the facia and built-in attachments for safety harness are provided.

A surprisingly roomy luggage boot houses the spare wheel vertically beneath a plastic cover. The two keys provided—one for the ignition and doors, the other for boot and fuel filler flap—have blue and white plastic grips respectively for easy identification. Exterior paint finish is excellent, while its smooth shape and low build make it easy to wash.

Under the bonnet one finds plenty of evidence of typical Lancia engineering detail, and all the accessories are obviously good quality products. Twelve fuses protect the electrical circuits, and are housed in a convenient box below the dash on the passenger's side.

At £2,736 (including P.T.) the Zagato Sport is beyond the pockets of many who would appreciate its strong character and special qualities. For that money, of course, one could buy cars that are faster, quieter, roomier, more luxurious—what you will. However, the world has not yet run out of wealthy connoisseurs with an appreciative eye for the highly individualistic products for which the Lancia factory has long been renowned.

Specification: Lancia Flavia Zagato Sport

PERFORMANCE DATA
Top gear m.p.h. per 1,000 r.p.m. ..... 19·5
Mean piston speed at max. power ..... 2,520 ft/min.
Engine revs. at mean max. speed ..... 5,800 r.p.m.
B.h.p. per ton laden ..... 84·8

ENGINE
Cylinders ... 4, horizontally opposed
Cooling system ... Water: pump, fan and thermostat, automatic radiator shutters
Bore ... 88mm (3·46in.)
Stroke ... 74mm (2·91in.)
Displacement ... 1,800 c.c. (109·8 cu. in.)
Valve gear ... Overhead, pushrods and rockers, two camshafts
Compression ratio ... 9·0-to-1
Carburettors ... Two Solex twin-choke C32PAIA8
Fuel pump ... Bendix electric
Oil filter ... Fram full-flow, renewable element
Max. power ... 100 b.h.p. (net) at 5,200 r.p.m.
Max. torque ... 120 lb. ft. (net) at 3,000 r.p.m.

TRANSMISSION
Clutch ... Fichtel and Sachs s.d.p., 8 in. dia.
Gearbox ... Four-speed, all-synchromesh
Gear ratios ... Top 1·0, Third 1·39, Second 1·86, First 3·33, Reverse 3·71
Final drive ... Hypoid bevel, 3·82-to-1

CHASSIS
Construction ... Integral, with aluminium body panels on steel frame

SUSPENSION
Front ... Double wishbones, transverse leaf spring, de Carbon telescopic dampers, anti-roll bar
Rear ... Beam axle, half-elliptic leaf springs, de Carbon telescopic dampers, anti-roll bar
Steering ... Gemmer-France, worm and roller
Turns ... Lock-to-lock 3·8. Wheel dia. 16in.

BRAKES
Make and Type ... Dunlop discs F and R, with Lancia vacuum servo. Independent circuits F and R
Dimensions ... F and R 11in. dia.
Total swept area ... 496 sq. in. (421 sq. in. per ton laden)

WHEELS
Type ... Pressed steel with perforated discs, four studs. 4·5in. wide rim
Tyres ... 165—15in. Michelin X with tubes

EQUIPMENT
Battery ... 12-volt 42-amp. hr.
Generator ... Marelli 62F 300W
Headlamps ... Carello dual system, 40-45 watt
Reversing lamps ... Two, standard
Electric fuses ... 12
Screen wipers ... Single-speed self-parking
Screen washer ... Trico suction, standard
Interior heater ... Fresh air, standard
Safety belts ... Extra, anchorages provided
Interior trim ... P.v.c. seats, cloth headlining
Floor covering ... Carpet
Starting handle ... No provision
Jack ... Scissors type
Jacking points ... Two each side in body sills

MAINTENANCE
Fuel tank ... 10·5 Imp. gallons (48 litres) (with low-level warning lamp)
Cooling system ... 14 pints (7·8 litres) (including heater)
Engine sump ... 12 pints (7·1 litres) SAE 10W30. Change oil every 2,500 miles. Change filter element every 5,000 miles
Gearbox and Final Drive ... 4·5 pints SAE EP 90. Change oil every 7,500 miles
Grease ... 11 points every 2,500 miles
Tyre pressures ... F 27, R 30 p.s.i. (all conditions)

▼ Scale: 0·3in. to 1ft. Cushions uncompressed.

LANCIA FLAMINIA G.T.

Slide into the shapely leather seat, swing shut the close-fitting aluminum door, fire up the unique V6 and discover how elegant earthbound motion can become.

▶ Lancia of Italy builds expensive, luxurious cars, famed for sure-footed road manners and perfection of detail. In its largest series, the 2½-liter V6 Flaminia, there are five body styles to choose from. There is the factory's own Pininfarina-designed four-door sedan, while on a 4¾-inch-shorter wheelbase Pininfarina builds a crisp, comfortable coupe which looks as closely related to the sedan as it is. On a wheelbase shorter by another 9 inches and with the same 131 bhp version of the V6, Touring builds the chic, elegant G.T. coupe (the subject of our test) and the delightfully handsome convertible while Zagato prepares the racily light and lively Sport coupes with their famous double-noggin notches. Though we put in some city driving on both Pininfarina models, we lived with the Touring G.T. coupe for more than 500 miles over the terrain where Lancias shine best: twisting, mountainous secondary roads.

Each of these body types is notable for fine finish and a luxurious leather interior, with chair-height seating in the Pininfarina designs and sports-car-like "channeled" seating in the others. The G.T.'s seats have widely splayed backs but are quite easy to slip in and out of. All three cars were commendably untiring.

Today's Flaminia is a direct descendant of the much-admired Aurelia, the one single car which gave birth to the term *Gran Turismo* in the early postwar era. Some Aurelia features remain, while some have disappeared in the course of development. Remaining, of course, are its heart, soul and skeleton; the aluminum V6 with its longitudinally in-

Lancia's famed transaxle features wonderfully effective Dunlop disc brakes and lightweight de Dion axle. Latter combines both comfort and handling.

clined valves and the rear-mounted clutch and transaxle (only the name is new) at the ends of a frameless chassis. The vintage sliding pillar front suspension has been bequeathed to Morgan in favor of coil springs and unequal wishbones but the de Dion axle with leaf springs of the later Aurelias remains.

The Flaminia's rear axle-mounted gearbox has synchromesh on all of its four forward speeds. The floor-shift lever is a large-diameter steel tube cranked so that your hand falls on it naturally. A spring load must be overcome to place the lever in first or second positions; it is heavy but not as heavy as that which protects reverse, off to the lower right of the H pattern. The synchromesh is infallible but the overcentering spring of the easily depressed clutch pedal seems to delay fast engagement during rapid shifts.

The V6 engine is very smooth throughout its range. It develops peak bhp at 5100 rpm and will go well beyond that although noisily. Such is the flatness of its torque curve that the car will accelerate smoothly in *any* gear from idle. The gear ratios are very well chosen and provide great flexibility. Third, with its range from 18 to 80 mph, is marvelously useful and pleasant.

Even with its 165 x 400 Michelin X tires (the sedans use 175 x 400) inflated to 30 psi, the G.T. coupe's worm and roller steering is heavy under parking conditions. This becomes light as soon as the car is rolling and is one of the world's best systems at speed. The car tracks superbly at 90 mph, asking to be driven all day long at that level. Only above 100 mph does slight wander set in.

Unmistakably Italian in layout and fine finish, the Lancia G.T. has deep leather seats, sturdy four-speed all-synchro gears, vertical wheel.

ROAD TEST:

LANCIA FLAMINIA G. T.

Price as tested: $6847 POE

Importer: Hoffman Motors Corporation
443 Park Ave., New York 22, N.Y.
9130 Wilshire Blvd., Beverly Hills, Calif.

ENGINE:

Displacement ....150.0 cu in, 2458 cc
Dimensions ..Six cyl, 3.15 in bore, 3.21 in stroke
Valve gear: pushrod overhead valves, inclined in longitudinal plane, bell-crank rockers.
Compression ratio ....9.0 to one
Power (SAE) ....131 bhp @ 5100 rpm
Torque ....137 lb-ft @ 3500 rpm
Usable range of engine speeds .....900-5600 rpm
Corrected piston speed @ 5100 rpm ...2700 fpm
Fuel recommended ....Premium
Mileage ....17-20 mpg
Range on 18.5-gallon tank ....310-370 miles

CHASSIS:

Wheelbase ....99.2 in
Tread ....F 53.8, R 50.0 in
Length ....177.4 in
Ground clearance ....4.3 in
Suspension: F, ind., coil, wishbones; R, de Dion axle, semi-elliptic leaf springs, Panhard rod.
Turns, lock to lock 4.0
Turning circle diameter between curbs ......40 ft
Tire and rim size ....165 x 400 (both)
Pressures recommended..........F 28, R 30 psi
Brakes; type, swept area: F 11½ in, R 12 in discs; 511 sq in
Curb weight (full tank) ....2940 lbs
Percentage on driving wheels 50%

DRIVE TRAIN:

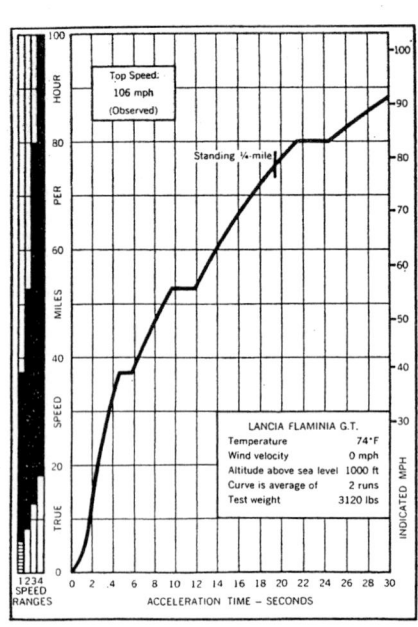

Gear	Synchro?	Ratio	Step	Overall	Mph per 1000 rpm
Rev	No	3.35	—	12.79	-6.0
1st	Yes	3.09	51%	11.80	6.5
2nd	Yes	2.05	45%	7.82	9.8
3rd	Yes	1.41	41%	5.38	14.3
4th	Yes	1.00		3.82	20.1

Final Drive Ratio: 3.82 to one. (3.92 with wider ratio gears in Pininfarina-bodied cars.)

LANCIA FLAVIA SPORT

"Idiosyncratic" is a description often applied to Zagato designs and, indeed, they are frequently distinctively unusual. However, this individuality does not arise through perversity or whimsy but is based on a logical approach to car design. The brief which Zagato set themselves in the case of the Flavia was to produce a car with a sporting character in a lightweight body with good aerodynamic qualities.

Viewed in this light, the final design is one which satisfies the requirements in a very effective manner. The aerodynamic design with its low nose, rounded sides, and deeply-curved windscreen meets all the criteria which have been derived during the years since the car was built; even to the extent that the earliest version, as shown in the heading, had semi-enclosed rear wheels. A further logical feature in the design was the use of rear side windows which extended into the roofline, as in Zagato's earlier "Panoramica" models. Inevitably in a streamlined 2 plus 2 coupé the rear seat passengers are enclosed to an almost claustrophobic extent; the enlarged windows help to give more light in the car. The logic is taken further in that sun-visors are provided for these rear side windows to alleviate the effect of the Italian sun.

Possibly the most unusual feature of the Flavia sport was the electrically-operated opening of the top-hinged rear window. This, again, shows the Zagato's understanding of aerodynamics; the air pressure outside the rear window is lower than that inside the car when the vehicle is moving thus the opening rear window provides an extraction system which is easily controlled by the driver.

In addition to having a more penetrative shape than the Coupé, which in general shared the same mechanicals, the Sport was appreciably lighter, mainly through the use of aluminium panels. These features gave the 1500 Sport an advantage over the Coupé in terms both of maximum speed and fuel consumption. Although nominally a 1500, all the Flavia Sports of this designation incorporated the Nardi-developed *Variante* 1005 of the 1500 engine, which had a capacity of 1727ccs. The later 1800 Sports, whether in carburetted or fuel injection form, also had higher-geared final drive ratios than the contemporary Coupés, which maintained the edge in performance.

The performance of the Sport was utilised in competition, both by the factory-supported HF Squadra Corse and by private entrants. However, although these cars were lighter than contemporary Lancia designs they were heavy in comparison with other makes and their relatively poor power-to-weight ratio counted against them, but some modest successes were achieved.

In summary, the Flavia Sport was a characteristically distinctive, almost flamboyant, Zagato design on running gear which was advanced for its time. Whilst its aesthetics were, and are, the subject of differing viewpoints there was no disagreement on the fact that the car was very well built and finished. Produced by a specialist *carrozzeria* in very small numbers, the Sport was virtually a hand-built car but was not extortionately expensive and brought exclusive and satisfying motoring to many motorists who could never aspire to one of the better-known "supercars".

LANCIA FLAMINIA vs LANCIA FLAVIA

Two lovelies from Lancia—with widely varied mechanical approaches to the same general objective—delightful transportation

The name Lancia is one of the oldest and most honored in the motoring world, and the firm's cars have always managed to combine solid practical virtues with a degree of individuality which is unusual in quantity-produced vehicles. The latest offerings from Torino's Via Vincenzo Lancia more than maintain this tradition, especially now that their power units have been enlarged to give more torque and greater flexibility.

The cars featured in this combined test report are examples of Lancia's more sporting products. Although only one is designated "GT," both are Grand Touring cars in the proper sense of the word—that is, they are suitable for touring countryside and cities, not just race tracks. Both are also available in sedan and convertible form—*and* in each case the general mechanical layout in common to the whole range.

Ideally, both cars are two-seaters with lots of luggage space. Both have "occasional" rear seats—even more occasional on the Flaminia than on the Flavia—but in each case coupe styling and a short wheelbase render the rear compartment more suitable for children than full-grown adults; getting in and out of the back seats is another hazard in this connection, though the front seat backrests do fold down to permit such maneuvers.

In this, and in their degree of equipment—exemplified by things like red lights in the rear edge of the doors, which come on automatically when the doors are opened—the two cars have a lot in common. In basic design, however, they are poles apart, almost the only unifying feature being the use of four wheels. The V-6 Flaminia can be described as advanced conventional; to the customary expedient of front engine and rear drive it adds a de Dion axle, inboard discs, and clutch and gearbox in unit with the differential—all of which makes the weight distribution virtually 50/50.

By contrast, the Flavia has a flat four engine mounted ahead of the driven front wheels, with the gearbox just behind them. Suspension in this case is by double wishbones and transverse spring at the front, with a beam axle on semi-elliptic springs at the rear. The only real criticism which can be made of this layout is that the engine and gearbox take up far more room than the British Motor Corporation's transverse-triplane arrangement.

The outstanding feature of the Flaminia is its ability to cruise effortlessly at 100 mph. David Phipps collected the car in Turin, drove straight out to the Autostrada, and let it find its own cruising speed. For about 50 kilometers his wife sat completely unconcerned, taking in the scenery with never a care in the world, but when he drew her attention to the speedometer, steady at 160 kmh, she started to look for seat belts. She need not have worried; the car ran "hands off" for over a kilometer and did not deviate an inch; Phipps tooted the horn gently at an indecisive Fiat, and a truck half a mile ahead pulled smartly in; and later, when a German-registered Mercedes veered out in front, he needed only to *rest* his foot on the brake pedal. Subsequently they got into a gigantic Milanese traffic jam, but the engine showed no sign of overheating or fouling plugs—probably because it is designed to run warm all the time. The car felt a little cumbersome (and more than a little vulnerable) under conditions like making U-turns, but at anything more than a crawl the steering is acceptably light, beautifully precise and completely free from kick-back. The shift is not the lightest in the world, but it is reasonably quick and seems absolutely fool-proof—which is more than can be said for some ultra-remote control mechanisms.

The seats are extremely comfortable, both in town and on the autostrada, and the combination of longer-than-average fore-and-aft travel, finely adjustable back-rests and a telescopic steering column should make it possible for anyone to find a suitable driving position; this range of adjustments also helps the driver to offset the fatigue of a set position on a long run. Add to this an almost vertical steering wheel, and matching tach and speedometer, you have a car that makes you feel good every time you get into it. It also gives you a feeling that you do not need to rush or force your way through traffic to make your next appointment. It will get you there quickly—very quickly if necessary—but it will not encourage you to take risks or to throw it about. This is not to suggest that it doesn't handle well. Its Michelin X tires stay glued to the road whatever the weather, it goes just where it is pointed, and it stops time after time in a manner which Detroit can only dream about. But it is not a Sprite, and its very size and weight dictate a certain amount of caution.

Complementing the overall character of the Flaminia, the 150-cubic-inch, 150-bhp V-6 engine makes very thoroughbred noises, suitably muffled, and seems to be just as happy at 5000 rpm as at any lower speed. It starts readily, warms up fairly quickly, and tells the driver how it feels via a full complement of gauges (oil pressure, oil temperature, water temperature) recessed into the two major dials; it also has such refinements as warning lights for choke and low fuel level. In view of all this, the pull-out handbrake under the dash seems somewhat out of character. A new owner could also be baffled by the array of six identical but unmarked control knobs for wipers, cigar lighter, lights, panel lights, interior lights, and heater fan (the latter four in a row) plus stalks for turn indicators/dimmer and headlamp flasher—not to mention the six or seven different knobs and levers for the very comprehensive heating/ventilating system.

PHOTOGRAPHY: PHIPPS

Front-wheel drive plus front-mounted transmission in a single unit dictate the layout of the controls on the 1800cc Lancia Flavia.

Flaminia can go more the conventional GT car route—except that the rear-mounted transmission necessitates remote gear change.

Lancia Flavia Coupe

Importer: Hoffman Motor Corporation
443 Park Avenue
New York 22, N.Y.
Hoffman Motor Corporation
9130 Wilshire Boulevard
Beverly Hills, California
Price as tested: $4715 POE N.Y.

ACCELERATION

Zero to	Seconds
30 mph	4.5
40 mph	7.2
50 mph	10.2
60 mph	14.2
70 mph	18.5
80 mph	24.0
Standing ¼ mile	73 mph in 20.0

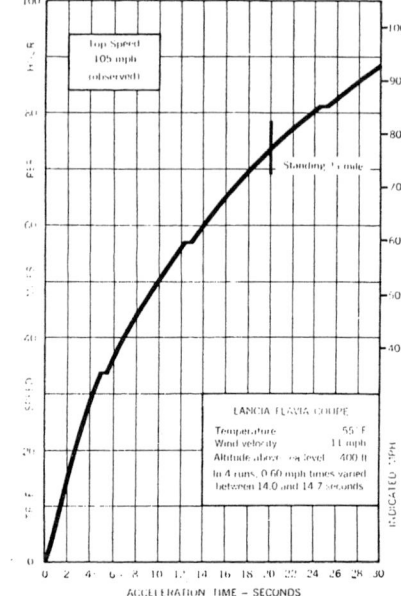

Top Speed 105 mph (observed)

LANCIA FLAVIA COUPE
Temperature 55 F
Wind velocity 11 mph
Altitude above sea level 400 ft
In 4 runs, 0-60 mph times varied between 14.0 and 14.7 seconds

ENGINE
Water-cooled flat-four aluminum block, 3 main bearings
Bore x stroke . . . . . 3.464 x 2.913 in, 88 x 74 mm
Displacement . . . . 109.8 cu in, 1800 cc
Compression ratio . . . . 9.0 to one
Carburetion . . . . Single Solex C 32 PAIA 8
Valve gear . . . . Pushrod-operated inclined overhead valves
Power (SAE) . . . . 106 bhp @ 5500 rpm
Torque . . . . 108 lb-ft @ 3000 rpm
Specific power output . . 0.965 bhp per cu in, 59 bhp per liter
Usable range of engine speeds . . 800–6000 rpm
Electrical system . . . . 12-volt, 42 amp-hr battery
Fuel recommended . . . . Premium
Mileage . . . . 22–30 mpg
Range on 13-gallon tank . . . . . . 285–390 miles

DRIVE TRAIN
Clutch . . . . 8-inch single dry plate
Transmission . . . . . 4-speed all-synchro gearbox

Gear	Ratio	Over-all	mph/1000 rpm	Max mph
Rev	3.70	14.46	-5.1	-30.6
1st	3.33	13.02	5.7	34.2
2nd	1.97	7.70	9.6	57.6
3rd	1.39	5.43	13.7	82.2
4th	1.00	3.91	19.0	105.0

Final drive ratio . . . . 3.91 to one

CHASSIS
Unit-construction, all-steel structure.
Wheelbase . . . . 97.6 in
Track . . . . F 51.2 R 50.4 in
Length . . . . 176.5 in
Width . . . . 63.4 in
Height . . . . 53.1 in
Ground clearance . . . . 5.0 in
Curb weight . . . . 2532 lbs
Test weight . . . . 2770 lbs
Weight distribution front/rear % 69/31
Pounds per bhp (test weight) 26.13
Suspension: F: Ind., unequal-length wishbones, transverse leaf spring, anti-roll bar, oleo-pneumatic dampers.
R: Dead axle, semi-elliptic leaf springs, anti-roll bar, oleo-pneumatic dampers.
Brakes . . 11-in discs front and rear (power assist), 496 sq in swept area
Steering . . . . Worm and roller
Turns lock to lock 4½
Turning circle . . . . 34 ft
Tires . . . . 165 x 15
Revs per mile 808

CHECK LIST
Rated on a basis of 0-to-10, with a score of 10 being excellent.

ENGINE
Starting 8
Responsiveness 7
Noise 7
Vibration 4

DRIVE TRAIN
Clutch action 7
Transmission linkage 5
Syncromesh action 8
Power-to-ground transmission 9

BRAKES
Responsiveness 8
Pedal pressure 5
Fade resistance 9
Smoothness 7
Directional stability 9

STEERING
Responsiveness 8
Accuracy 9
Feedback 7
Road Feel 5

SUSPENSION
Harshness control 8
Roll stiffness 7
Tracking 9
Pitch control 7
Shock damping 9

CONTROLS
Location 5
Relationship 7
Small controls 6

INTERIOR
Visibility 7
Instrumentation 5
Lighting 7
Entry/exit 8
Front seating comfort 8
Front seating room 8
Rear seating comfort 4
Rear seating room 2
Storage space 7
Wind noise 10
Road noise 10

WEATHER PROTECTION
Heater 4
Defroster 3
Ventilation 5
Weather sealing 5
Windshield wiper action 5

QUALITY CONTROL
Materials, exterior 9
Materials, interior 9
Exterior finish 9
Interior finish 9
Hardware and trim 8

GENERAL
Service accessibility 5
Luggage space 4
Bumper protection 5
Exterior lighting 8

Our first impressions of the Flavia coupe were that it was something of a ladies' car, but it subsequently proved to combine docility in town with a very virile performance on the autostrada, accelerating briskly both through the gears and in top, and cruising comfortably at anything up to 90 mph. Above 5000 rpm, however, the engine begins to get a little fussy, and several times one finds oneself trying to change up into a fifth gear which is not there.

A lot of people could drive the Flavia a long way without realizing it has front wheel drive. There is certainly nothing in the transmission to give away the secret, except for a squeak from the front tires during a really violent takeoff. The steering is light and precise (though rather devoid of "feel") under all conditions, and there is very little change of attitude between power-on and power-off.

In the wet, which it was most of the time we had the Flavia, the combination of Michelin X tires and insensitive steering did not encourage exploration of the limits of the car's roadholding capabilities—mainly because they are very high, and an accident at high speed usually hurts! Suffice to say that it took us far and fast on both wet and dry roads without ever getting out of shape, and that with longer acquaintance we might well have been able to eradicate any suspicions about the tires and steering.

After the Flaminia, the Flavia seems to have rather small seats, which are somewhat short in the cushion and do not offer very much in the way of lateral support. However, they go back far enough to provide adequate leg-room for tall people, and adjustable backrests allow one to adopt Jim Clark or Vintage driving positions at will.

The gearshift on the Flavia is not particularly sporting, but it is precise and reasonably quick. On the test car the only possible shortcoming of the transmission was a trace of clutch slip during performance testing, a phenomenon which did not recur in normal use. The intermediate ratios are much better spaced than on the original 1500cc car, giving top speeds of 32, 55 and 78 mph, and 105 mph in top.

As on the Flaminia, the minor controls (in this case piano-key switches for lights, wipers and heater fan) are not labeled, but this is unlikely to worry most owners after the first few thousand miles! Some, however, might be concerned by the height of the brake and clutch pedals from the floor, and by the amount of knob-twisting required to get the heater temperature just right.

The instruments—an accurate ribbon speedometer, a circular tachometer and indicators (rather than gauges) for oil pressure, water temperature, fuel level and battery charge—are housed in a large hooded nacelle. The horn is in the center of the steering wheel, with a button in the middle of it which flashes the headlights, and the dip-switch resides in the end of the turn-indicator stalk. As on the Flaminia, the choke control is hidden away under the dash, but is equipped with a bright red warning light which encourages you to weaken the mixture at the earliest possible opportunity; in this case the warning light is also wired to the handbrake, which is ideally placed between the seats. (In both cars you start the engine by turning the ignition key and then pressing it in.) All-round visibility is good, except that the mirror creates an unusually large blind spot, and the car is reasonably quiet with the windows closed; this is made possible by fresh air nozzles at either end of the dash.

There are lots of little things about the Flavia coupe which help to give it an atmosphere of quality; the trunk lid falls shut with a muted clunk; little leaf springs bear against the front edge of the hood to make sure it does not rattle; the lockable parcel tray beneath the dash slides silently in and out on roller-bearings; and the ashtray is spring-loaded, popping out at the slightest touch.

Esthetically, the two cars do not have much in common. The Flaminia (body by Carrozzeria Touring of Milan) looks like a spyder with an added hard-top, while the Pininfarina-bodied Flavia has a fully integrated coupe design.

Like their sedan and convertible counterparts, both of these cars have a definite niche in the market: the Flavia as a most attractive, unmistakably Italian coupe, the Flaminia as a Grand Touring car which anybody would be proud to own. Of the two, the long-striding Flaminia is rather better-suited to American conditions, but the Flavia clearly has a lot to offer where the roads are wet, twisty, mountainous or a combination of all three. And both give the impression that they will last for a long, long time.

The 1800cc flat-four Flavia is aluminum, with pushrod operated overhead valves—it makes a neatly compact unit, but doesn't compare with the BMC Minis on that score.

Flaminia engine is also pushrod ohv in design, a very compact little V-6 of 2775cc.

Lancia Flaminia 3C GT

Importer: Hoffman Motor Corporation
443 Park Avenue
New York 22, N.Y.
Hoffman Motor Corporation
9130 Wilshire Boulevard
Beverly Hills, California
Price as tested: $7200 POE N.Y.

ACCELERATION

Zero to	Seconds
30 mph	4.0
40 mph	5.8
50 mph	8.2
60 mph	10.8
70 mph	14.4
80 mph	18.3
90 mph	23.0
100 mph	29.5
Standing ¼ mile	78 mph in 17.7

Top Speed 125 mph (observed)

Temperature 63° F
Wind velocity 7 mph
Altitude above sea level 200 ft
In 4 runs, 0-60 mph times varied between 10.6 and 11.3 seconds

ENGINE
Water-cooled V-6, aluminum block, 4 main bearings
Bore x stroke....3.346 x 3.208 in, 85 x 81.5 mm
Displacement............169.3 cu in, 2775 cc
Compression ratio.................9.0 to one
Carburetion....One Weber 35 DCNL/3 and two Weber 35 DCNL/2
Valve gear....Pushrod-operated inclined overhead valves
Power (SAE)............165 bhp @ 5400 rpm
Torque.............165 lb-ft @ 3500 rpm
Specific power output......0.975 bhp per cu in, 59.5 bhp per liter
Usable range of engine speeds...1000–6000 rpm
Electrical system....12-volt, 45 amp-hr battery, generator
Fuel recommended ....Premium
Mileage...........................16–24 mpg
Range on 14.6-gallon tank......235–350 miles

DRIVE TRAIN
Clutch................9-inch single dry plate
Transmission......4-speed all-synchro gearbox

Gear	Ratio	Over-all	mph/1000 rpm	Max mph
Rev	3.03	10.73	−7.1	−42.6
1st	2.80	9.91	7.7	46.2
2nd	1.86	6.58	11.6	69.6
3rd	1.28	4.53	16.9	101.4
4th	1.00	3.54	21.6	125.0

Final drive ratio....................3.54 to one

CHASSIS
Platform steel frame, all-steel body.
Wheelbase ....102.4 in
Track....................F 53.8 R 53.9 in
Length ....178.3 in
Width ....65.4 in
Height ....54 in
Ground clearance ....5.0 in
Curb weight ....3090 lbs
Test weight ....3436 lbs
Weight distribution front/rear %....50.5/49.5
Pounds per bhp (test weight).........20.82
Suspension: F: Ind., unequal-length wishbones, coil springs, anti-roll bar
R: de Dion axle, semi-elliptic leaf springs, panhard rod
Brakes....11½-in discs front, 12-in discs rear, 436 sq in swept area
Steering ....Worm and roller
Turns lock to lock.....................4½
Turning circle......................36 ft
Tires ....165 x 400
Revs per mile........................785

CHECK LIST
Rated on a basis of 0-to-10, with a score of 10 being excellent.

ENGINE
Starting.........................8
Responsiveness...................8
Noise............................7
Vibration........................8

DRIVE TRAIN
Clutch action....................8
Transmission linkage.............7
Syncromesh action................7
Power-to-ground transmission....10

BRAKES
Responsiveness...................8
Pedal pressure...................5
Fade resistance.................10
Smoothness.......................8
Directional stability...........10

STEERING
Responsiveness...................8
Accuracy........................10
Feedback.........................7
Road Feel........................8

SUSPENSION
Harshness control................8
Roll stiffness...................9
Tracking........................10
Pitch control...................10
Shock damping....................9

CONTROLS
Location.........................7
Relationship.....................7
Small controls...................6

INTERIOR
Visibility.......................6
Instrumentation..................8
Lighting.........................8
Entry/exit.......................8
Front seating comfort...........10
Front seating room...............8
Rear seating comfort.............—
Rear seating room................—
Storage space...................10
Wind noise.......................7
Road noise.......................6

WEATHER PROTECTION
Heater...........................4
Defroster........................3
Ventilation......................4
Weather sealing..................3
Windshield wiper action..........5

QUALITY CONTROL
Materials, exterior..............9
Materials, interior..............9
Exterior finish..................8
Interior finish..................9
Hardware and trim................8

GENERAL
Service accessibility............4
Luggage space....................9
Bumper protection................4
Exterior lighting................8

LANCIA FLAVIA

ITALY'S FIRST FRONT-WHEEL-DRIVE CAR: 1½-LITRE HORIZONTALLY OPPOSED FOUR CYLINDER ENGINE

EVER since the foundation of the Lancia company in 1908 by Vincenzo Lancia—originally a well-known racing driver and engineer with the F.I.A.T. company—they have enjoyed a reputation for sound engineering, and the courage to adopt an unorthodox approach to engineering matters if it were theoretically desirable. Cost often seemed a secondary consideration. Although some of this tradition might have departed when the company passed out of the hands of the Lancia family, this, in fact, has not occurred. It is not surprising, therefore, that with this background, Lancia are the first Italian company to go into production with a front-wheel-drive car, to be known as the Flavia. This title is in line with the policy of using names of highways into Rome for model designation; the roads themselves are named after Roman statesmen.

The Flavia has a flat-four, horizontally opposed, water-cooled 1½-litre engine mounted forward of the front wheels. From the clutch the drive passes through the hollow hypoid pinion of the final drive to a pair of single helical gears, mounted outside the gearbox portion of the transmission. All four gears, each having synchromesh of the baulk ring type, are thus indirect. The drive shafts, which have Rzeppa type constant velocity joints at each end, with ball-and-groove sliding splines, are supplied by Hardy Spicer Ltd. This is in line with established Lancia policy of obtaining the best equipment, irrespective of the country of origin. Other British components used are Vandervell bearings and bushings (which Lancia have fitted on all models since 1954), Dunlop disc brakes at front and rear, and a Hobourn-Eaton internal rotor oil pump.

Design of the Flavia is the work of Professor Fessia, who joined Lancia during the period that the Flaminia was under development, and was responsible for the substitution of wishbone suspension for the company's traditional sliding pillar type on that car. Professor Fessia was with Fiat pre-war, and designed the famous Topolino. He left them and produced the Cemsa-Caproni, a front-wheel-drive car with a 1,100 c.c. horizontally opposed, four-cylinder engine which appeared as a prototype in 1948. Its object was to utilize the surplus capacity of the Caproni aircraft factory during the post-war years, but the design did not proceed beyond the prototype stage. Returning to Fiat, he produced a similar layout for the Fiat 600, in parallel with Dr. Giacosa's rear engine design, which was ultimately adopted when the car went into production. It is a logical evolution that Professor Fessia should now propound and develop his ideas for the Flavia.

Right-hand-drive versions of the car will be available immediately production commences; this is expected to be in full swing by the end of the year. Prices were not available at the time of writing, but were to be announced at the opening of the Turin Show yesterday, and will be given in the report on that Show in next week's issue. It is expected that the price will be between 1,700,000 and 1,800,000 lire, equal to £1,000 to £1,060.

With a wheelbase of 8ft 8·33in. and a widest track of 4ft 3·2in., in conjunction with mounting of the engine forward of the front wheels, the Flavia is a very roomy car in the 1½-litre class. Three adults can sit abreast on the rear seat, which has a maximum width between trim

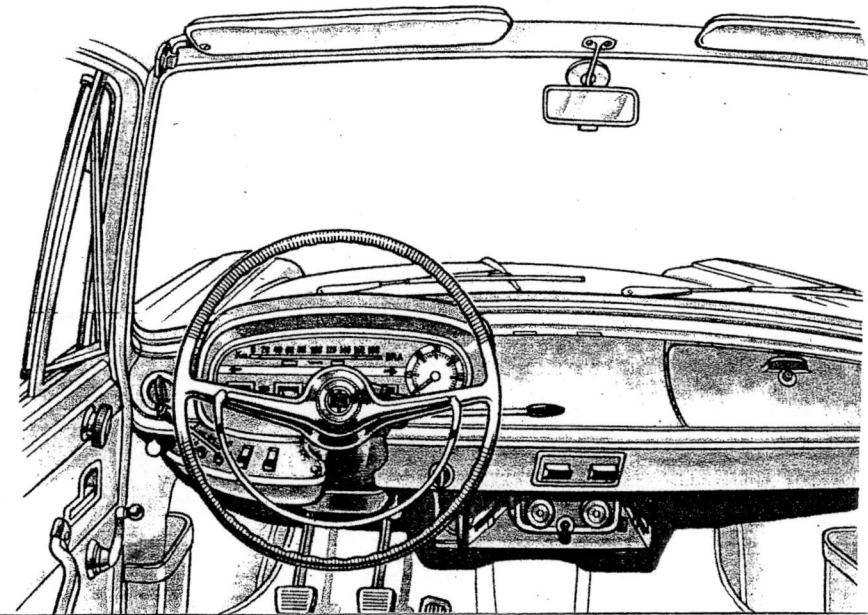

Control switches are mounted on an arcuate panel blending with the facia and steering column. Gear change lever is to the right and the turn indicator lever to the left; this layout will be interchanged on right-hand-drive cars

LANCIA FLAVIA...

At the rear there is an unusual "fold" in the body styling which seems out of balance with the main contour. Twin light clusters contain turn indicators, parking and stop and reversing lamps. Overriders have twin reflectors and there is a number plate lamp in the bumper

panels of 4ft 5in.; the corresponding width at the front is 1·25in. greater. With a vertical height of 2ft 10in. measured from the uncompressed seat cushion to the roof lining—an identical dimension front and rear—and with 6·5in. knee room for the rear passengers when the front seat is in its rearmost position, the car is commodious for its size.

Upholstery is carried out in cloth and Vinyl, over foam rubber cushions and squabs. Floors are covered with rubber mats front and rear. There is an armrest on each door but, rather surprisingly, not one of the folding type for the front or rear seats. Small parcel stowage is provided in the form of a lockable cubby hole on the facia and a container at each side adjacent to the toeboard for front passengers. Rear passengers have the use of an elastic map pocket in the front seat back, and a deep rear window parcel shelf.

Fully Equipped

Swivelling quarter ventilators are fitted to each front door; they are operated by a worm-and-nut mechanism having a circular operating knob so that they can be finely adjusted and secured in any desired position; this is also a useful thief-resisting provision. The facia is covered with imitation leather, underlaid with a shockproof foam material.

Set in a cowled panel in line with the steering wheel, instruments comprise a ribbon-type speedometer with trip and total distance recorders, and a circular rev-counter. Beneath the speedometer scale are rectangular instruments for fuel contents, water temperature and oil pressure, and an ammeter. There are, in addition, warning lights for excessive water temperature, fuel reserve, low oil pressure, headlamp main beam, parking lamps, and a combined one for parking brake and carburettor choke, which is hand operated.

Control switches are in an auxiliary arcuate panel on the lower edge of the facia, between the steering wheel and the driver's door. From left to right these switches, which are of the tilting touch-button type, are for electric screen washer, two-speed screen wiper and lamps. Next come the direction indicator lever, instrument panel light and parking light.

Dual headlamps, using 5·75in. diameter sealed beam units, are standard fittings. After bringing these into circuit by the main switch, changeover from main to dipped beam is obtained by a touch on the button on the end of the turn indicator lever. This operates a solenoid which selects each of the beams in sequence; the wiring is arranged so that the meeting beam is always obtained first when the headlamps are switched on.

In the centre of the steering wheel there is a press button for headlamp flashing, the horn being operated by a half-ring. Courtesy lights, operated when any of the four doors are opened, are located on the upper part of each door pillar. Desirable safety features are red marker lamps fitted to the rear edge of each front door, with automatic switching coupled to the courtesy lights. In addition, operated automatically as the respective lids are raised, there are two lights in the engine compartment and one in the luggage locker (which is very capacious, with the spare wheel mounted vertically on one side).

A comprehensive heating and ventilation system is part of the standard equipment. There is a fresh-air intake on the right front side of the car, with a butterfly regulator valve. A separate control is provided for the degree of heat and for distribution to either of the two outlets for general interior heating or for screen defrosting; there are 10 slots extending across the width of the screen at its base. This circuit includes two butterfly controls on each side of the facia, which be used for defrosting the side windo Air flow can be boosted, if required, a single-speed fan.

The pressed-steel body hull follo normal practice for this integral type construction. Beam strength is provi in two deep and wide sills at each si They merge into the rear seat pan str ture, shallow channel section floor tun which houses the exhaust pipe, and scuttle assembly which in turn mer into the wing valances; from these wheelbarrow box-section arm proje forward at each side. There is a rem able front sub-frame attached at rubber mountings; this unit can detached and wheeled away compl

The sliding, full width front seat has an adjustable and fully tilting backrest, in the rear of which is a map pocket and central ashtray. Each door, with flush-fitting pull-out handles, has an armrest and a plastic combined door pull and grab handle

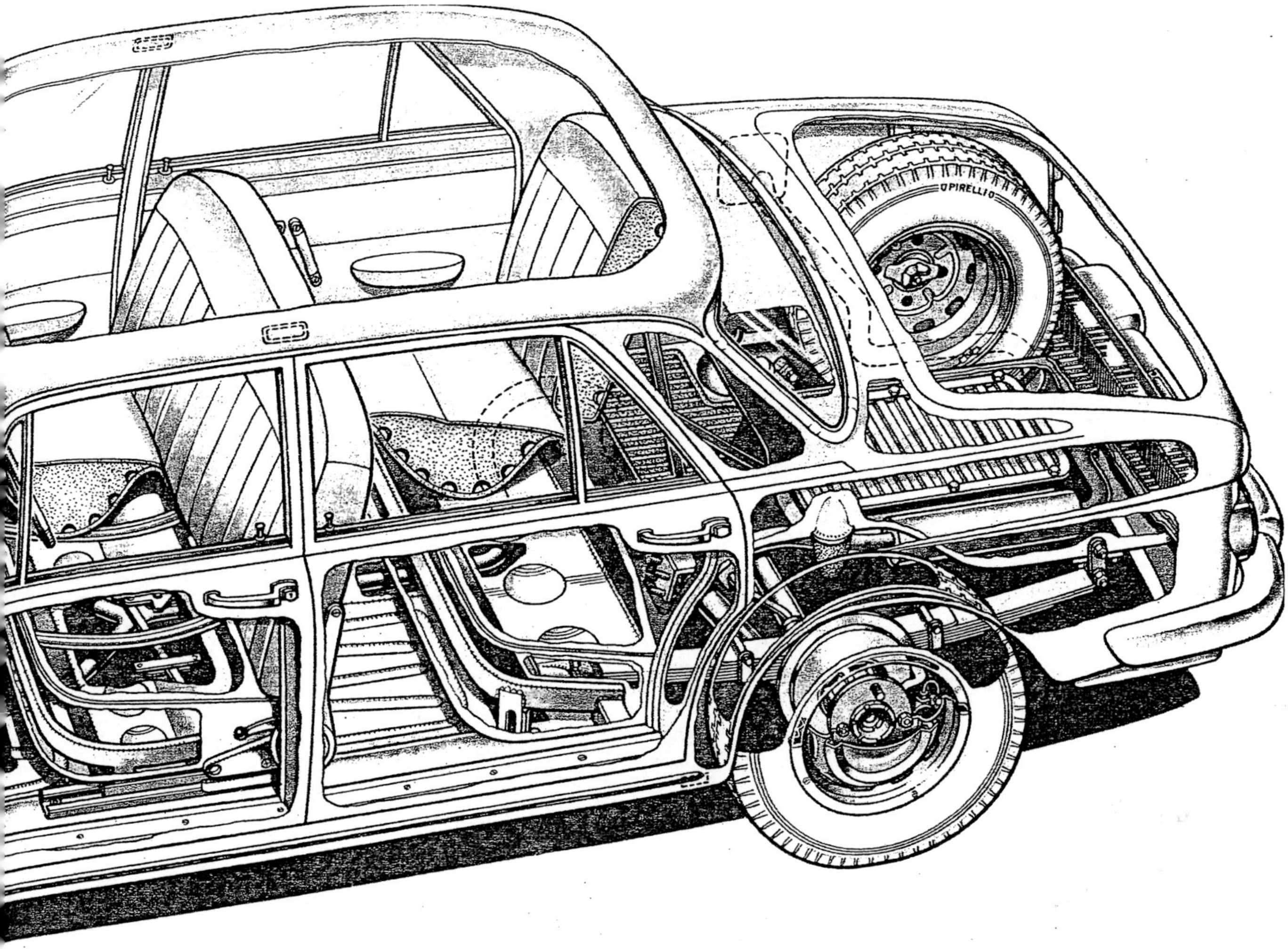

with the engine, transmission, suspension and steering linkages. Such a construction has the advantage of unit assembly during manufacture, and aids service at major overhauls.

The front sub-frame consists of two box-section side members joined front and rear by cross members of the same dimensions. Bolted to this welded sub-frame is a substantial aluminium casting at each side, to which the wishbones, steering box and idler lever are also attached. These castings are braced with three steel channel-section members across the upper and lower extremities. The upper one forms the saddle mounting for the transverse leaf spring, which at each outer end is attached to its upper wishbone by a substantial rubber bobbin. The use of a leaf spring is undoubtedly related to the front-wheel drive layout, for it is quite difficult to utilize coil springs and avoid the wheel drive-shafts without having an offset load on the wishbones or a high reaction point for the springs, if mounted above them.

Each wishbone has tubular arms, copper-brazed to forged steel ends. Rubber bushings are used at the inboard attachments to the aluminium casting and they are noticeable for their very wide spacing. Ball pivots, 1·5in. dia. spaced at 10·25in., are used top and bottom for the outer swivel joints. Each is sealed with a rubber gaiter and has a lubrication point. Typical of the attention to detail is the upper ball joint which, on the Flavia, takes the greatest load. It is in two halves, with a ball thrust race between them to lighten steering loads. A de Carbon telescopic damper is mounted to the rear of each lower wishbone.

Expense has been subordinated to ideal design in the construction of the Hardy Spicer front-wheel drive-shafts, which are often the Achilles heel of such a layout. A constant velocity Rzeppa-type joint of approximately 3·25in. dia. is used inboard and outboard. The outer case of the inner one is formed with six equally spaced semi-circular grooves, matching with similar ones in the surrounding pot joint. In each of these grooves five 0·375in. dia. balls are trapped in position. These accommodate endwise movement of the shaft arising from wheel movements, and virtually eliminate sliding friction. Each joint is gaitered and sealed with lubricant for life. An anti-roll bar, connected to the lower wishbones, passes beneath the side members of the sub-frame.

Steering is by a rear-mounted, three-piece track rod system, such that the steering box, which is of the worm and roller type, can be interchanged with the idler lever for either right- or left-hand drive. In the shaft between the box and the steering wheel there is a rubberized fabric coupling.

Several types of rear suspension, including independent, were tried on the prototype car before the choice settled on a tubular steel beam attached to a half-elliptic leaf spring at each side. It was considered by Professor Fessia that the best compromise of handling characteristics was obtained with this light beam. Coil springs and radius arms, in conjunction with the tubular beam, were considered, but the leaf spring arrangement made least intrusion into luggage space.

Dunlop disc brakes—of the same size as are used on the Mark II Jaguars—are fitted to all wheels. They are servo-assisted, with separate front and rear hydraulic circuits. This independence is achieved by the use of a tandem master cylinder, each half having its own circuit

Front-wheel-drive permits a clean under tray, with a minimum ground clearance of 5in. in the unladen condition. Wheels are 15in. diameter

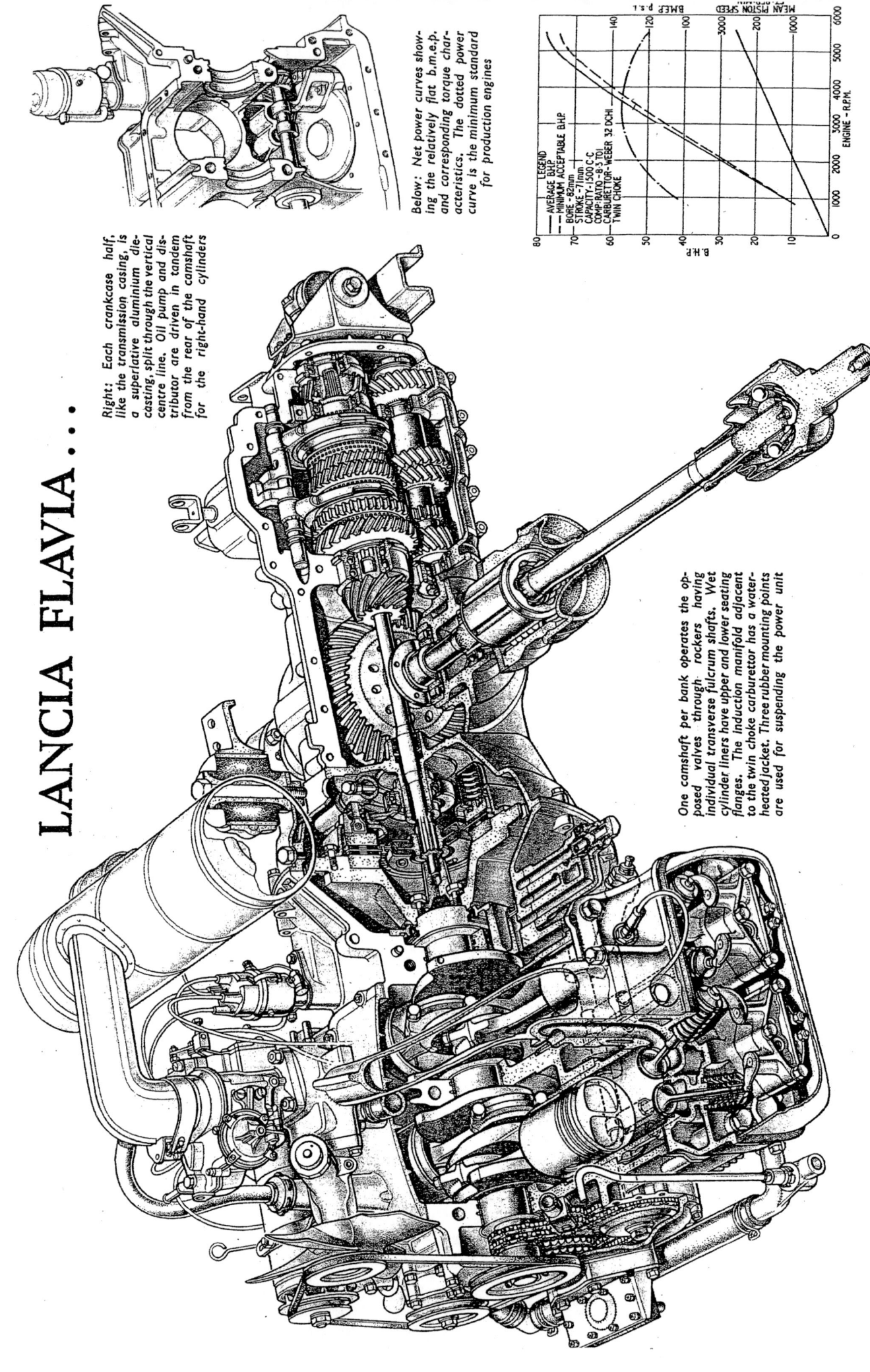

LANCIA FLAVIA...

Below: Net power curves showing the relatively flat b.m.e.p. and corresponding torque characteristics. The dotted power curve is the minimum standard for production engines

Right: Each crankcase half, like the transmission casing, is a superlative aluminium diecasting, split through the vertical centre line. Oil pump and distributor are driven in tandem from the rear of the camshaft for the right-hand cylinders

One camshaft per bank operates the opposed valves through rockers having individual transverse fulcrum shafts. Wet cylinder liners have upper and lower seating flanges. The induction manifold adjacent to the twin choke carburettor has a water-heated jacket. Three rubber mounting points are used for suspending the power unit

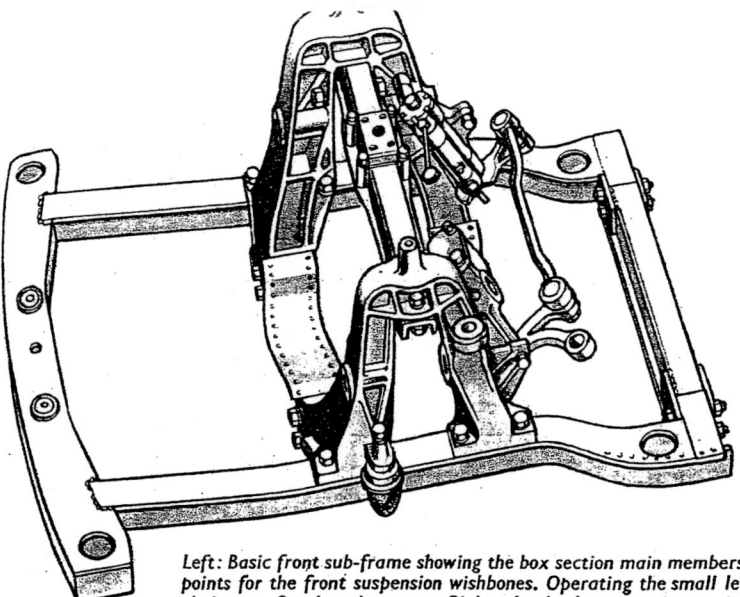

Left: Basic front sub-frame showing the box section main members and two aluminium castings bolted to it, which form the attachment points for the front suspension wishbones. Operating the small lever adjacent to the steering lever bearing restricts wheel lock when chains are fitted to the tyres. Right: A wheel-away unit—engine, transmission and suspension assembled on their sub-frame—is attached to the body hull by a rubber bobbin mounting at each corner and a similar one at the top of each aluminium casting

to the servo unit. Like the clutch, the brakes are operated by a pendant pedal; the throttle pedal is of organ type. Parking brakes with cable operation to the rear wheels are operated by a lever under the instrument panel.

There are many attractions in a horizontally opposed four-cylinder layout; there are also some shortcomings if the main advantages are exploited to the full. It is almost certainly more expensive than an in-line arrangement; if its virtue of compactness is applied, bearing sizes and crankweb thicknesses can be marginal. Lancia have avoided the snags, and accepted the greater cost.

Most horizontal cylinder layouts use a single camshaft in the plane of the crankshaft, but this calls for long pushrods with high reciprocating masses, and thus valve gear heavily stressed at high speeds. The Flavia uses two camshafts to overcome this defect, so that its maximum power at 78 b.h.p. net is produced at 5,200 r.p.m., and the engine is capable of revving up to 6,000 r.p.m. The two camshafts are driven by a duplex roller chain from the crankshaft, the chain incorporating a hydraulic tensioner. The pushrods have a duralumin tubular centre section to match the expansion rates of the aluminium crankcase and cylinder heads.

If the adjacent cylinders are spaced to use a minimum fire joint between the block and the head, crankshaft scantlings and bearings are of meagre proportions. In the Flavia the design seems to have been centred initially around the crankshaft and its bearings, for the cylinders are much wider than they need be for gasket width or water space between the cylinders. Another factor was undoubtedly the use of opposed valves in a hemispherical combustion chamber; they have an included angle of 39 degrees, which gives just sufficient clearance for the valve springs on the adjacent inlet valves, as seen on the cross-section drawing.

This opposed valve arrangement is made possible by the use of individual transverse fulcrum shafts, as first applied on the Aurelia. Individual inlet ports are uppermost on the cylinder head, the exhaust ports projecting downwards to separate flanges on the underside of each head. Valve head diameters are 38mm (1·496in.) for the inlet and 33mm (1·300in.) for the exhaust; these are large by current standards, indicative of good breathing over a wide speed range. The valves seat on cast-in iron inserts.

Crankshaft bearings are massive by any standards, the mains having a diameter of 2·375in., and widths of 1·06in., 0·93in. and 1·375in. for the front, intermediate and rear respectively. Like the mains, the big ends are Vandervell indium-infused lead-bronze type, with a diameter of 1·937in. and a width of 0·875in. Crankweb thicknesses adjacent to each main bearing are 0·5 in., the intermediate flying webs being 0·75in.

Bearing lubrication is from a Hobourn-Eaton internal rotor oil pump with a gauze pick-up filter, and a circuit through a full-flow filter before the oil is fed to a drilled gallery in the left crankcase half. Connecting rods have an angular serrated faced joint and 1in. dia., fully floating gudgeon pins. The German Mahle pistons, which have two compression rings and an oil control ring above the gudgeon pin, are noticeable for deep recesses in the crowns. These are not required for valve clearance at top dead centre, but are undoubtedly provided for increasing compression ratio at some future date.

The combined crankcase and cylinder block is split on its vertical centre line like the transmission casing. A great deal of thought has been put into these components, and they are produced as aluminium die-castings with open sides so that loose pieces in the internal cores are avoided throughout. The sump, with its cooling fins, is integral with each crankcase half, access to the oil pump

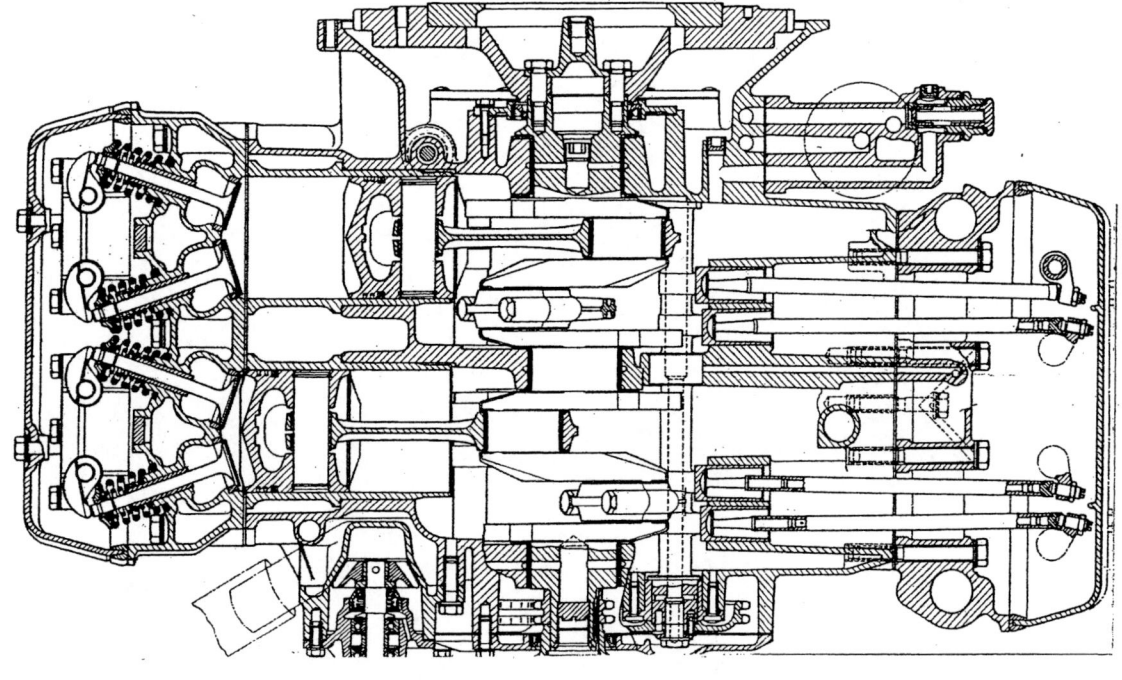

Cylinder block construction consists of two aluminium die-cast halves with wet cylinder liners. Camshafts and their tappets run direct in the aluminium casting. Individual transverse rocker shafts and pushrods—an arrangement first used on the Aurelia—provide for a neat layout of opposed valves in a hemispherical chamber

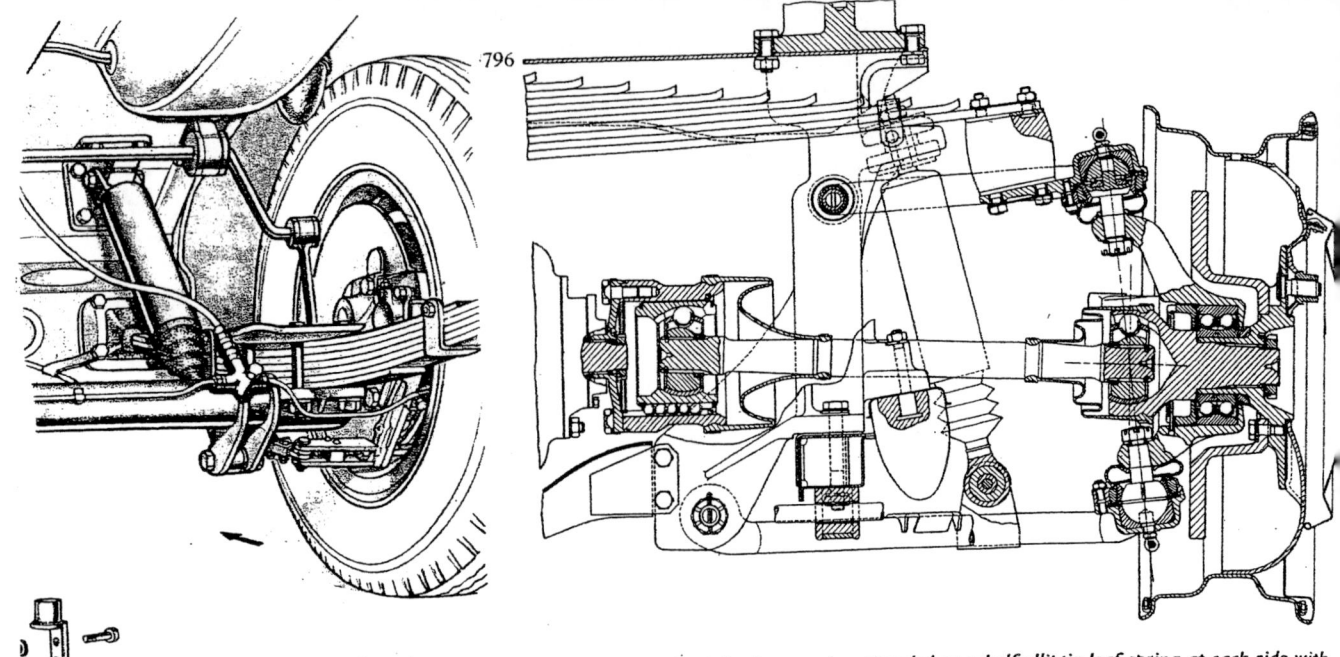

Above left: Rear suspension consists of a dead tubular beam axle suspended on a half-elliptic leaf spring at each side with forward-facing telescopic dampers and an anti-roll bar. Left: Rear spring shackle with its trunnion mounting and nylon bushes clamped in a rubber housing. Above: Front suspension consists of double wishbones with ball pivots at each side, and an upper transverse leaf spring with a rubber cushion block at the outer attachment point to each upper wishbone. Changes in drive-shaft length are accommodated in sliding ball splines on the outside of the inner constant velocity joint

LANCIA FLAVIA ...

and its pick-up filter being through a separate inspection cover. The halves are held together by set bolts on either side of each main bearing; Helicoil inserts are used in the female threads. There is, in addition, a series of bolts around the periphery of the joint face.

The wet cylinder liners are held in compression. The amount of nip is controlled solely by the depth of the recess in the casing and the distance between the two flanges on the liner; in other words, no shims are used. A rubber ring, fitting into the chamfer of the lower seating flange, forms the water seal. Between cylinder head, liner and crankcase there is a copper asbestos gasket with a machined concentric V-section groove in the liner top face and around the combustion chamber in the cylinder head. A single water pump, with split outlet to each cylinder bank, is belt-driven from the crank in a four-point drive which includes the dynamo (hinged for adjustment) and an aluminium cooling fan.

Carburation is either by a downdraught twin-choke Solex or a Weber instrument. The two chokes lead into a common water-jacketed hot spot, from which individual pipes merge into separate intake ports on each cylinder head.

From the Fichtel and Sachs clutch, which incorporates a patented Lancia cushion drive plate, the drive is taken through the hollow hypoid pinion shaft to a pair of helical gears at the rear of the main gearbox casing. All gears are in constant mesh with helical teeth, except for reverse; this is a separate train of straight spur gears placed between first and second. All forward ratios have synchromesh of baulk ring type; selection is by a column-mounted lever.

Road Impressions

During investigation into the technicalities of the Flavia, an early prototype was placed at our disposal for opinion and impressions, during which it was possible to cover some 50 miles in the hilly district around Turin. Throughout this short test there were five occupants, the three at the rear commenting favourably on the comfort of the seats and the amount of room. The front passengers would have preferred a central armrest or some slight curvature of the seat squab to provide support during severe cornering.

The driving position is excellent, with a well-raked wheel which does not intrude into the line of vision, and good all-round visibility. Pedal relationship to the seat is good and the pendant pedals are not difficult to operate—unlike many with this type of layout. Gear change lever movements are short and light, and the touch-button change-over switch for the dual headlamps is a clever innovation. Road noise has been well suppressed, and it was not possible to detect any body vibration or resonance when fully laden. Once one becomes familiar with the position of the controls on the switch panel, they are easy to find and operate.

Without previous knowledge that a front-wheel-drive layout had been utilized, it would be difficult to detect any characteristic revealing this feature. There is a degree of understeer, but no kickback at the steering wheel or change in attitude in cornering on hard lock with the engine alternating between drive and overrun.

The smoothness and tractability of the engine are memorable. Several times the car was taken up to 5,500 r.p.m. in the gears and it remained unobtrusive. Lancia claim a maximum speed of 92 m.p.h. It would need quite a long run to achieve this figure and, with full load, the acceleration was not outstandingly lively, but for 1½-litre it is rather a heavy car at 24 cwt. It is, nevertheless, very refined in all that it does, and in its appointments

SPECIFICATION

ENGINE

No. of cylinders	4 horizontally opposed water cooled
Bore and stroke	82 × 71 mm (3·23 × 2·79in.)
Displacement	1,500 c.c. (91.6 cu in.)
Valve position	Overhead, pushrods and rockers
Compression ratio	8·3 to 1
Max. b.h.p. (net)	78 at 5,200 r.p.m.
Max. b.m.e.p. (net)	135 p.s.i. at 3,500 r.p.m.
Max. torque (net)	82 lb ft at 3,500 r.p.m.
Carburettor	Twin choke Weber 32DCHI or Solex 32PAIA3
Fuel pump	Bendix electric
Tank capacity	10·5 Imp. gallons (48 litres), including reserve
Sump capacity	11 pints (6·24 litres)
Oil filter	Full flow
Cooling system	Pressurized, pump, fan and thermostat
Battery	12 volt 40 amp. hr.

TRANSMISSION

Clutch	Single dry plate, 7·87in. dia.
Gearbox	Four speeds; synchromesh on all forward ratios; steering column lever
Overall ratios	Top 4·09; 3rd 6·71; 2nd 9·53; 1st 16·16; reverse 18·00 to 1
Final drive	Hypoid bevel, ratio 4·09 to 1

CHASSIS

Brakes	Dunlop disc, vacuum servo assistance
Suspension: front	Independent, double wishbones with transverse leaf spring and anti-roll bar
rear	Dead axle, with half-elliptic leaf springs and anti-roll bar
Dampers	de Carbon telescopic
Wheels	Pressed steel (4·5in. wide rims)
Tyres size	6.50—15
Steering	Worm and roller
Steering wheel	Two-spoke, 15·5in. dia.
Turns, lock to lock	2·5

DIMENSIONS (Manufacturer's figures)

Wheelbase	8ft 8·33in. (265 cm)
Track: front	4ft 3·18in. (130 cm)
rear	4ft 2·39in. (128 cm)
Overall length	15ft 0·24in. (458 cm)
Overall width	5ft 3·23in. (161 cm)
Overall height	4ft 11·06in. (150 cm)
Ground clearance (laden)	5in. (13 cm)
Turning circle	36ft (11·0m)
Kerb weight	2,698 lb, 24 cwt (1,210 kg)

PERFORMANCE DATA

Top gear m.p.h. at 1,000 r.p.m.	18·1
Torque lb ft per cu in. engine capacity	0·89
Brake surface area swept by linings	496 sq in total
Weight distribution (kerb weight)	F. 60 per cent R. 40 per cent

The Flavorous Flavia

A personal experience of the breed by *John Whitehouse*

My introduction to the Lancia marque was with a Flavia, — a 1500 Berlina, bought from a wily ladybird. It was fairly tatty, needing a lot of paintwork smartening up and new sills, all of which were done, and it was resprayed a non-Lancia bright red. Many members of the L.M.C. will not have experienced the Flavia Berlina. It is a six-seater with a bench front seat, a column gear change and a set of switches that look like a mini-piano. It is a very comfortable car, with the front seat fully reclining giving a flat area of six feet by five, and with back window curtains it has been described as a double bed on wheels. My car was WMP 75G. Type number 815.01. (Did you know that there are 27 versions of the Flavia 815?). It was first registered in 1969 in this country but turned out to be a 1962 car imported privately by a Mr. Scheldt with a second owner given as a Mr. Pettet (no, I'm not advertising — no commercial connections) or so the log book says.

This car was also responsible for my introduction to the Lancia Motor Club. I was at the local car breakers one day (not looking for Lancia parts) when all of a sudden there was this idiot asking the yard if my car was for breaking — and it was showing six months to go on a tax disc too — he was driving one of the three Appias then resident in Holmer Green. It was Nigel Hargreaves, then on the Club Committee and constantly looking for recruits.

The Berlina was a nice car to drive. The flat four configuration gave a lower than average bonnet line resulting in good manoeuvrability, though as the engine is mounted in front of the front wheels, this creates a considerable front overhang. The car had one of the biggest front windscreens I had ever come across, and the all round view was excellent.

With time the snags became apparent. One Boxing Day I got water in the oil. The Flavia engine has wet liners, that are set 1.5 thou. proud. In long use these tend to sink into the engine, so that the head gasket can no longer keep the two liquids from mixing. The liners have to be extracted, and shimmed so that the proudness is restored. (The same problem occurs on Flaminia engines and, I'm told, Aurelia engines). I told you that the car was resprayed, but I used ordinary Triumph paint, which on Lancia lacquer eventually crazes and lifts in fantastic patterns. It began to look odd, then the engine went completely. We decided to replace the 1.5 engine with a 1.8 that Harry just happened to have handy. The clearances for lifting the engine out are less than half an inch and even that is with the engine tilted. In the factory the engine was mounted on the subframe and the body was then lowered on to the subframe. Do not try reversing the procedure, as on jacking the body off the subframe the former tends to warp and twist. Additionally, the 1.8 engine has an oil cooler which the 1.5 does not, so that a means of mounting the cooler has to be found.

My second Flavia was a RHD 1.8 Pininfarina Coupé, 815.331, made in 1964 which I bought for £100. It suffered one defect, water came up through the floor as the tin worm had been at it. It had been sprayed pink at some time (a Jaguar colour) so that it was distinctive. There are quite a number of differences between the saloon and the coupé, apart from the obvious one of the number of doors. The coupé was much more aesthetically pleasing with its greater delicacy of rounded curves but the seating was much harder and nothing like so comfortable. To get into the coupé there was a sense of lowering oneself into the driving seat. It had individual front seats both of which were tippable to give access to the rear, and a long floor mounted gear stick. The handbrake was between the front seats whilst on the saloon it was beneath the dashboard, out of view, and had to be groped for.

The 815 Flavia had four different body shells — the Berlina (or saloon), Pininfarina coupé, Vignale convertible and the Zagato (or Sport). Apart from certain engine parts these bodies have no common interchangeable parts. Lancia don't change, in Betas how many interchangeable body parts are there between the saloon, coupé, HPE and the Trevi? The Flavia coupé had a standard circular speedo and rev. counter whilst the saloon had a ribbon type speedo. The saloon, Vignale and Zagato have identical looking rear light clusters. The lenses were the same but the holders in each case are very slightly different. Saloon rear light clusters do not fit the Vignale as the radius of curvature of the latter is less. Even the Flavia badges on the boot lid of the Berlina and Vignale are not interchangeable despite their similar appearance.

To return to the Coupé. Time took its toll. The rear springs parted from the body, and that was that. It had to be broken. Both the Flavias were worked hard and frequently well loaded, so they had done well.

Another of my Flavias was a left-hand drive Vignale, though I never owned it as a wholly road-going vehicle, except for the 400 miles I drove it home on acquisition, the rest of the time it spent as a restoration project. I bought it through the L.M.C. News Sheet six months after the advertisement appeared. I had to go to the wilds of Kirkcudbright to collect it (the last time I went on a train). The car was a runner with an M.o.T. only 10 days out of date. I say a runner, if it could be got to start, as the starting motor was not working. After spending time trying to make the starter work, I left for home after dark, still with no starter motor. No Flavia will do 400 miles on one tankful of petrol, and have you ever tried to find a filling station on a motorway with a slope to bump start a car on? With luck, I got a push start from a police patrol car despite having no tax, etc.

The 820 Berlina could have either carburettor or fuel injection, and either have four or five speed gearboxes. Mine is five speed. Trying to compare the Flavia 815 saloon and the 2000 820 saloon is difficult, both are large roomy cars with flat four engines, but the 820 has individual, partially-reclining front seats, a floor mounted gear change, power assisted steering and electric windows. The Flavia had never seemed to have heavy steering — until trying to drive one immediately after driving the 2000.

The 2000 is a very nice, fast, comfortable car. Eighteen months ago, the handbrake failed on a slope (I know it should have been left in gear) and it rolled driverless to demolish a rear wing. It took six months to get a new wing out of Lancia U.K. but it was managed, and eventually returned to the road. Its major snag is the fuel injection system, when this goes wrong it is difficult to get it put right. I drove it through a puddle in the road, and got the engine wet. The water has made something go in the electronics, and at the moment nothing will make the car go. I hope I have been able to obtain a secondhand injection system, and I will just have to swop parts till it decides to go again. I am looking forward to the 2000 returning to the road, so that I can dispose of the Beta HPE I am currently driving. The 2000 is a far superior car. ∎

Summary Data

BERLINA

DESCRIPTION	CHASSIS IDENTIFICATION	CHASSIS SERIAL NUMBERS	DATES OF BUILD	ENGINE TYPE	CAPACITY (ccs)	POWER/RPM (HP DIN)	KERB WEIGHT (Kg)	MAX. SPEED (KPH)
Flavia 1500	815.00 (LHD) 01 (RHD)	1001 - 29362	1961-63	815.00	1500	78/5200	1190	148
	815.103 (RHD) (for South Africa)	1001 - 1072	1963	815.00	1500	78/5200	1190	148
Flavia 1500	815.200 (LHD) 201 (RHD)	29363 - 32601	1963-66	815.200	1488	80/5600	1190	150
Flavia 1800	815.300 (LHD) 301 (RHD)	1001 - 10557	1963-67	815.300	1800	92/5200	1190	160
	815.305 (RHD) (for South Africa)	1001 - 1240	1964	815.300	1800	92/5200	1190	160
Flavia 1800 Iniezione	815.400 (LHD) 401 (RHD)	80001 - 80826 81001 - 81138	1965-66	815.400	1800	102/5200	1190	168
Flavia 1500	819.200 (LHD) 201 (RHD)	1001 - 3350	1967-70	819.200 or 819.202	As 815.200 1490	80/5600	1190	152
Flavia 1800	819.300 (LHD) 301 (RHD)	1001 - 5334 column gearchange	1967-70	819.300 or 819.302	As 815.300 1816	92/5200	1190	165
	310 (LHD) 311 (RHD)	1001 - 6796 floor gearchange						
Flavia 2000LX	819.610 (LHD) 611 (RHD)	1001 - 5457	1969-70	820.000	1991	114/5400	1240	175
Flavia 1800 Iniezione	819.400 (LHD) 401 (RHD)	1001 - 2611 column gearchange	1967-70	819.400	As 815.400		1200	170
	410 (LHD) 411 (RHD)	1001 - 2374 floor gearchange						
Flavia 2000LX Iniezione	819.810 (LHD) 811 (RHD)	1001 - 1483	1969-70	820.400	1991	126/5600	1250	180
Flavia 2000LX	820.010 (LHD) 011 (RHD)	1001 - 1639	1970-71	820.000	1991	114/5400	1240	175
Flavia 2000LX Iniezione	820.410 (LHD) 411 (RHD)	1001 - 1067	1970-71	820.400	1991	126/5600	1250	180
2000	820.210 (LHD) 211 (RHD)	1001 - 9844	1971-74	820.200	1991	115/5800	1235	175
2000 I.E.	820.416 (LHD) 417 (RHD)	1001 - 6475	1971-73	820.406	1991	125/5800	1235	180

COUPÉ

DESCRIPTION	CHASSIS IDENTIFICATION	CHASSIS SERIAL NUMBERS	DATES OF BUILD	ENGINE TYPE	CAPACITY (ccs)	POWER/RPM (HP DIN)	KERB WEIGHT (Kg)	MAX. SPEED (KPH)
Flavia 1500	815.130 (LHD) 131 (RHD)	1001 - 4725	1962-63	815.100 or 815.100 Var 1005	1500 1727	90/5800 92/5200	1160	171
Flavia 1800	815.330 (LHD) 331 (RHD)	1001 - 16568	1963-68	815.300	1800	92/5200	1160	173
Flavia 1800 Iniezione	815.430 (LHD) 431 (RHD)	Shared with 330/331 series[1]	1963-68	815.400	1800	102/5200	1160	180
Flavia 2000	820.030 (LHD) 031 (RHD)	1001 - 4458	1969-71	820.000	1991	114/5400	1190	185
Flavia 2000 Iniezione	820.430 (LHD) 431 (RHD)	1001 - 1705	1969-71	820.400	1991	126/5600	1200	190
2000	820.230 (LHD) 231 (RHD)	1001 - 2399	1971-73	820.200	1991	115/5800	1200	185
2000 HF	820.436 (LHD) 437 (RHD)	1001 - 2229	1971-73	820.406	1991	125/5800	1205	195

Note: [1] Approximately 2150 cars supplied with fuel injection

SPORT

DESCRIPTION	CHASSIS IDENTIFICATION	CHASSIS SERIAL NUMBERS	DATES OF BUILD	ENGINE TYPE	CAPACITY (ccs)	POWER/RPM (HP DIN)	KERB WEIGHT (Kg)	MAX. SPEED (KPH)
Flavia 1500	815.132 (LHD)	1001 - 1098	1963	815.100 Var 1005	1727	92/5200	1060	178
Flavia 1800	815.532 (LHD) 533 (RHD)	1001 - 1626	1963-67	815.500	1800	100/5800[1] 105/5800[2]	1060	180[3] 187[4]
Flavia 1800 Iniezione	815.432 (LHD) 433 (RHD)	Shared with 532/533 series[5]	1963-67	815.400	1800	102/5200	1060	188

Notes: [1] Up to chassis No. 1512 (with two Solex double choke carburettors)
[2] From chassis No. 1513 (with two Weber double choke carburettors)
[3] Up to chassis No. 1496 (with 11/42 final drive)
[4] From chassis No. 1497 (with 10/37 final drive)
[5] 32 cars supplied with fuel injection

CONVERTIBLE

DESCRIPTION	CHASSIS IDENTIFICATION	CHASSIS SERIAL NUMBERS	DATES OF BUILD	ENGINE TYPE	CAPACITY (ccs)	POWER/RPM (HP DIN)	KERB WEIGHT (Kg)	MAX. SPEED (KPH)
Flavia 1500	815.134 (LHD) 135 (RHD)	1001 - 1724	1962-63	815.100 Var 1005	1727	92/5200	1150	171
Flavia 1800	815.334 (LHD) 335 (RHD)	1725 - 2601	1963-64	815.300	1800	92/5200	1150	173
Flavia 1800 Iniezione	815.434 (LHD) 435 (RHD)	Shared with 334/335 series[1]	1963-64	815.400	1800	102/5200	1150	180

Lavish Lancia

Reprinted from *Australian Motor*

SIMON FORD *tries a car on which Zagato let his flair for design run riot. You mightn't like it but you'll certainly notice it go by.*

Judging from comments I overheard around the Lancia display at the Sydney Motor Show, some onlookers thought the Flavia Sport's appearance was particularly attractive and some felt otherwise. Either way, though, nobody ignored the "Sport".

Whether you like the styling or not, you must admit that it is uniquely distinctive. And controversial! But Zagato probably had just that in mind when creating the Sport — to produce a body which was not only aerodynamically efficient, but also sufficiently individual to stand out in any company. Both aims have obviously been achieved.

Proof of the body's aerodynamic efficiency is found in the car's performance. Although frontal area is quite substantial the relatively modest power output provides speeds in excess of 115 mph; 30 mpg fuel consumption also confirms the efficiency of the styling.

I was especially interested in examining and driving the Sport, not only because it was the first of its kind to reach Australia, but also because it gave me the opportunity to experience the Kugelfischer fuel injection system which is now optional throughout the range of Flavia models.

The fuel injection adds $640 to the cost of the Sport, raising the total outlay to $7,740. This sum includes $240 for the optional Borrani wheels. These will be standard on Flavia Sports imported by Lambda Motor Co. in the future unless the client specifically deletes them in favour of the stock steel wheels.

Unusually, the injected engine, with 102 bhp (DIN) at 5,200 rpm and 113 lbs/ft. torque at 3,500 rpm, is less powerful than the carburetted engine it supplements. With two dual-throat Webers the unit produces 105 bhp (DIN) at 5,600 rpm and 116.4 lbs/ft. torque at 3,500 rpm. The explanation probably lies in the fact that the carburetted flat-four, as fitted to the Sport, represents the top of the line in its existing form. The caburetted Flavia sedan version, for example, delivers 92 bhp and 105.6 lbs/ft., while the coupé and convertible models have the same bhp with 107.7 lbs/ft. torque. Thus there are three different stages of tune for the carburetted plant. With fuel injection aboard, however, all four models share the same engine. So, while the Sport loses a little in sheer output with injection, the others gain.

Advantages of the injection system are not entirely evident from the specifications alone. Among the other benefits are improved starting and fuel economy, with increased flexibility and faster acceleration.

The FI engine can also readily digest fuel of lower octane rating than can the carburetted versions.

The first thing noticed when driving the "Iniezione"-engined Lancia is that it fires up almost, it seems, before the starter dog has fully engaged with the ring gear. And from that moment the car will pull away as cleanly as one could wish for — and as fast, if the driver chooses to ignore the cold engine. This he should not do, of course, and particularly not if he has read the instruction manual.

Although the FI system will not wash the cylinder bores to the same extent as a choked carburettor, the factory recommends that in cold weather the engine be run without load at 1,500 rpm for a minute or two before taking off, and that full acceleration be avoided until the tempera-

ture gauge's needle is in the white sector — corresponding 149 deg F. Rapid warm-up is assured, as on the carburette models, with thermostatically controlled shutters regula ing the amount of air able to pass through the radiator.

In cold weather the preliminary starting procedure is th same as for typical automatically choked carburetted e gines. Before the engine is started, the accelerator pedal fully depressed, then allowed to return to the rest position.

An orange light on the dash panel warns if fuel pressure low from the electric pump. The light must shine when t ignition is turned on and be extinguished after four or fi seconds. In the unlikely event that the pump has drain and is unable to prime itself, due, for example, to the c having stood unused for an extended period, the warni light will not go out and the pump must be primed by po ing fuel into the main fuel filter.

There are four filters throughout the fuel system for t purpose of keeping foreign matter from the injector nozzles. T injectors are, of course, situated in the ports i mediately upstream from the inlet valves. The corre quantity of fuel and its moment of injection are dictated the belt-driven mechanical pump operating in conjunctic with a butterfly valve which regulates the intake of air.

This provides the optimum fuel/air ratio for any and conditions and, naturally, promotes improved output a economy. Consumption is further reduced because no fu is delivered if, on over-run, the accelerator pedal is release and engine speed exceeds about 2000 rpm.

I have dealt with some of the less familiar aspects of t injected engine, because such units are all the mo interesting due to their comparative scarcity. Even today, wh FI has been proved practical for 10 years or more, the numb of makers employing it on production cars can be counted the fingers of one hand.

Though lacking first-hand experience with the carbure ed Flavia Sport, I have no reason to doubt Lancia's clai that the injected model is superior in all respects. Fuel consum tion of the FI Sport, for example, is stated to be 30 mpg based the Italian CUNA standard, whereas the carburetted job, und identical conditions, returns 27.3 mpg.